GAMES IN EDUCATION AND DEVELOPMENT

GAMES
IN EDUCATION
AND DEVELOPMENT

Edited By

LOYDA M. SHEARS, Ph.D.

Clinical Psychologist
Marymount Mental Health Center
Garfield Heights, Ohio

and

ELI M. BOWER, Ed.D.

Professor of Education
School of Education
University of California at Berkeley
Berkeley, California

C H A R L E S   C   T H O M A S   •   P U B L I S H E R
Springfield • Illinois • U.S.A. 1974

Published and Distributed Throughout the World by
CHARLES C THOMAS • PUBLISHER
BANNERSTONE HOUSE
301-327 East Lawrence Avenue, Springfield, Illinois, U.S.A.

©*1974, by* CHARLES C THOMAS • PUBLISHER
ISBN 0-398-02608-4
Library of Congress Catalog Card Number: 72-93229

With THOMAS BOOKS *careful attention is given to all details of
manufacturing and design. It is the Publisher's desire to present books
that are satisfactory as to their physical qualities and artistic possibilities
and appropriate for their particular use.* THOMAS BOOKS *will be true
to those laws of quality that assure a good name and good will.*

Library of Congress Catalog Card Number: 72-93229
Shears, L.M. & Bower, E.M.
    Games in education and development
Springfield, Ill.   Charles C Thomas
1972   ISBN 0-398-02608-4
                                                10-18-72

Printed in the United States of America
A-2

CONTRIBUTORS

LAYMAN E. ALLEN, M.P.A., LL.B.
Professor of Law and Research Social Scientist
University of Michigan
Ann Arbor, Michigan

FRANZ ARMBRUSTER
Founder and President
Products of the Behavioral Sciences, Inc.
Campbell, California

ELI M. BOWER, Ed.D.
Professor of Education
School of Education
University of California at Berkeley
Berkeley, California

DENNIS C. DOBBS
Simulation Designer
Real World Learning, Inc.
Teacher
Hillsborough, California

RIVKA R. EIFERMANN
Professor
Psychology Department
Hebrew University in Jerusalem
Jerusalem, Israel

DINA FEITELSON, Ph.D.
Hebrew University of Jerusalem
Jerusalem, Israel

v

ROBERT W. FREEMAN, Ph.D.
Director of the Parent Consultation and Child Evaluation Service
University of Maryland Counseling Center
College Park, Maryland

ROSE FRUTCHEY, M.ED.
Organizer
Border Crafts of Thailand

PERRY GILLESPIE, Ph.D.
Professor of Education
University of Lethbridge
Lethbridge, Alberta, Canada

CAROL GUYTON GOODELL
Simulation Designer
President
Real World Learning, Inc.
San Carlos, California

BESS LOMAX HAWES
Associate Professor
California State University at Northridge
Northridge, California

ROBERT F. HILL
Simulation Designer
Real World Learning, Inc.
Teacher
Palo Alto, California

JAMES H. HUMPHREY
Professor of Physical Education and Health
University of Maryland
College Park, Maryland

RICHARD MOON
Columnist
San Mateo Times
San Mateo, California

DIANE REARDON, Ph.D.
Department of Psychiatry
University of California
School of Medicine
The Center for the Health Sciences
Los Angeles, California

JOAN K. ROSS, M.SC.
Mental Health Research Institute
University of Michigan
Ann Arbor, Michigan

LOYDA M. SHEARS, Ph.D.
Clinical Psychologist
Marymount Mental Health Center
Garfield Heights, Ohio

BRIAN SUTTON-SMITH, Ph.D.
Program Head of Developmental and Educational Psychology
Teachers College, Columbia University
New York, New York

INTRODUCTION

The overall objective of this volume is to encourage the wider use of games as teaching devices in school settings. Games fit the life style of children, and they engage children in learning experiences. These learning experiences differ from those usually required of them at school, since ordinarily children are free to engage in games for their own private reasons. Furthermore, games can absorb the participants for extended periods without their seeming to be aware of the passage of time. All these observations point to the fact that for children games are *fun*.

At the same time that children are absorbed in the details that make up a game, they are learning or practicing something that interests them. This interest can be unrelated to school, and it often supports some nonacademic aspect of the child's socialization. However, when learning goals are related to the framework of a game, children may find them just as much fun and absorbing of their interest provided the participants become involved in the "game world." We do not suggest that games should be used exclusively as *the* teaching method, but games offer variety for the classroom and allow children to gain perspective on their real world events. The game-form allows the child to take and maintain an "as if" relationship to the problems that make up the momentary round of the game. Each child is free to "cut in" and "cut out" as his or her emotions and involvement ebb and flow during the game. These two aspects represent the unique qualities that games offer to the classroom teacher.

Before we launch into the contributions of the several authors it is appropriate to discuss some of the issues surrounding games and play as teaching devices. Although one of the contributors will deal explicitly with theories of play as they relate to child development, we need to note here that games are not traditionally thought of as appropriate to the serious business of training children. Our view of games as useful for instruction in academic subjects or in socializing children into useful citizens of tomorrow is relatively new. However, the use of games as simulations of real life problems is as old as Chess and Go. When children are invited to play as a part of the educational process, the usefulness of their activity is not always clearly understood by teachers, parents, and administrators.

Games and children playing games constitute potentially powerful educational tools. There is therefore a great responsibility by game-users and a need for care and skill as they use these dynamic tools. Games can have unwanted side effects in much the same way as valuable medical treatments do. They do not affect all students similarly or equally.

To gain perspective on the management of teaching games in the classroom, let us look at two of the patent objectives of their use. We may simply want children to practice using information that has already been presented in a usual way. Let's say we want them to practice their arithmetic combinations. If we can get the children to compete with each other using their knowledge, the practice time will pass more easily, and the children will do more of the work of teaching themselves than they would if their teacher led them in a drill session. On the other hand, we may want the game experience to lead the children to discover something for themselves. Let's say we want the children to deduce the mathematical principle that multiplication is the same as adding a number to itself a given number of times. For this purpose we may instruct them as teachers have done for many years, to add and add and add again. If we elect to use a game we can involve the children in a game of Two-deep or Three-deep or Four-deep, and tell them that each set of children in the game represents a particular digit. When required, each set of children must tell **what** their total numerical value is; that is, if the game is called Eights, $8 \times 2 = 16$ or $8 \times 4 = 32$. Presented in this fashion, games may yield *exercise* for the children and the children may be enjoying the game, but the teacher may not be convinced of the game's value as a teaching device over her usual academic teaching methods. The point of all this is that unless games are used in a way that motivates children in their own educational growth they may be of doubtful value to either the children or their **teachers.**

The goals and life style of children can be tapped to unlock the motivational potential in games. Children seek to develop themselves and to surpass their own previous performance. It is possible to describe this kind of activity as a solitary-player game in which the adversary is *nature*. Jacks, Hopscotch, and Golf are such games. When a child has gained a certain mastery over the game-technique, he or she may wish to draw a comparison between each performance and that of another child. At that point the competition shifts to the social realm, and a second childhood objective comes into the motivational scheme. This objective consists of seeking to locate one's unique niche in the social competence hierarchy among his or her peers. Games serve their most valuable developmental purpose when they present the game materials in such a way as to leave the outcome of any particular game or round of the game in doubt as long as possible. This state of affairs comes about when the outcome is dependent on the skill and strategy of the players as they manage the game elements. In order to make maximal use of games in learning, one or the other or both of these childhood objectives should be served as well as the teacher's objective to present academic information and practice with that information. The definition of the winner and the distribution of the payoff or reward becomes the teacher's role and stock-in-trade when teaching games are viewed from this vantage point.

The teacher's role shifts from that of direct source of information and reward to that of manager of the situation in which the hoped-for reward is to be secured by the players' skill or strategy or even by chance during their management of the game materials. In this new role the teacher sets up and arranges (when necessary to maintain the doubtful outcome) the rules of the game until the children begin to design their own rules and game materials. The climate in which these changes occur is called a metagame. Teachers have always managed the metagame in their classrooms. They simply did not identify it as such. When they managed the metagame, they organized the social interchange rules between themselves and their students and among the several students. They set the rules which defined the elites and the proscribed members of the classroom and school society. When games are used as teaching devices the nature of the "metagaming" role of the teacher becomes a little more explicit and, at the same time, less dictatorial and predetermined. One of the tenets of the metagame is that a specific game loses its interest for some or all of the players when the outcome of the game or round of the game is clear before it begins. In order to revive interest in that game or any other, confidence must be restored to the losers (and reduced in the winners) about the outcome of the activity. It is unfortunate that winning all the time can be as dull and unmotivating as losing all the time. When a game lacks the element of suspense it is not actually a game that induces children to play.

The remainder of this volume will contain a theoretical and an applied section. The theory associated with games and play will be accompanied by illustrative applications. On the practical side, games that have been observed, devised and altered as the student-players experienced them will be accompanied by theories that have helped to make them relevant to educational use. Here, the devices available to a teacher who wishes to design or redesign game materials will be included. Skill, alertness and, above all, timing are needed by game-users in order to maintain the motivationally dynamic attributes of games. Through them the children can be induced to take more and more responsibility for their own education. To this end the teacher can select and combine from the following chapters in whatever ways imagination and planning suggest to obtain the benefits of games and integrate them into the goals and practices of their profession.

Loyda M. Shears

CONTENTS

GAMES IN EDUCATION AND DEVELOPMENT

PART ONE

CHAPTER 1

PLAY'S THE THING
ELI M. BOWER[1]

INTRODUCTION

ELI BOWER, Bess Lomax Hawes, and Diane McGunigle Reardon have each dealt with the dimensions, effects and functions of play in human lives. In the first three chapters in this volume each author, in turn, documents the fundamental value of play in the lives of adults and children. Although games are mentioned these chapters are devoted chiefly to the topic of play.

Eli Bower discusses the creative and dynamic functions of play throughout the lives of human beings. He points out that as young creatures, whether human or animal, the serious business of survival seems to dictate a playful period in their development. It is of considerable interest that he finds it necessary to emphasize this issue, especially in connection with the concept of play in education. Adults who teach are not playing and the students in their classes are there "to work" and they "should tend to business." Bower deals with the often negative effects that can and do result when adults intrude upon the play of children, and he documents the positive effects that follow from allowing them to play. The implication of his discourse is that play belongs to childhood as a developmental tool, and it should be an integral part of a child's life inside as well as outside of school. To clinch his arguments he cites several adult activities that are highly valued in our culture

---

[1]Reprinted with permission of NEA Journal. From *Today's Education,* September 1968.

that fit the play definition. Since a playful attitude toward one's adult self-in-action seems to underlie creativity, the grim, non-playful attitude we are asked to assume in everyday life must be calculated to damage or destroy creative potential in school children. It seems to be a question of goals, both for educators and for the children they seek to educate.

—Editors

IT IS IMPORTANT, INDEED MANDATORY,
FOR ANIMAL AND HUMAN EXISTENCE

"Is a puzzlement," said the King of Siam. He could have been scratching his head at the average American who works less hours so he can have more time for play, only to find that he has to work twice as hard to enjoy it. The opportunities for fun and games are plentiful, yet we pursue them like frenzied housewives at a Macy's bargain basement sale.

Our basic approaches to play and work have become somewhat diffused and interwoven. If anything worth doing is worth doing well, then one must also learn to play well. Work values and goals become play values and goals, so that Americans will read, study, and work hard to be better golfers, better bridge partners—even better sex partners.

For example, numerous manuals aimed at helping married couples achieve optimum sexual adjustment make it quite clear that love is a job which can only be carried out successfully with study, training, and hard work. Wives especially are told that sex is too important to give it less effort and work than cooking, laundry, and other womanly activities. Lewis and Brissett, who did a study of 15 marriage manuals, comment wryly, "To the housewife's burden is added yet another chore."

Play starts with children. Children have little trouble finding opportunities to play if left alone. Our society, however, is moving rapidly toward a complete takeover of this traditional franchise of childhood. Increasing amounts of human effort and of local, state, and federal funds are being expended and expanded to get young children into planned preschool programs. Social and behavioral scientists have discovered how crucial this time of life can be for educational and social competence. Consequently, educators (and parents) conclude, the early years of childhood cannot be dissipated in aimless play. They begin to plan more meaningful activities for children.

While their intent is laudable, it is important to keep an ecological ear cocked for side effects. At present, most planned or operating preschool programs are conceptual hybrids of the older American middleclass nursery schools which provided individual and group play (often guided and supervised) and the nursery schools set up in Rome and other European cities by Maria Montessori and her followers to raise the personal and educational competence of slum children.

The latter schools most often concentrated on structured play- and task-oriented activities aimed at enhancing specific skills and learnings. At present, most preschool programs represent a marriage of the old world and the new, with the offspring somewhat unclear about their heritage or future.

The period between the birth of an animal and the time when he begins to assume task and role responsibilities is the golden age of play. All young animals play. Children and other animals relate to each other through play. Play is an idea or concept that gains its existence in the minds of children and higher animals. Careful observation of pups or kittens reveals that they can distinguish the idea of play from the idea of fight, although to the casual onlooker it is often difficult to decide if the pups or kittens are playing or fighting. Children and animals may play rough, but it's only when someone gets angry and moves into another communicational modality that play stops.

Play cannot be prescribed, assigned, or done to order. It is voluntary. It is fun. It is important, indeed mandatory, for animal and human existence.

Young monkeys deprived of play show more serious developmental and functional deficits than those deprived of mothering. Professor Harlow, who has experimented with monkeys for many years, concluded that, for young monkeys, play with peers seemed more necessary than mothering for the development of adult monkey competence.

One cannot work and play under the same conceptual banner. Some work or tasks may be fun to do and some fun may require hard work, but the idea and goal in each are qualitatively different. Essentially, play is a relationship with oneself or others which requires the skill of creating and becoming involved in illusions, of being able to step out of the real world and back again.

Man the explorer, the conceptualizer, the adventurer is man at play. The great scientific and social leaps that man has made in mastering his environment did not come about through hard work but through play. Man's major sources of food—agriculture and cattle raising—were probably not started to serve utilitarian reasons but as a source of fun for curious and imaginative men. At no time was Gregor Mendel doggedly pursuing the laws of genetics; he was simply playing around with garden peas and enjoying it. Blaise Pascal was enticed to develop theories of probability by some of his card-playing and crap-shooting friends. Nor did Orville and Wilbur Wright have any notion of providing public transportation for hordes of tourists when they started playing around with their flying machine.

A society concerned with producing a fair number of creative and imaginative adults must protect the play modalities of thinking developed in childhood. If children are required or ordered to play on behalf of adult aims or goals, the illusion of play and its magical thinking are destroyed. This does not mean that children cannot be helped to play or encouraged to try new, exciting, and stimulating modalities. But once prescribed, play is no longer play.

The play modality or relationship is utilized in what we call games. A game is a contest in which there are agreed upon rules and goals. It is a contrived social system with prescribed space and time boundaries.

An English historian suggested that cricket, a game that may take one to five days to complete, was invented by religious zealots to give the English some idea of eternity. To some extent, baseball does the same for Americans. Nevertheless, games constrict play through rules and clearly defined goals and by the implicit assumption that the relationships between opponents will be one of "fair play."

Both animals and humans can play, but only humans can play

human games. The game is probably the child's first social relationship with strangers and his first testing of self against others. To play, he needs to be able to conceptualize the notion of rules and the separateness of the game from real life. Children (and adults) who see winning or losing a game as a matter of life and death are not playing anything and have not been able to step out of reality to any great extent. Although much of the value of the game is dependent on its seriousness and concentration, such seriousness is relevant only in the way it enables one to enter into the game wholeheartedly.

It is characteristic of some children that the outcome of a game can so overwhelm the child's real world that play and reality become one and the same. On the other hand, some cannot leap comfortably into the true illusory world of play and therefore participate coldly and with little spirit. Children who live in poor or deprived homes and neighborhoods often face overwhelming survival problems and therefore may lack the psychological freedom or opportunity to play. In many cases, such children must grow up fast, care for siblings when mother is at work, become self-reliant fast because there are few adults about to rely on, and in general become adult before they are quite grown up.

Since many of these children lack experience with a mediating or conceptualizing adult, they often find it difficult to connect the real and imagined. Many disturbed and deprived children have difficulty in games, often demonstrating impatience with rules and taking defeat as a personal affront.

The middle-class child frequently faces a set of grim-faced parents determined to prove that the chip off the old block is a giant Sequoia. As the values and goals of success have been switched from acquisition of material things to educational and personal achievement, middle-class parents have become less and less patient with the "wastefulness" of play. Their attitude is that while it cannot be done away with entirely, it can be made to serve adult ends.

There is nothing amiss or subversive in widening children's play opportunities with games which require higher and more complex skills, provided that the fun, enthusiasm, and play are still in them for the child. If the child is to learn to differentiate between play-fun and play-work, he must learn to differentiate his goals from the goals of others. Play, like mathematics, has its own internal assumptions and is only valid if these assumptions are not disturbed. Play is for fun; if this is compromised, nothing will add up right.

Where game values and enjoyments have been subverted by other values, children grow up into adults who are unable to enter the game world in the spirit of play and fun. They will have little or no chance to connect their adult world to the more primitive, naturalistic world of the child that still lives in them. They become like Lennie in Steinbeck's *Of Mice and Men,* who wanted desperately to play but could do so only with tragic results.

In our society, hard-working adults often find it difficult to separate games from nongames. While the game spirit may pervade such contests as war, it is often impossible for the losers to replay the contest. In days of yore, wars were fought in gentlemanly fashion by gentleman knights on the basis of rules firmly and magnificently enforced by the age of chivalry.

It is interesting to note that the idea of war *as a game* still persists in the minds of children and adults. This is why our sense of fair play was as much outraged by the Japanese sneak attack on Pearl Harbor as by the death and destruction it caused. One just doesn't play the "game" that way. On the opposite end of this continuum is the example of the battle between the French and British at Fontenay in 1745. As the opposing lines faced each other, Lord Charles Hay of the British First Grenadiers called out, "Gentlemen of the French Guards, will you fire first?" The French commander, not to be outdone by this gesture, replied, "Après vous, messieurs les Anglais."

One can increase one's skills and enjoyment in games, since games can be played again and again. However, to become a better player, one needs to play against opponents who are more or less comparable in skill and power. To get fun out of games, one seeks opponents who can extend one's playing ability. There is little fun in annihilating opponents (as in war) and still less in being annihilated oneself.

Things done for fun may be disturbing to some adults, especially those permeated by the Puritan ethic, who see mirth as quickly gliding into sin. At times, in an effort to become completely rational, men seek to obliterate some of the more primitive irrational aspects of self. But completely rational, nonplaying men would be inhuman monsters. Despite his growth into adulthood, civilized man is able to maintain the wilderness play preserve of his mind and has ready access to it when he needs it. Our society cannot befoul or destroy these areas of experiencing without some risk.

Civilization is an argument to work, play, and interact according to rules and a sense of fair play. True play, like virtue, is its own reward. It cannot exist where opponents aim to destroy each other. Children can be helped to learn many things through play and games, but if they do not have fun in doing so, the game is over.

CHAPTER 2

LAW AND ORDER ON THE PLAYGROUND

(Some observations on stability and change in the traditional games of white middle-class children)

BESS LOMAX HAWES

INTRODUCTION

*I*T *IS immediately clear that Bess Lomax Hawes does not mean the legal and political connotations of* Law *and* Order *when she applies them to the playground. She is dealing with the notion that both stability and variability must coexist in every situation in order for human beings to learn to cope. She has identified an important paradox in human interactions with either nature or other human beings. The mechanism of coping seems to require the individuals to take an expanded view of each situation so that a portion of it may be altered to fit the whim or necessity of each participant. Hawes sees rules in their entirety as including those which are stable throughout and those open to negotiation as each game or play is undertaken. The negotiation segment of the rule system, in her view, provides the practice-ground on which social negotiation processes may be learned, practiced and carried out. The stable segment of the system provides the basic fabric of the interaction that allows each individual to learn what to expect when this or that game (or situation) is in progress. Hawes, like Bower, points out the often negative effects of adult interference with child's play. She further explicates this notion with some hunches about adult feelings as they encounter children in negotiations over rules. This volume with its objective of increasing game-*

usage in the classroom is enriched by this kind of insight, since it allows users to better understand themselves as they invite children to play games.

—Editors

S OME YEARS AGO on a weekday afternoon, I was passing by a Los Angeles elementary school when the final bell of the day rang, and the children began to pour out of the play-yard. Two little girls, aged perhaps eight or nine, walked past me, deep in conversation.

"Let's play *step on a crack, break your mother's back.*"

"Naw, let's play *monkey faces*; that's lots better. See, the good thing about *monkey faces* is you step on *all* the cracks! You can stomp on the cracks if you want to, or you can wipe your feet all over the cracks; the only thing is, you can't step on a square that's got a monkey face in it . . ."

Apparently, a "monkey face" was the contractor's symbol imprinted in the sidewalk cement, for the children jumped ceremoniously across a nearby square that contained such a marking; and I watched them walk away, stepping boldly on all the cracks they passed and now and again taking big running leaps across the tabued sections of pavement.

This everyday and essentially unremarkable incident seemed to me, on later reflection, to contain the most central of the elements that make the subject of play so intriguing and so complex. To use Caillois' formulation as a starting point, the episode included all those characteristics he describes as essential to the nature of play itself.[1]

First, the behavior was *free,* not forced; the children themselves elected to play, thus simultaneously restricting and limiting their own freedom of activity by their own free choice—an absolutely essential paradox. Secondly, the activity was *separate, not for real,* but distinguished from all the other methods of walking home by mutual agreement and shared knowledge of the limitations implicit

---

[1]Roger Caillois, *Man, Play and Games,* trans. Meyer Barish (New York: Free Press of Glencoe, 1961), pp. 3-10.

to this particular game. Thirdly, it was *uncertain* (though on a very simple level), the activity itself being unclear as to its outcome. And fourthly, it was *unproductive,* except insofar as the children presumably eventually reached their respective houses; however, as soon as the game began, their arrival home became not the essential objective of the activity but simply its terminal point.

Lastly[2], the activity was *governed by rules,* not the everyday traffic and behavioral rules, but special rules within which limits the children were free to improvise and innovate—indeed, to "play". As Caillois puts it,

> This latitude of the player . . . is equally accountable for the remarkable and meaningful uses of the term "play", such as are reflected in such expressions as the *playing* of a performer or the *play* of a gear, to designate in the one case the personal style of an interpreter, in the other, the range of movement of the parts of a machine.[3]

Each play situation, however, contains its own special complexities. As I watched the two little girls, it seemed plain that a large part of the pleasure they found in the activity stemmed from their realization that they were doing more than playing *monkey faces*; they were also *not* playing *step on a crack, break your mother's back.* Their particular emotional gratification hinged upon their knowledge of both games, not just the one they elected to play. Were there, indeed, two games, or was one possibly a reverse image of the other—in that sense, a permissable variation in the rules?

Folklorists tend to pose this kind of problem in terms of the twin factors of stability and variation in traditional forms. And, when dealing with children's traditional materials, one is almost always confronted by both dimensions stretched to their utmost. The historical continuity of childlore is one of the most remarkable aspects of the human condition. Revolutions, wars, vast migrations of peoples often seem to have had little or no effect upon the private world of the children involved. Some of the counting-

---

[2] I am deliberately omitting, as not germane to this argument, Caillois' sixth characteristic, *make-believe,* which he describes as functioning in alternation to the fifth, *governed by rules.* In other words, according to Caillois, play may contain rules or make-believe, but not both.

[3] Caillois, op. cit., p. 8.

out rhymes still chanted on twentieth century playgrounds can be traced to Celtic languages spoken by Britons in pre-Roman times. Spanish-speaking children in the new world still play the singing games that their old-world cousins play, though an ocean and a two-hundred year time span lie between. Marbles, kites, cats cradle and hopscotch go back before recorded history, and, as a child in Texas, I used to thump on my brother's back in a guessing game mentioned by Petronius[4].

At the same time, variation is apparently as essential as stability. One of the perplexing difficulties encountered in dealing with children's lore is that out of a hundred renditions of the "same" counting-out rhyme, for example, almost no two will be exactly identical. And when adult intervention, print and other stabilizing forces enter the picture—as in the case of the nursery or "Mother Goose" rhymes—then the parodies begin.

> Hickory dickory dock
> Two mice ran up the clock.
> The clock struck one,
> And the other one got away.

> Hickory dickory dock
> The mouse ran up the clock.
> The clock struck three
> So he ran home
> So his mother would not spank him.

> Hickory dickory dock
> Three mice ran up the clock.
> The clock struck one,
> And the rest escaped with minor injuries.

> Little Miss Muffett
> Sat on a tuffett
> Eating her curds and whey.
> Along came a spider
> And sat down beside her
> And she ate that, too.

---

[4]Paul G. Brewster, "Some Notes on the Guessing Game: How Many Horns Has the Buck?," *The Study of Folklore.* ed. Alan Dundes (Englewood Cliffs, N.J., Prentice Hall, Inc., 1965), pp. 338-368.

Little Miss Muffett
Sat on a tuffett
Eating her curds and whey.
Along came a spider
And sat down beside her
And she beat the heck out of him with her spoon.

Rub a dub dub
Three men in a tub
Isn't that unsanitary?

Again, the pleasure intrinsic to parody—which is only a kind of variation, after all—seems to lie in a sort of double vision; one must know the original in order to savor the adventuresomeness of the variation, and thus, to some extent, both are reinforced. In this sense, it seems quite possible that only those cultural items which are susceptible to variation have much chance of survival, and this may in part account for the longevity of the child's own tradition wherein variation flourishes.

I am suggesting, then, that the apparently paradoxical co-existence of rules and innovation within play may be analagous to the co-existence of stability and variation within oral tradition. This thesis may be explored in greater detail by an examination of those play activities sometimes referred to as "games of individual skill", such as jacks, ball bouncing and hopscotch. These games parallel the jokes, nonsense rhymes and tongue-twisters of childlore in at least two critical dimensions: they circulate primarily among the seven to twelve-year-old peer group, and they are generally learned informally, by simply watching and listening to other children at play.

Most of the games of individual skill are extremely tightly structured. To take jacks as an example, each player in turn must maneuver through a lengthy sequence of orderly and highly restricted movements, any variation in which requires the player to give up his turn to the next player. In actual play, however, in spite of the large number of stringent requirements on which agreement is general: (a player may not move any jack except the one in play; all jacks must be picked up first one at a time, then two at a time and so forth; a player who doesn't catch the ball after one bounce has "missed", etc.), there are a large number of variables which are free-floating and considered open to discussion.

The order in which the various moves, or sub-games, are made is a case in point. Most children start with "babies" (or "plainsies") in which each jack is simply picked up without additional flourishes, but after the first round, any or all of the following moves may be required:

Pigs in the pen
Eggs in the basket
Upsies
Downsies
Pick the cherry, eat the cherry, throw the pit away
Babies in the high chair
Babies in the low chair
Through the Golden Gate
Around the world
Rolling down Broadway
Shooting stars
Up quicks
Down quicks
No bouncies
    Etc.

The order in which these various sub-games are played has varied with almost every game reported to me; it is apparently negotiable each time a round of jacks is proposed.

And when the sequence has been agreed upon, there are still a number of points of play that are open to a number of kinds of settlement. What is to be done about "kissies" (two jacks that land touching each other) or "haystacks" (one jack on top of another)? Sometimes such jacks alone may be rethrown; sometimes all the jacks must be rethrown; sometimes the situation is considered a "miss", and the thrower loses his turn. Can you play "cart before the horse", in which a player working on his "foursies" is allowed to pick up the ten jacks in the order of two, four and four, rather four, four and two? In between games, do you have to "graduate" by throwing the jacks in the air and catching as many as possible on the back of the hand?

The significant point is that agreement on all these questions is only temporary; all such rules are considered to be in effect only for the duration of the particular play session about to begin. Although children who often play together may evolve a mutually acceptable routine, should one or the other grow bored with the

the issue. Not infrequently it can be observed that a group will use the entire time available for play in a bitter—but apparently refreshing—discussion over the "rules". No one seems to mind, really, that the game never gets played. No wonder the decibel rate of our schoolyards is so high; floating over our playgrounds are the shrill intense voices of a thousand decision-makers at work—testing, probing, re-arranging, counter-posing—all very exhausting and unnecessary to a tidier-minded adult world.

For variation is frequently productive of uproar; there is absolutely no doubt about that. However, it can also promote flexibility and the knack of achieving compromise. Our children appear to have taken their cultural stance; they will cheerfully risk chaos any day in order to preserve a satisfactory degree of group or individual autonomy. And theirs is a more sophisticated position than first may appear; for by the time children have reached the game-playing age they have, by definition, learned that there are some immutables, some rules that cannot be challenged, or there is no game at all. It is the area in which change is possible that interests them most—and quite properly so.

It is, after all, possible that the children are right, that in terms of the democratic life style it is far more important for them to practice reaching and working within a temporary consensus than to learn obedience to an unchanging set of requirements. And so, from the perspective of the playground, "lawandorder" appear not as a static, monolithic, single unit but as "law" and "order", alternative and complementary processes, twin channels through which the human control of the human destiny may flow.

It is easy to theorize about the necessity for flexibility in American adult role behavior and the temporary nature of our decision-making and codification processes. It is harder—and much more wearing on the nerves—to listen to the battle being fought out under the classroom window, or in the streets, for that matter. However, if the foregoing observations are accurate—and I believe they are—it is plain that there are deep cultural forces at work in our childrens' apparently off-hand selection not only of what games they will play, but, more critically, how they will play them. It seems that we should try to comprehend these processes better before we so casually—and so ineffectually—interfere by administrative fiat, invention or codification. As adults, we stand to learn much; for clearly our children, as they play, are themselves grappling with an issue of central importance to a democratic society—the interlock of order and flexibility, individual freedom and group consensus, stability and change.

REFERENCES

All citations of game rules and direct quotations of childlore appearing in this article were taken from the California State University at Northridge Folklore Archives, to which some ten academic generations of student collectors have contributed. I owe them all thanks. Parallel data demonstrating the longevity and variation to be found in the folkloric tradition of the child may be found in such published sources as:

Abrahams, Roger D.: *Jump Rope Rhymes: A Dictionary*. American Folklore Society Bibliographical and Special Series, Vol. 20. Austin, University of Texas Press, 1969.

Bolton, Henry Carrington: *The Counting-Out Rhymes of Children: Their Antiquity, Origin and Wide Distribution. A Study in Folk-Lore*. New York, D. Appleton Co., 1888.

Brewster, Paul G.: *American Nonsinging Games*. Norman, University of Oklahoma Press, 1953.

Brewster, Paul G.: "Some Notes on the Guessing Game: How Many Horns Has the Buck?" Originally printed in *Bealoideas: Journal of the Folklore of Ireland Society*. Vol. 12 (1942), 40-78. Reprinted in Dundes, Alan (ed.), *The Study of Folklore*. Englewood Cliffs, N.J., Prentice Hall, Inc., 1965.

Brown, Frank, C.: Collection of *North Carolina Folklore*. Vol. I, edited by Paul Brewster. Durham, North Carolina, University of North Carolina Press, 1952, pps. 29-219.

Emrich, Duncan: *The Nonsense Book of Riddles, Rhymes, Tongue Twisters, Puzzles and Jokes from American Folklore*. New York, Four Winds Press, 1970.

Evans, Patricia: *Rimbles, a Book of Children's Classic Games, Rhymes, Songs and Sayings*. New York, Doubleday and Co., 1961.

Gomme, Alice Bertha: *The Traditional Games of England, Scotland and Ireland*. New York, Dover, 1964. (Two volumes.) Originally published as Part I, *Dictionary of British Folklore*. London, 1894 and 1898.

Hickerson, Joseph and Dundes, Alan: "Mother Goose Vice Verse," *J Am Folklore*, 75:249-259, 1962.

Howard, Dorothy: *Childlore: (Folklore in the Elementary Schools, Vol. VI)*.

Tri-University Project in Elementary Education. Lincoln, University of Nebraska Center, 1968.

Newell, William Wells: *Games and Songs of American Children.* New York, Dover Press, 1963. First published in New York: 1883; revised in 1903.

Opie, Iona and Peter: *The Lore and Language of School Children.* Oxford, Clarendon Press, 1959.

Other references important to the preparation of this paper include:

Caillois, Roger: *Man, Play and Games.* New York, Free Press of Glencoe, 1961. Translated by Meyer Barash. Original edition, Paris, Librarie Gallimard, 1958.

Erikson, Eric F.: *Childhood and Society.* New York, W.W. Norton, 1963.

Piaget, Jean: *The Moral Judgment of the Child.* Translated by Marjorie Gabain. Glencoe, Illinois, The Free Press, 1948.

Sutton-Smith, Brian and Rosenberg, J.C.: "Sixty Years of Historical Change in the Game Preferences of American Children," *J Am Folklore, 74*: 17-46, 1961.

CHAPTER 3

THE PLIGHT OF FREE PLAY

Diane F. Reardon

INTRODUCTION

In this final chapter devoted chiefly to play, Diane Reardon has summarized some of the literature on play. She raises the theoretical question of whether or not play is one or several entities of events in human lives. Is it possible that each theory of play can stand for a specific concept in development and/or mental health terms? Reardon asks whether a multifaceted approach to play may not make a global concept of play unnecessary. She counters this possibility with her own careful definition of play which rests on a single phenomenon in the human condition— playfulness as a subjective, internally controlled event in the life of the playing individual. The content of play and the age of the child would be irrelevant in her scheme; only the subjective attitude of the child towards the activity that is internally directed and undertaken for its own sake would define play.

After a careful examination of theoretical positions about play and a survey of the observational and experimental literature devoted to play, Reardon has proposed an experimental paradigm that would yield answers to the questions that teachers ask; "What will the effect of my intervention in a child's play be?" She leaves us with the problem of separating play from non-play and the challenge to make the best and most appropriate use of playfulness in bridging the gap between the inner life of each child and the reality of the world. —Editors

INTRODUCTION

T HE PLAY OF YOUNG CHILDREN has been described from a wide variety of viewpoints and *investigated* on many levels. A theoretical framework to relate the many facets of free play in a consistent way is conspicuously lacking. This chapter has two goals: to review the patchwork of existing theoretical attempts to develop such a framework, and to point out some of the problematic issues that seem to repeatedly plague efforts to conceptualize play in a meaningful way.

One of the more obvious obstacles to meaningful formulations of play is the attempt to include the playful activities of adults, children, and animals in a single conceptualization. Even excluding adults, neither Millar (1968) nor Berlyne (1969) concluded that play is a useful concept for study. The present paper is thus restricted to the free play of young children. Such play is assumed to exclude Little League games, Brownie meetings, and the like which begin to bring a semblance of formality to play patterns.

Following a statement of the present author's general approach and a review of early formulations, the two most extensive theoretical treatments of play are discussed. The first derives from the psychodynamic theory of development while the second is based on Piaget's theory of cognitive development. The third section relates the available empirical research to the author's proposed theoretical framework. The emphasis is on integrating previous findings. We intend to highlight areas that provide guidelines needed by teachers who wish to use play activities in the school setting.

Treatments of Play

While children have provided a wide variety of explanations and descriptions of play (Cousinet, 1951; McCullough, 1957), most adult formulations seem to have been colored by the Protestant ethic and its emphasis on the virtues of work. Erikson (1950, p. 187) points out that "adults . . . invent theories which show either that childhood play is really work (life preparation) or that it does not count (a slightly sinful pleasure)." It would seem that the poetic opinion of Schiller, that man is "fully human only when he plays" was offered before the advent of Calvinism (Schiller, 1875).

Beyond this similarity among adult perspectives, there are wide differences in the treatments of play. They can be classified along two main dimensions, those of psychological time and psychological space. In terms of time, explanatory factors are drawn from past racial history, present environmental conditions, or the assumed consequences (future) of play. Ultimately, each view is answering a different question—what causes play in general (past), what causes play in a specific situation (present), and what play is *for* (future). The past and future orientations are mainly characteristic of the early formulations.

The two poles on the space dimension are emphases on aspects of play that are 1) internal or 2) external to the psychological state of the player. In the early 1930's, observational studies of nursery school children were carried out with toys—an external approach. More recently, the differentiation of play from non-play is generally felt to require assumptions about the player's internal psychological state. As Tyler (1951) has phrased it, the presence of play "depends not upon the activity itself but upon the individual's attitude toward it." Hurlock (1964, p. 442) also emphasized the individual's non-observable motivations: "It (play) is any activity engaged in for the enjoyment it gives," rather than for an end result or due to demands of other people. This internal-external dimension is a psychological one rather than one within or without the physical person. For example, play explained by physiological factors would reflect an external rather than internal orientation. Very few treatments of play make it clear whether play is considered to be defined by observed behaviors (external) or by an inferred quality of behavior (internal). In the absence of explicit definitions, the underlying assumptions of each approach must be examined to define its position on this dimension of psychological space.

Finally, the views of play differ in their choice of types of behavior involved in the conceptualization. The psychoanalysts, of course, relate play to anxiety, conflict, and the psychosexual stages of the child described by Freud. Piaget, on the other hand, relates play to the cognitive changes during the development of the child's intellectual capacities. Some approach play from the philosophical or anthropological view (Burgers, 1966; Roberts *et al,* 1959).

Others highlight the social (Johnson, 1957) or motor aspects (Jones, 1939). The alternatives vary widely precisely because play is not limited to one form of overt behavior. Almost all of the preschool child's behavior seems to be play, for it gives no indication of a purposeful goal in adult terms. Yet the child does many other things as he plays; he is never "just playing", but always perceiving, moving, expressing himself, or learning about himself and the things of his world. Approaches differ in their emphasis on these various facets of playful behavior.

Definition and Other Theoretical Matters

In spite of the seemingly obvious variety of play behavior, the early writers in the area usually attempted to frame one criterion for distinguishing play from other activities. Such unidimensional criteria of play cannot hope to substantially clarify relations among the many subgroupings of play. Slobin (1964) has, in fact, eschewed the necessity of proposing a formal definition of play. He uses Wittgenstein's description of games as a family . . . "Family resemblance is hard to define . . . but is a network of similarities."

The definition offered below is a theoretical one, based on states of the player that must be inferred. In terms of the two dimensions of psychological time and space, this definition is an internal one, and the primary motivation for playing is in the present (i.e. the play itself). Such theoretical guidelines, however, do not provide means of identifying the "network of similarities" that makes us call certain observable behaviors "playing". In the section on empirical work, characteristics of the child and of the environment that affect play will be considered as parts of this network of observable similarities among types of play.

A Definition

Play is actively changing the elements of a potentially controllable and predictable sequence of events so that a relatively new pattern occurs. The first element of this definition is that the player is active. It is he that initiates the changes in the situation. The second element is that the player has potential control of the situation, including relinquishing control at will. Falling down is fun if you mean to; "letting" brother push you down *can* be fun.

Control in this definition has a particular meaning. Saying that the player has control or can do anything he wishes, implies he has a choice, has alternatives at many points in the process to actively choose from many possibilities. This does not mean he knows what the outcome of his actions will be—such uncertainty of what will happen provides part of the motivation. Whatever does happen, however, the player always has a choice of what to do next. Burgers (1966) has similarly characterized play as the process of maximizing one's alternatives. One alternative always available to the player is stopping at any time. Although play may be terminated by calls to supper, bedtime, and other interruptions, it cannot be extended by external consequences such as pleasing a teacher or parent. This point is also applicable to adult play. Even though we may thoroughly enjoy many of our tasks, they are usually part of the web of commitments we weave around our time. I am not playing when I cook dinner or write about play because these activities have definite end goals to which I have committed myself, albeit some time ago. Any activity serving some future goal or past commitment cannot be stopped without external consequences and thus is not play.

The third element of the definition is that play is self-motivating, i.e. motivated by the changing patterns that occur. In other words, the player doesn't have to do anything but only what he wants to do, and he can change his mind at any time to maximize his enjoyment. If his activities are carried out mainly for adult approval (a future consequence) or to fulfill previous promises or rules (past commitment), they do not fit this definition of play.

Finally, this definition serves to distinguish play from some types of aesthetic enjoyment[1] and games. Aesthetic pursuits are either passive as in visiting a museum or, if active, as in painting a picture, are not play insofar as the final product has importance to the artist. Games are self-motivating and active, but the control element is relinquished as soon as the game starts; games have rules

---

[1]The changing processes of the art world are increasingly inviting the "audience" to "play" with the changing reflections and patterns of objects determined by the position of the viewer. Experimental theater, "happenings", and other innovations similarly invite active rather than passive aesthetic enjoyment.

before they begin, either from tradition or group consensus. In play, the rules may be made up and changed as it happens along, and no one hollers "No fair!" Also, the player may choose to keep or not to keep score, and may change the scoring system at will.

Leaving further discussion of the proposed definition and how one applies it to observable behavior for a later section, let us look briefly at earlier attempts to define and explain play.

Early Efforts

Slobin (1964) has considered the literature in terms of the answers it provides to seven questions he poses. Briefly:

1. Where does energy for play come from?
2. What, if any, is the biologic function of play?
3. How does play aid the child in future development?
4. Why does play occur rather than nothing or some other kind of behavior?
5. What is the motivation for choosing a given game to play?
6. Why does a child continue to play once he has started?
7. Why does society provide the child with a given subset of all possible games?[2]

The early writings on play are concerned with the first three of Slobin's questions. The energy theories focus on the energy and biological factors (questions 1 and 2) while the functional theories focus on the future consequences of play (question 3).

Energy Theories

Schiller (1875) described the play behavior of both animals and men as "the aimless expenditure of exuberant energy", occurring with freedom from any definite external necessity. His example is at best a picturesque analogy "When hunger no longer torments the lion . . . (he) roars with the mere joy of existence." Tinklepaugh (1942) and Spencer (1873) present similar formulations, noting that children's energy is available because their "needs" are met by parents. During this same period, Lazarus (1883) proposed the opposite hypothesis, that play satisfies the physiological need for relaxation. Tolman (1932) provided a compromise interpretation

---

[2]The question of cultural effects on play will not be considered here since the work in the area emphasizes organized games rather than the more spontaneous play under consideration (cf. Sutton-Smith, 1959; Roberts and Sutton-Smith, 1962).

of the two energy views by careful wording: "Such exercise (play) will gently tire him (the player) and bring him into the demanded state of physiological quiescence." Both Tolman and Lazarus are interjecting a new dimension here by proposing that play has a useful physiological function rather than being "aimless activity". Whether play is its own end or whether it is a means to an end is not clear. "The outstanding feature (is) that the final activity is done for its own sake, or rather for its own immediate physiological results and not as a means to the satisfaction of some more ultimate appetite or aversion."

In these views, the cause or source of play is external on the dimension of psychological space. The point may become debatable as psychophysiological research forges links between the physical and psychological aspects of motivation, but these early authors clearly ignore the internal psychological state. On the time dimension, these formulations emphasize factors present while playing. Little attempt is made to relate play to other behaviors.

Functional Theory

In the functional theory of Groos, play is seen as an instinct occurring primarily *for* future utility. All play is pre-exercise, contributing to the development of functions whose maturity is reached only at the end of childhood (Groos, 1901). In his words: "A child was made by nature to go through a period of childhood in order that he may play and thus prepare himself for adult activities." Besides the future utility of play, Groos does note aspects of play occurring during the activity. As the psychological criterion of play he proposes "an act performed solely for the pleasure it affords." From the limited data available at the time he wrote, he recognized the "infant's unmistakeable happiness with contact," the circular reaction (currently a Piagetian notion), and the "pleasure of being the cause", all still generally accepted as mechanisms central to the description of play.

The functional differs from the energy theories not only on the dimension of time as described, but also on the dimension of psychological space. Groos sees play both as an activity for its own sake (internal) and as a means to an end (external). In general, it seems that these views seek an explanation of play not in the player's internal motivations, but in the physiological and genetic theories in the minds of the authors, who seek to justify play by some "rational" or external explanation.

Finally, one of the more extreme formulations places the mainspring of play far back in the player's history with no mention of individual internal motivations. For G. Stanley Hall, "Play is not doing things to be useful later, but it is rehearsing racial history." (Hall, 1922) Once again, this view is only an offshoot from the author's theory of behavior in general.

How and When Play Occurs

In these early formulations, the internal attitude of the player is not considered in depth. Basically, although physiological factors are called on for their facade of explanatory power, the "causes" of play are external to the psyche of the player. In more current views, the internal psychological state of the player is of prime importance. This is especially true of the psychoanalytic view. Both the psychoanalytic and the Piagetian conceptualizations address themselves to the fourth, fifth, and sixth of Slobin's questions—When is behavior play vs. non-play? What is the motivation for play's form? and why does play continue once it is begun?

The how and when of play can only be studied within the context of a developmental theory, since the forms of play are dictated to a great extent by the changing social, cognitive, emotional, and motor abilities of the growing child. Both the psychoanalytic ideas and the pictures of play offered by Piaget arise from their theories of development emphasizing the emotional and symbolic aspects and the sensory-motor cognitive factors respectively. In spite of their relevance to the topic at hand, it should be remembered that neither set out to write a theory of play.

The Psychoanalytic View

Cohn has put it, "For historical reasons, psychoanalytic childhood theories emphasize regression rather than progressive phenomena," (in Woltmann, 1955). Consequently, this approach, coming largely from the play therapy room, focuses on the role of play in reducing anxiety rather than in promoting growth. Although the reduction of anxiety places the approach on the internal end of the psychological space dimension, the present author feels that play influenced by anxiety, at some point of severity, ceases to be under the conscious control of the player and is thus no longer play but serving needs beyond the player's control. On the time dimension, the analytical view traces determinants of play to events in the child's past, typically some anxiety-producing traumatic event, which the therapist hopes to help unearth and resolve. Often in reports of play therapy with disturbed children, it is clear that the player is not free to do what he wants, to change his mind, or to explore freely, being restricted by his efforts to avoid direct portrayal of an anxiety-producing situation.

The first psychoanalytic view of play, beyond the comments and implications in Freud's writings, was written in 1932 by Waelder. The main function of play is the gradual assimilation, piece-meal, of anxiety connected with an experience that was too overwhelming to be assimilated immediately. This is accomplished by the defense mechanisms occurring in play: omnipotence, wish fulfillment, repetition compulsion, transformation from the passive to the active role, leave of absence from reality and from the superego, and fantasies about real objects. Although Waelder is aware of the view that play is an end unto itself, mentioning Charlotte Buhler's concept of functional pleasure (*Funktionslust*; Buhler, 1933), his prime focus is on anxiety reduction.

The myopia of the psychoanalytic view of play is the assumption that anxiety-reduction is peculiar to play or that all play is anxiety-reducing. Children spend a large portion of time playing, anxious or not, just as adults spend the major portion of their time working and talking, whether anxious or not. The use of play therapy in treating children tells us no more about play than the use of verbal therapy tells us about adult verbal interaction. Even though the psychoanalytic view of play is thus restricted, the hours of watching children play in therapy situations have resulted in interesting generalizations about play.

There are three main aspects of play that have been identified as putting psychological distance between the child and an anxiety-producing situation: the taking of various roles, the use of symbolic fantasy, and the displacement of situations in time.

Roles

Peller (1952) feels that even children's most forthright physical explorations of the environment and playful repetitions are related to their emotional needs. Taking examples of seemingly pure manipulative play, she illustrates how "when the emotional problems are known, it appears that the manipulative activity carried out with innumerable repetitions was not chosen at random." She further presents ten models of play and shows how they are related to emotional needs. These models may be divided into three classes: 1) taking omnipotence roles (imitating an admired person, dominating an imaginary or inanimate object, happy ending fantasies, "magic" rituals such as peek-a-boo); 2) changing from the passive to the active role (imitating a feared person, choosing the role of baby or under-dog purposely, choosing to be laughed at by clowning); and 3) displacing aggression (expected punishment aimed at himself, retaliation deflected to toys, and so forth). The first two groups illustrate the variety of roles possible in play. Further patterns are simultaneously playing two roles or oscillating among several roles.

The child in control can "play" with a variety of roles; a child restricted by emotional needs has a limited repertoire. One purpose of play therapy is to provide a supportive atmosphere where the anxious child can increase this repertoire to normal breadth and gain the control described in the author's definition of play.

Symbolism and Abstraction

By projecting meaning onto objects and onto his playful creations, the child can express aspects of an anxiety-producing situation while keeping a safe emotional distance. The interpretation of these symbols and abstractions by the play therapist may be drawn from the most general symbolic vocabulary started by Freud or from knowledge of the particular child's past history. The usefulness of such interpretations is determined by the reactions of the child; many instances of increased ability to verbalize feelings and anxieties as a result of insightful interpretations are reported in the literature (cf. Kardos and Peto, 1956; Moustakas and Schalock, 1955; Klein, 1955). Often, however, the therapist seems to be aware of more meaning than the child. Bender cautions "There is a tendency for . . . an observer to feel omnipotent because of the amazing things he observes in children in a play situation of his own making. We tend to forget that the child is doing these things and believes that we have done them, and we call such sessions "therapeutic" (1955).

Time Displacement

Greenacre (1959) points out that play may be made up of more than anxiety-reducing defense mechanisms and may in fact be a "dress rehearsal" for future experiences. Further "it seems to me that frequently some residue of the anxiety contributes to the fun and excitement of play." The fact that the child may be preparing for an anticipated experience he is anxious about does not substantially change the anxiety-reduction position of the classical Freudian interpretation of play. The comment does underline the flexibility of the psychodynamic position on the dimension of psychological time. Even if the child is somewhat constrained by the presence of anxiety he is able to shift his time dimension during play to keep a safe distance from the panic point, shifting from past traumas to current problems and future fears as his emotional needs dictate.

Neo-Freudian Approaches

There are psychodynamic approaches that do not support an anxiety-reducing interpretation of play. Erikson's main theme of child development, which he also applies to play, is the child's drive to achieve mastery. "Play is a function of the ego, yet the emphasis should be on the ego's need to master areas of life, especially those in which the individual finds his self, his body, and his social role wanting" (1950, p. 184).

It is not hard, when regarding these theoretical positions to consider anxiety-reduction and mastery as two sides of the same coin. Alexander (1958) sees the common element in the two emphases as problem-solving. "If one includes in the category of functional pleasure the gratification derived from the mastery of the unresolved threat of a past situation, the contradiction disappears." This line of reasoning can also account for the most frightening play activities children evolve when one assumes that the child has always before him the goal of mastery, anxiety-reduction, or problem-solving. Although anxiety-reduction and mastery may occur in play, the author feels that they are not more crucial to play than the exercise of muscles, the spending of energy, or the many other aspects of behavior that are present in and during play. Each, at various times, may provide the focus, but not the differentiating characteristic of play.

The Cognitive View of Piaget

In the psychoanalytic approach to child development and play, the child is typified as reacting to the stresses and trauma of successive psycho-sexual stages. In the cognitive theory of Piaget, the child is cast as a more active participant in his world. Play has a specific role in this theory of intellectual development. It is closely related to "adaptation", the process primarily responsible for cognitive development in Piaget's scheme of things. Adaptation is a balance between two major subprocesses—assimilation and accommodation. Assimilation of experience might best be compared to the intake of food, where, regardless of the form and character of the material assimilated, the body makes use of it according to its needs. This is illustrated behaviorally during the stage when infants literally put everything in their mouths. Accommodation, on the other hand, is the process of interaction with the environment in which the form and limitations of the material itself dictate the process; the organism modifies its behaviors to accommodate the material. In adaptation, both processes are in balance with "potentially slavish and naively realistic accommodations to reality . . . effectively held in check by an assimilatory process which can organize and direct accommodations, and in which assimilation is kept from being riotously autistic by a sufficiency of continuing accommodatory adjustments to the real world" (Flavell, 1963; p. 65). It is only periodically that the two processes are in balance and this adaptation occurs. Similarly occasions do occur when either assimilation or accommodation processes predominate. For Piaget, the patterns that are primarily asimilative are play. "In play, the primary object is to mold reality to the whim of the cognizer, in other words, to assimilate reality to various schemas with little concern for precise accommodation to that reality" (op.

cit.). Situations where accomodation is predominant, on the other hand, are labeled imitation in this theory.

Before discussing the implications of this theoretical statement, let us look at the stages of the development of play as described by Piaget. The major periods of intellectual development are the sensory-motor (0-2 years), the pre-operational period (2-8 years), the period of concrete operations (8-11 years), and the period of formal operations (11-14 years). Of interest here are the sensory-motor period consisting of six stages and that of pre-operational thought (three stages). Play in the last two periods (8-14 years) consists mainly of Piaget's "games with rules." (Although these are considered in depth in relation to the development of morality (Piaget, 1932), they will not be considered here).

Detailed descriptions of the beginnings of play during the first two years of life are derived from Piaget's observations of his own children (Piaget, 1951). In the first stage, accommodation and assimilation are just beginning to become differentiated (0-1 month), so that "primitive play begins by being almost identical with the set of sensory-motor behaviors." In stage two (1-4½ months) such behaviors as motion for the sake of motion do not constitute play since almost everything the child does at this stage has this quality. At the end of stage three (4½-9 months) play begins to develop as the child assimilates a limited number of objects into his activities. Three further qualities emerge at the fourth stage (8-11 months). Previously functional patterns of behavior are carried out for pleasure; the patterns are applied to many objects(including seemingly inappropriate ones; patterns begin to take on a ritualistic quality connected with reality (beddy-bye, pouring tea, etc). It is in the fifth stage (11-18 months) that these rituals are applied nonsensically to many situations accompanied by laughter and some awareness of their *silliness*. Finally in the sixth stage (18-24 months) the element of make-believe is fully developed and play extends to functionally irrelevant objects with no practical purpose or goal.

It is in the fourth stage that Piaget sees the firm establishment of the assimilatory behaviors and thus play, as he defines it; the child applies his ritualistic patterns of behavior to a wide range of objects with little accommodation to their proper use. His terms for this type of play during the sensory-motor period are exercise or practice play. From the ages of two to approximately eight years (the pre-operation sub-period) the appearance of symbolic play dominates the scene. (Practice play is reduced gradually in frequency, although never completely.) This is the "let's pretend" era, developing into more and more complex patterns as the child incorporates a growing facility with language and representational thought into his play. The final stage of this period is marked by the beginnings of stated regulations for make-believe play that lead into the more formal games-with-rules of the concrete operations period.

Sutton-Smith (1966) has criticized the relation of Piaget's stages to his theoretical definition of play. First, Piaget clearly implies that play decreases with age "Rule games . . . mark the decline of children's games and the transition to adult play, which ceases to be a vital function of the mind when the individual is socialized" (1951 p. 168). Sutton-Smith holds that play only becomes more differentiated with age. If one considers play as a behavior, Piaget is in fact right that children spend more of their waking hours in play than adults do. Since play is defined as the predominance of assimilation over accommodation, however, Sutton-Smith feels that fantasy and undirected thought also fit the definition and that these modes of thought do not decrease with age.

Secondly, Sutton-Smith protests relegating play to a cognitive function in the development of cognitive abilities. In his words, Piaget "uses games to illustrate the development of morality while he uses play to illustrate the development of thought. Neither time does he deal systematically with the peculiar functions of games or play in human development." Both of these criticisms, however, are based on Piaget's unconcern with non-directed thinking, fantasy, and affect. In his rejoinder to Sutton-Smith, Piaget (1966) does not defend this emphasis in his theory, which, in point of fact, was not written about play, but about cognitive development.

Sutton-Smith does try to establish that Piaget's treatment of play leads to contradictions *within his own theory*. The gist of his point is that Piaget has placed play and imitation in opposition to each other as predominating assimilation and accommodation respectively, but has given the lion's share of the work of intellectual development to the imitation-accommodation function. "Imitation is an essential factor in the constitution of representative activity, whereas play is not. It has no essential role in the structure of intellect as conceived by Piaget" (Sutton-Smith, 1966). Piaget replies that "play fits into this system without becoming subordinated to accommodative imitation. Imitation only plays the role of symbolic instrument from the moment that sensory-motor play becomes symbolic." In general, Piaget feels that his ideas have been misinterpreted (which is not a difficult achievement).

Piaget presents a paradox to these interested in play. His observations, even if leaning far to the cognitive side, have provided one of the clearest pictures of play behavior in early childhood. When one attempts to use his theoretical definitions for one's own observations, however, the translation of assimilation and accommodation to behavioral patterns is difficult at best. Further, the placing of play and imitation at opposite ends of the theoretical continuum leads to confusion in observational work. A little girl setting a play table for dinner is both "playing" house and imitating what she has seen. In this case, imitation "plays (*sic*) the role of symbolic instrument" according to Piaget. But one cannot tell behaviorally whether play or imitation is predominant. In Piaget's system it is impossible for a child to both play and imitate equally; both ends of the assimilation-accommodation see-saw cannot be down at once. By way of a wary conclusion it would obviously be wise for further investigators of play to consider the role of imitations in play and vice versa, so as to shed some behavioral light on this theoretical controversy.

Empirical Studies

Although the concepts above provide raw material for a theoretical framework covering many aspects of play, no integration will be helpful unless it is formulated in a testable way. With that in mind, the next section will provide a review of the several islands of observational and experimental work in the literature. An arbitrary distinction has been made between the effects of the child and environmental factors on play. The literature is quite rich as it relates to the first type of evidence, largely because the age of the child has long been a potent variable in developmental studies, and of course is important for play. The effects of environmental factors on play have received somewhat less attention. The problems of studying a class of behaviors that rest on assumptions about internal states that must be inferred are sidestepped by most of these studies; play is not defined with any regularity by most of the investigators but is assumed to occur in specified (usually toy-filled) situations.

Characteristics of the Child, the Player

Developmental Level or Age

Part of the theoretical difficulty in defining a "universal criterion of play" is that children's play can only be considered realistically within the changes of the developmental process. As Heathers (1955) has pointed out in discussing emotional dependence in nursery school play, "the same day he (a child) is learning emotional dependence in one situation, he is learning emotional independence in another." Similarly, the same behavior that is being seriously practiced one day becomes play behavior a week later (when the child has achieved some degree of control).

With this warning that the age-stage lines change and vary from child to child and for a given child, depending on the situation, let us look at the age-related data available.[3]

Considerable data on age differences in play were collected during the 1930's in observational studies of nursery school children. Practically theory-free, and using only the most rudimentary statistical techniques, these studies typically focus on one aspect of play (e.g. social, choice of toys, motor play). Since, as the child's age increases, his play gradually expands from motor and sensory activities to include the social sphere, the studies below have been arranged in this order insofar as possible.

Although materials rich in sensory possibilities have often been used by clinicians (Murphy, 1941) and IQ tests incorporate motor tasks, little experimental work has been done to verify Piaget's description of play in the sensory-motor stage. Manipulative play and

---

[3]Hurlock (1964) gives a descriptive picture of the typical play activities for different age groups.

watching others have been shown to be more frequent in two than in three-year-olds' free play, while three-year-olds show more verbal imaginative and group play (Manwell and Mangret, 1934; Parten, 1933). McDowell (1937) in a similar study found no difference between two and three-year-olds in type of play, but points out that the methods used did not reflect the different ways in which toys were manipulated. "A child of two is likely to play with dishes by crowding onto a table all of the dishes possible, with no apparent order or purpose. At three, he is likely to set the table in an orderly manner, playing at having a meal." A study by Cockrell (1935) offers support to the age differences found by Manwell and Mangret and notes further the greater number of repetitious activities of two-year-olds as compared to older children.

The vigorousness of play, rather than just the amount, shows a tendency to decrease with age, although this is most likely due to changes in types of activity (Fales, 1937). Koch and Streit (1932) found that although activity level varied with the type of activity engaged in, there were no changes due to age within the same type of activity.

The amount of empirical work on social factors in relation to play contrasts sharply with the dearth of social concepts in theoretical treatments. Even before play between children begins to emerge, the first social games occur between a mother and her child. Peek-a-boo, for example, begins in a simple form at about three months of age and has continued interest value until well past four years when it is played with peers (Maurer, 1967). The development of mother-child interactions, although not often focusing on play *per se* includes many relevant patterns of synchrony and reciprocal interaction that occur before the age of two (Sander, 1962; Call and Marschak, 1966; Lewis and Goldberg, 1969; Kogan, Wimberger, and Bobbitt, 1969b; Fineman, 1962).

Maudry and Nekula (1939) do not agree with those who find social play among peers emerging around two years of age (Ames, 1952). Although they found a play partner was treated "about the same as play material" up to the age of one year, at this age they report high frequencies of social interaction. This social play, however, consisted mainly of fights and quarrels over the use of materials, with cooperation only becoming the dominant mode at

1½ years of age. Green (1933) found both quarrels and cooperation appearing later than in the Maudry and Nekula study.
Further, quarrels were mostly physical until the age of three when
verbal "fighting" predominated.

Both the proportion of time spent playing and the proportion of
social play have been shown to increase with age (Heathers, 1955).
The most frequent size of social group for children two to five
years of age consists of two children with the probability of being
in larger groups (up to five children) increasing with age. In
two-thirds of the dyads observed by Parten (1933), the partners
were of the same sex.

Although these observational studies provide general information about developmental norms as related to play, it is clear that
having posed no specific questions or hypotheses they do not
answer any of the problems implied in the theoretical writings.
The use of specific categories of observation related to previous
research or theoretical concepts is minimal. The amount of time
spent in a broadly defined activity can at best provide general
data; delineation of types of cooperative social play and the particular use made of manipulable materials should highlight differences
due to developmental age. Further, some areas have received little
attention. The skills of fine and gross motor activities and the
use of language in play as compared to non-play have not been
investigated.

Intelligence

In those studies where the IQ scores of normal children have
been related to play, few differences have been reported. Intelligence has little effect on choice of playmates (Parten, 1933;
Challman, 1932) or activity level (Koch and Streit, 1932). Boys
who play together are somewhat closer in IQ score than girl friends
(Wellman, 1931). Research comparing the play stages of the
mentally retarded to those proposed by Piaget have shown conflicting results (Capobianco, 1960; Rosenzweig, 1954; Woodward,
1963).

Sex

The role of sex differences has received much attention in the developmental literature and much of the data has been collected in free situations (Sears, 1951; Sears and Pintler, 1947; Lewis and Goldberg, 1969a). Since sex differences are typically analyzed as a matter of course in developmental studies, this literature is a rich source of hypotheses. For example, since two-thirds of two to five-year-olds' play partners are of the same sex, one might ask how their play differs from that of mixed pairs. In the realm of imitation, the sex of the model as related to sex of the subject has been shown to be crucial (see Flanders, 1968 for review of imitation research), as well as the sex appropriateness of the behavior being modeled (Freyear and Thelen, 1969). Further, the development of varying sex-role expectations may affect play as much as the child's actual sex; creativity has been related to sex-role in this way by Biller, Singer and Fullerton (1969).

Differences in play styles of girls and boys have also been described and studied by play therapists (Erikson, 1951) and in research using doll play (Levin and Wardwell, 1962). In doll play, for example, boys are in general found to be more aggressive than girls; the more precise finding is that this is true only for physical aggression, with girls exhibiting more verbal aggression (Johnson, 1951).

Personality and Affective Behavior

The possible relations of free play to personality characteristics are a complex network. Lieberman's factor analytic work resulted in a major factor of playfulness (spontaneity, manifest joy, and sense of humor) which was in turn related to divergent thinking. She hypothesized that this trait found in kindergarten samples develops into a personality trait in later life (Lieberman, 1965; 1966).

Rather than using playfulness as a measure of one aspect of personality, play therapy is sometimes used as a means of personality assessment, as well as for diagnosis and treatment of childhood disorders. Klein emphasizes the substitution of free play for the free association techniques used in therapy with adults (1955).

Research on affective aspects of play have included variables such as compliance, aggression, affection, stereotyped (routine) play, family relations, and racial prejudice. The types of play recorded may be analyzed in and of themselves or related to teacher or parent ratings of the child, or observations of the child in another situation. Levin and Wardwell (1962) have reviewed the research using doll play situations and point out one major problem in interpretation—how to tell when the play observed is a replication of the child's daily experience and when it is an expression of fantasy or wish fulfillment. He notes four criteria for play to be accepted as "wish fulfilling fantasy": 1) evidence that there are in "real life" some restraints against the expression of the behavior in question; 2) a desire for such expression; 3) little overt manifestation of the behavior; and 4) the appearance of the behavior in fantasy. He concludes that few studies fulfill these criteria and suggests ways of classifying play responses and manipulating antecedent conditions to overcome this problem.

Since play is assumed (by the psychoanalysts) to reveal personality through expression of fantasy material, the relation of play (observable) to fantasy (unobservable) is of concern. This issue will be postponed until the final section for lack of empirical data.

The Effects of Environmental Factors on Play

Although age differences have been discussed above, there is a further relation between level of development and play, mediated by the environment. Much information on early development of sensory and motor skills is available in the child development literature. For example, the bulk of research on vision and touch and their coordination at one time implied that tactual perception developed first. Pick *et al.* (1969) have begun revising our ideas in this matter, however, with results that show vision to be operative earlier than had been thought. Flavell and Hill agree that "it is vision rather than touch that appears to be the developmentally precocious dominant source of perceptual information" (1969, p. 9).

Similar research on the learning and performance capacities of young children provide much information that is indispensible to a developmental understanding of play. Normative and experimental data on visual attention to novel and incongruous stimuli (Lewis and Goldberg, 1969b), the role of eye contact in social behavior (Robson, 1967) and peer interaction patterns (Caldwell,

1962; Madsen, 1969; Doland and Adelberg, 1967; Bandura and Whalen, 1966) provide developmental norms for behaviors that often appear in play.

There are specific aspects of the environment, however, that have been studied in direct relation to play. The novelty and complexity of toys, their feedback potential, and stress-inducing manipulations.

Novelty

Both Millar (1968) and Berlyne (1969) have provided critical reviews on this aspect of play. Much of the evidence presented derives from the exploratory behavior of animals and is related, in Berlyne's case, to hypotheses concerning the arousal value of novel, complex and incongruous stimuli. In brief, he proposes that the amount of exploration is greatest when the arousal value of the stimulus is optimal; familiar objects do not provide sufficient stimulation to elicit play and a very strange or complex object is too arousing, provoking fear and avoidance, rather than exploration or play.

Novelty, however, is used in diverse ways by various investigators. Included are novelty (no previous experience), surprise (violation of expectations), complexity (number of elements) and uncertainty (conflicting stimulus elements). (Berlyne has pointed out similar distinctions.) In terms of studying the effects of these variables on play, novelty has received the most attention. Mendel (1965) found that novel toys elicited more play than familiar ones. (Gilmore (1966) found similar overwhelming choices of novel toys, although in his studies, the novel toys were compared to simple rather than familiar toys.

Novelty literature on visual attention to stimuli varying in complexity, and so forth, does not provide a perfect analogy for the effects of these variables on play; play is active and in play the child is acting on something or someone. The consequences of his actions vary widely according to the properties of the play object's feedback potential.

Of course, the highest potential occurs when the play object is another person. The effects of feedback in this situation have been neatly illustrated by Wahler (1967). The social reinforcer of peer attention was changed from baseline rates by instructing the subject's playmates to respond only when the subject was carrying out specific types of play. The play categories shifted in each case to those resulting in reinforcement by peers. The similar power of adult reinforcement has been used to treat a variety of clinical problems (Krasner and Ullman, 1965).

Leuba and Friedlander (1968) have shown the eliciting power of audio-visual feedback using automated *toys*. In an earlier study, higher rates of response occurred when the visual feedback was spatially variable than when it appeared consistently at the same place.

Although observational studies have compared the amount of time spent with various toys (McDowell, 1937; Parten, 1933; Koch and Streit, 1932; Beiser, 1955), the results provide little more than rank order preferences for specific objects. One area of investigation necessary is the investigation of the relative play time with toys having differing degrees of each of the following qualities: novelty, complexity, uncertainty, and feedback potential and variability. Beyond, counting the number of seconds spent with a given toy, the number of different uses occurring will provide needed information on the non-exploratory aspects of play. Previous work on the preferability of stimulus dimensions may be generalizable to earlier manipulatory and exploratory play, but further work is necessary on the effects of stimulus dimensions on symbolic play. Phillips (1945), for example, has shown that realistic dolls evoke more exploratory than symbolic play when compared to simple figures. Similarly, confronted with irregular arrangements of doll house furniture, children tend to spend more time in "organizational" play than when presented with a more regular arrangement (Pintler, 1945).

Such organizational manipulation is usually coded as stereotyped play, which is typically exhibited in early doll play sessions and by anxious subjects. Conceivably, the amount of explorations elicited by a toy might be complementary to the amount of symbolic play evoked. Does the perennial popularity of empty boxes as toys reflect the added degrees of freedom of non-realistic materials having no specified function or use? Many such experimental questions come to mind. How do anxious children react to such toys? Will a complex toy evoke symbolic play after a period of exploration? (Perhaps toys that break down early are assumed by toy companies to be useless after this exploration phase.) What kinds of feedback uncertainty are optimal for various response classes at various ages?

Temporary Affective States

Studies of the effects of various stressful manipulations on children's play are few but well-integrated with theoretical hypotheses. The Gilmore experiments (1966) mentioned earlier varied anxiety of subjects (children waiting for tonsillectomies compared to school children) and measured the time spent with toys relevant and irrelevant to the hospital setting. In two further experiments he manipulated the expectancies of painful auditory or visual overstimulation and presented toys that were novel or simple and auditory or visual. Regardless of anxiety level, he found consistent choices of novel over simple toys, and a greater preference for novelty among the anxious children. In Mendel's study, children from three to five years of age also played more with novel than with familiar toys but the differences were greater for the less anxious subjects (1965). Whether the different effects of anxiety in the two studies are due to age differences or the use of simple vs. complex stimuli as comparisons for the novel toys is not clear. The differences due to anxiety alone in Gilmore's study were themselves complex. He proposed that, at moderate levels of anxiety, play is counterphobic, i.e. children play more with toys related to their anxiety while at extreme levels of anxiety, reactions to such relevant toys were phobic, i.e. they were avoided.

The slightly threatening situation of having mothers leave the room decreased play activity in one and two and one-half year-old children, more so for the younger group (Cox and Campbell, 1958). In another study, the presence of a relative stranger inhibited fear responses to sudden events and resulted in more play than when the child's mother was present (Schwartz, 1968). A possible relation of fear to play activity is offered in Bronson's analysis of fear as a reaction to novel visual patterns (1968).

A classic study in the developmental literature offers a final example of the technique of manipulating affective states and measuring the effects on play. The investigators (Barker, Dembo and Lewin, 1941) simply placed a wire screen between the child and highly attractive toys he had played with briefly. Regression of play activity (less constructiveness) was predicted to result from this frustration. Although the results confirm their hypothesis, a range of individual differences prompted Block and Martin (1954) to repeat the study using children differing in ego control, as rated independently in behavior observations. They found that constructiveness in the face of frustration was significantly correlated with ego control ratings.

Although no experimental manipulations are used in doll play, many studies have attempted to relate aggressiveness to a variety of factors (Levin and Wardwell, 1962). In the face of differences in rating methods and the vagueness of fantasy aggression's relation to life experience, these studies provide more questions than clues to the role of aggression in play. Experimental work on modeling has teased out many of the important factors determining the imitation of aggressive behaviors (Bandura, 1962).

Singularly lacking are studies of the effects of positive affect on play or the expression of such affect during play. Although many smiles and laughs of children have been analyzed, they are typically used as measures of "sense of humor" (Young and Frye, 1966). Are there systematic differences in play that is accompanied by smiling, laughing, and other signs of positive affect? Research on humor has emphasized its cognitive aspects (Zigler, Levine and Gould, 1966; 1967) and the role of the social setting (Henker and Kosslyn, 1970). Certainly the cognitive and social correlates of smiling and laughing in play also deserve investigation.

Play as a Concept

It is clear from the preceding sections that there has been little communication between those offering theoretical thoughts on play and those collecting the data. Exceptions are the work of Sutton-Smith and that of Gilmore, in which both the theoretical and empirical aspects of play are considered. Because of the variety of approaches, many only considering play as part of a larger theoretical problem, little agreement has evolved as to the usefulness of the concept.

In 7947, Schlosberg passed a judgment on the conceptual value of play that has yet to be successfully challenged: "Play is a totally vague, scientifically useless concept. It covers a motley of behaviors which ought to be investigated separately." As indicated above, the recent empirical studies of developmental psychologists follow this suggestion, providing data on play in the course of investigations of other childhood behaviors. Further, recent reviews (Millar, 1968; Berlyne, 1969) offer little support for considering play as an area of conceptual value, although the continued publication of such reviews indicates a paradoxical degree of interest in the problem.

Restricting this chapter to the free play of children and defining play in terms of internal psychological states only somewhat reduces Schlosberg's "motley of behaviors". If further work on children's play is not to add to the confusion, three definitional issues must be considered. First, the study of the motivational aspects of play as opposed to those of nonplay is necessary. New ways of assessing motivation will be helpful if play is to be considered a class of behaviors defined by inferences about internal psychological states. Secondly, the relation of play to development in general must be clarified. If most of children's behavior is play, there is little to be gained in separating play from other behaviors occurring during development. Finally, the relation of play to fantasy and "reality-based" behaviors remains the focus of some controversy.

The Question of Motivation in Play

Defining play as self-motivating does not solve the motivational question, but admittedly raises further theoretical and empirical problems. As Berlyne has pointed out, to say that a behavior provides its own reinforcement is only to say that the reinforcement is internal; this concept of intrinsic motivation leaves room for a variety of interpretations. The dynamics of such reinforcements proposed by psychology in general vary widely. Internal reinforcements have been interpreted as the reduction of uncertainty or anxiety, feelings of mastery, success at problem-solving, keeping arousal at the optimal level, and effectance motivation. Klinger (1969) has discussed many of these motivational constructs and concludes that none has been sufficiently substantiated as the motivational basis of play.[4]

None of these concepts is peculiar to play. Any may or may not be present depending on individual and situational differences. Such motivational states may affect many types of behavior. The effects of manipulations used to vary anxiety, uncertainty, mastery, etc., might tell us something about motives operating in particular play situations, but not about the peculiar motivational qualities of play that distinguish it from non-play.

It is proposed here that there are two levels of motivation going on in play. Any of the same motivations that affect behavior in general may affect play activity, but they are subordinate to the primary motivational quality of play—that the player is in control of his own actions and free to play according to his moment-to moment whims.

There is little choice or control and, consequently, little play, when children are confronted by a task having implicit or explicit instructions to solve a problem or learn the material. In all such cases, adult approval is given on a contingency basis. In play, the judgments of the adult world are kept at bay. A limited area is marked out in which the child himself decides not only what he will do, but what it means and what it is worth. Although the deterministic position of psychology in general offers some concepts of "intrinsic motivation" as mentioned, the field is poor in concepts to describe behaviors that serve no "useful" purpose or fill no existing need. Only the existential therapies deal with the problem of freedom as such and the choice of goals. The functional autonomy of Gordon Allport and other such fringe concepts might be considered in relation to the motivational bases of play.

Such a theoretical formulation of the motivational quirks of play, however, must be applicable to empirical investigations, if play is characterized by the player's freedom, how can it be studied using controlled experimental conditions? There is a set of paradigms that offers some hope for exploring this motivational question. These designs would study the effects of differing amounts

---

[4]Piaget, it should be noted, *assumes* that all organisms are motivated to behave, but does not discuss why organisms are motivated to behave in different ways at different times.

of freedom on the quality and quantity of behavior to substantiate or disconfirm the proposal that freedom significantly increases the play-like quality of behavior.

An example of such a design is the following. Three randomly selected groups of four-year-olds would spend ten minutes with the same collection of toys. Subjects in the first group are left free to do as they please, although an adult is in the room reading. The second group is introduced to the same situation but suggestions are made throughout the ten minutes that each subject do what one of the children in the first group did, at the same time in the session that the first child did it. (Why don't you build a tower with the blocks now? or have you tried the wind-up toy yet? Why don't you try it now?) Finally, the situation is presented to the third group of children as a series of formal tasks, perhaps even as a test.

Similar designs using induced anxiety, failure-rigged toys, or varying levels of arousal (physiological and behavioral) would clarify how free play differs from play restricted by these various manipulations. Of crucial importance in this type of paradigm is the selection of meaningful dependent variables. With the assistance of video tape and computer analyses, exploratory efforts could include measures along a variety of dimensions. Preliminary work of the author with retarded children has indicated the importance of including measures of affective, attentional, and linguistic behaviors as well as information on patterns of mobility and general activity level.

The motivational question in play has implications for psychology in general. Few studies have been designed to elicit data tied to theoretical concepts while at the same time leaving the subject completely free in the situation. It is probable, in fact, that adults cannot be entirely free from their assumptions about any experimental setting; they tend to be restricted by what they deduce the purpose of the study to be. Non-purposeful behavior has not been studied well in psychology and we have few concepts for thinking about *fun* activities such as loafing, fooling around, taking a drive. In the case of play, it will be very useful to determine how children act under varying degrees of restriction. If the definition of play based on active, potentially controllable and self-motivation qual-

for mother to find, and finally as a formal group of hide-and-seek. Thus different forms of behavior may express similar types of play, while the same behavior may change from non-play to play and back again to non-play as development progresses.

Play, Fantasy, and Reality-Based Behavior

The third issue underlying controversies about a definition of play is its degree of "reality". On the one hand, play has been described as "a leave of absence from reality as well as from the superego" (Waelder, 1932). On the other hand it "binds the individual more closely to reality" (Holmes, 1965). If the definition proposed at the beginning of the chapter is accepted, the player is free to play with either the very real qualities of sand and mud or play with his imaginary companions. He can recreate situations that actually did occur or create totally new situations. The possibilities are wide and can be conceptualized as shown in Table 3-I.

TABLE 3-I

REALITY ORIENTATION DIMENSION IN RELATION TO PLAYING
WITH THINGS AND PEOPLE, AND NON-PLAYING WITH THOUGHTS

Object		*Orientation*			
Referent	*Reality*				*Idiosyncracy*
(Play)					Free
People	Imitation	Role-playing			interaction
Things	Exploration	Construction			Creation of
(Non-play)					new things
None	Thinking	Planning	Musing	Dreaming	Fantasy

This conceptualization of play as spanning degrees of reality orientation does not take into account the concepts of either the Freudian or Piagetian approaches. Only the imitation entry would be excluded by Piaget's theory, since imitation is accommodation in his scheme of things, and the opposite of play. Fantasy and dreaming would be classed as assimilation processes by his definitions, although Piaget himself does not relate these activities to play or assimilation explicitly. The other entries would be classified according to the processes involved, any given instance being classed as either predominantly assimilatory or accommodatory.

Those using the Freudian approach to play bring up further questions in the area of reality orientation. Their emphasis on the expression of internal motivations in play is not limited to the categories of fantasy and dreaming. Many psychodynamic adherents extract full interpretations of idiosyncratic needs and anxieties from the most "reality-oriented" activities, such as exploration of interesting toys. Thus, from their view, it would seem that all play should be classified under the idiosyncratic end of the reality orientation dimension.

Other issues, although not crucial to the conception of play proposed in this chapter, are presumably crucial to the psychodynamic approach and should be included in their treatments of play. Is most play expressing anxieties or resolving unconscious conflicts? Is a successful resolution of problems through play intentional or unconscious? The questions of consciousness and intention in play are problematic. Like many psychodynamic concepts they are not easy to operationalize or put into testable statements. They are merely indicated here as problems within Freudian theory for their treatment of play.

*   *   *

These issues of the role of motivation, developmental changes, and orientations to reality have been quietly tabled by many authors. Typically the assumptions about these matters are implicit, especially in theoretical writings, and these assumptions predetermine one's view of play. The proposed definition of play in this paper is only that—a proposal—but one that attempts to be specific in its assumptions relevant to such issues. Suggestions have been made for experimental designs that could transform the proposal into an hypothesis. If the hypothesis is supported, certain aspects of the motivation, developmental, and reality issues will have been clarified, and play, a concept describing a class of behaviors, will merit further specific study. Until that time, the best source of information on what children do in their free time is the general research literature of those studying child development.

REFERENCES

Alexander, F.: A contribution to the theory of play. *Psychoanalytic Quarterly, 27,* 175-193, 1958.
Ames, L. B.: The sense of self of nursery school children as manifested by their verbal behavior. *J of Genet Psychol, 81,* 193-232, 1952.
Bandura, A.: Social learning through imitation. In Jones, M. R. (Ed.)

Nebraska Symposium on Motivation, Lincoln, University of Nebraska Press, 1962.

Bandura, A. and Whalen, C. R.: The influence of antecedent reinforcement and divergent modeling cues on patterns of self-reward. *J Pers Soc Psychol, 3,* 373-382, 1966.

Barker, R. B., Dembo, T. and Lewin, R.: Frustration and regression: An experiment with young children. *University of Iowa Studies in Child Welfare, 18,* 1-314, 1941.

Beiser, H. R.: Play equipment for diagnosis and therapy. *Am J Orthopsychiatry, 25,* 761-770, 1955.

Bender, L.: Therapeutic play techniques. *Am J Orthopsychiatry, 25,* 784-787, 1955.

Berlyne, D. E.: Laughter, humor, and play. In Lindzey, G. and Aronson, E. (Eds.), *The Handbook of Social Psychology, Vol. 2.* Reading, Mass., Addison-Wesley, 1969.

Biller, H. B., Singer, D. L. and Fullerton, M.: Sex-role development and creative potential in kindergarten-age boys. *Developmental Psychology, 1,* 291-296, 1969.

Block, J. and Martin, B.: Predicting the behavior of children under frustration. Paper presented at the meeting of the Midwestern Psychological Association, Columbus, 1954.

Bronson, G.: The development of fear in man and other animals. *Child Dev, 39,* 409-432, 1968.

Buhler, C.: The social behavior of children. In Murchison, C. (Ed.), *Handbook of Child Psychology,* Worchester, Clark University Press, 1933.

Burgers, J. M.: Curiosity and play: Factors in the development of life. *Science, 154,* 1680-1681, 1966.

Caldwell, B. M.: The usefulness of the critical period hypothesis in the study of filiative behavior. *Merrill-Palmer Quarterly of Behavioral Development, 8,* 229-242, 1962.

Call, J. D. and Marschak, M.: Styles and games in infancy. *J Am Acad Child Psychiatry, 6,* 193-210, 1966.

Capobianco, R. J. and Cole, D. A.: Social behavior of mentally retarded children. *Am J of Ment Defic, 64,* 638-651, 1960.

Challman, R. C.: Factors influencing friendships among preschool children. *Child Dev, 3,* 146-158, 1932.

Cockrell, D. L.: A study of play of children of preschool age by an unobserved observer. *General Psychology Monographs, 17,* 377-469, 1935.

Cousinet, R.: Investigation of what students think of play and work. *Journal of Psychology and Pathology, 44,* 556-568, 1951.

Cox, F. N. and Campbell, D.: Young children in a new situation with and without their mothers. *Child Dev, 39,* 123-131, 1958.

Doland, D. J. and Adelberg, R.: The learning of sharing behavior. *Child Dev, 38,* 695-700, 1967.

Erikson, E. H.: *Childhood and Society.* New York, Norton, 1950.

Erikson, E. H.: Sex differences in the play configurations of preadolescents. *Am J Orthopsychiatry, 21,* 667-692, 1951.

Fales, E.: A comparison of vigourousness of play activities of preschool boys and girls. *Child Dev, 8,* 144-158, 1937.

Fineman, J.: Observations on the development of imaginative play in early childhood. *J Am Acad Child Psychiatry, 1,* 167-181, 1962.

Flanders, J. P.: A review of research on imitative behavior. *Psychol Bull, 69,* 316-337, 1968.

Flavell, J.: *The Developmental Psychology of Jean Piaget.* Princeton, Van Nostrand, 1963.

Flavell, J. H. and Hill, J. P.: Developmental psychology. *Ann Rev Psychol, 20,* 1-55, 1969.

Freyear, J. L. and Thelen, M. H.: The effect of sex of model and sex of observer on the imitation of affectionate behavior. *Developmental Psychology, 1,* 298, 1969.

Gilmore, J. B.: The role of anxiety and cognitive factors in children's play behavior. *Child Dev, 37,* 397-416, 1966.

Green, E. H.: Group play and quarreling among preschool children. *Child Dev, 4,* 302-307, 1933.

Greenacre, P.: Play in relation to creative imagination. *Psychoanal Study Child, 14,* 61-80, 1959.

Groos, K.: *The Play of Man.* London, Wm. Heineman, 1901.

Hall, G. S.: *Youth: Its Education, Regimen, and Hygiene.* New York, D. Appleton, 1922.

Henker, B. A. and Kosslyn, S.: Social influences on children's humor responses. Paper presented at meeting of the California State Psychological Association, Monterey, 1970.

Heathers, G.: Emotional dependence and independence in nursery school play. *J Genet Psychol, 87,* 37-57, 1955.

Holmes, Douglas: A contribution to a psychoanalytic theory of work. *Psychoanal Study Child, 20,* 384-393, 1965.

Hurlock, E. B.: *Child Development.* New York, Fourth Edition, McGraw-Hill, 1964.

Johnson, E.: Attitudes of children toward authority as projected in their doll play at two age levels. Unpublished Doctoral Dissertation, Harvard University, 1951.

Johnson, L. V.: A study of socialization in block play. *Journal of Educational Research, 50,* 623-626, 1957.

Jones, T. D.: *The Development of Certain Motor Skills and Play Activities on Young Children.* New York, Teachers College, 1939.

Kardos, E. and Peto, A.: Contributions to the theory of play. *Br J Med Psychol, 29,* 100-112, 1956.

Klein, M.: The psychoanalytic play technique. *Am J Orthopsychiatry, 25,* 223-237, 1955.

Sutton-Smith, B.: Piaget on play: A critique. *Psychol Rev, 173,* 104-110, 1966.

Tinkelpaugh, L. L.: Social behavior of animals. In Moss, F. A. (Ed.), *Comparative Psychology.* New York, Prentice-Hall, 1942.

Tolman, E. C.: *Purposive Behavior in Animals and Men.* New York, Century, 1932.

Tyler, L. E.: The relationship of interests to abilities and reputation among first-grade children. *Educational Psychology Measurement, 11,* 255-264, 1951.

Waelder, R.: The psychoanalytic theory of play. *Psychoanal Q, 2,* 208-224, 1932.

Wahler, R. G.: Peer reinforcement control in a free play setting. Paper presented at the meeting of the Society for Research in Child Development, New York, March 1967.

Wellman, B.: The school child's choice of companions. *Journal of Educational Research, 24,* 126-132, 1931.

Woltman, A. G.: Concepts of play therapy techniques. *Am J Orthopsychiatry, 25,* 771-783, 1955.

Woodward, M.: The application of Piaget's theory to research in mental deficiency. In Ellis, N. R. (Ed.), *Handbook of Mental Deficiency,* New York, McGraw-Hill, 1963.

Young, R. D. and Frye, M.: Some are laughing: Some are not—why? *Psychological Reports, 18,* 747-754, 1966.

Zigler, E., Levine, J. and Gould, L.: Cognitive process in the development of children's appreciation of humor. *Child Dev, 37,* 507-518, 1966.

Zigler, E., Levine, J. and Gould, L.: Cognitive challenge as a factor in children's humor appreciation. *J Pers Soc Psychol, 6,* 332-336, 1967.

CHAPTER 4

RULES AND FREEDOM: GAMES AS A MECHANISM FOR EGO DEVELOPMENT IN CHILDREN AND ADOLESCENTS

LAYMAN E. ALLEN[1]

INTRODUCTION

A NEW PHASE of Part I begins with this chapter by Layman Allen. The chief difference between the earlier and the later chapters lies in an emphasis first on play, then later on games. Allen summarized the proceedings of a "Rules and Freedom" conference that had been set up by Dr. Eli Bower with the intention of bringing together professional people having a wide variety of backgrounds. In many cases practitioners in one field did not know about the interest in and uses by practitioners in another. In a situation conducive to free exchange of orientations and objectives, the assembled professionals expressed their own positions and explored the implications of positions held by the others. In each case the emphasis was on games as devices to achieve some goal for the participants. It became clear that the game referrents themselves varied considerably, but an even greater variety of views of games and play were held by the professionals of different discip-

[1]Report on Workshop F, 44th Annual Meeting of the American Orthopsychiatric Association, Washington, D.C., March 23, 1967. Dr. Eli M. Bower of the National Institute of Mental Health organized and served as Chairman of the workshop. Resource Participants were Professors Layman E. Allen of the University of Michigan, Nadine M. Lambert of the University of California at Berkeley, and Loyda M. Shears of the Claremont Graduate School.

lines. Some of the variety arose from the use to be made of the games-in-situation by the child-participants who were to be treated, taught or simply entertained.

Definitions of game and play occupied the conference at some length, and the role-playing that characterizes both emerged as a third entity in its own right in some orientations. Allen noted that the group recommended an empirical study should be undertaken to describe and predict the effects of adult intervention on games and game participants. Such study could be directed toward a better understanding of the game-play continuum as it changes over the developmental sequence. It was emphasized that it was not clear at what level of skill or maturity it would be appropriate to initiate the next level of the sequence. However, it seemed clear that the participant's relationship to rules was central to development and emerging maturity. For example cheating seems to precede negotiated changes in the rules. The urgency of a user's need for the knowledge that such research would yield was highlighted by the conference members' concern for the effects of any new intervention that they might undertake and/or the effect of their usual procedures with different populations or ages of children. They wanted guidelines as they ventured out to improve the welfare and maturational development of children through each child's game-play life. The three following chapters represent efforts to fill the need for descriptive and predictive research findings.
—Editors

T HE GROWING INTEREST in games and game-like situations as learning and therapeutic devices in a wide variety of fields of application is reflected in the diversity of the participants in the Second Annual Workshop on Games sponsored by the American Orthopsychiatric Association. Among the sixty participants were representatives from education (university, secondary, and elementary), law, nursing, psychiatry, psychology, recreational directors from hospitals and other institutions, and social work.

A general characterization of the aspects of games that participants were invited to explore is contained in the description of the workshop in the 1967 AOA Program:

Games, like life, are arrangements among persons in which one is free to respond or act within limits set by rules. Since participation in games is voluntary (prescribed play ceases to be play), they are accompanied by pleasurable, absorptive and possibly ego-enhancing separations from life. Games for children are societies in miniature. In the game the child strives for goals against peers based on time and space limitations and agreed upon rules. Yet game's essence is its safety and freedom for individuals and groups to try something new within fair-play rules or limits. Children's adaptability to specific social institutions requires specific game skills to function in that institution. To help lower-class children to be increasingly successful in school, can such functioning (learning to use symbols, work in groups, relate to adults, etc.) be enhanced and developed through use of games or game-like experiences? Can transition from one social setting (deprived home) to another (middle-class school) be bridged more effectively and economically by use of games? Specific examples of attempts to enhance ego processes in managing school-related activities through games use will be presented and discussed.

The discussion at the workshop centered around several general themes. The features that distinguish games from play and the relationship of both to role playing were explored at the outset with some consideration given to why it is important to distinguish games from play. The absence of a developmental sequence of games in the literature on games and discussion of the need for more information of this type was then considered. The next topic that emerged in the discussions dealt with the need to clarify the purposes of using games, with emphasis on their role as ego-enhancing activities. Some of the problems of introducing games into various institutional settings were explored, and finally, games that various participants found useful for various purposes were listed and described briefly.

I. Games, Play, and Role Playing

In characterizing games and distinguishing them from play and role playing, at least seven different kinds of games were identified: recreational, pedagogical, therapeutic, role-playing, human interaction, negotiation, and those that serve as a basis for a mathematical theory of strategy. Although there was no express reference to the characterization of a game given by Anatol Rapoport in *Two-Person Game Theory—The Essential Ideas* (1966), the properties there stipulated as essential for a game from the viewpoint of the

Theory of Games were all discussed. Rapoport lists six properties and suggests (pp.17-21) that a game is the totality of rules which define these six essential properties for that particular game:

1. There are at least two bona fide players.
2. The activity begins by a choice by one or more players among a number of specified alternatives ("move").
3. Resulting from this first choice is a situation which determines
   (a) who is to make the next move, and
   (b) what alternatives are open to him.
4. Choices made by the players may or may not become known. (All choices known to everyone as soon as made constitutes a game of perfect information.)
5. There is a termination rule.
6. Every play of a game ends in a situation which determines a payoff to each bona fide player.

From this point of view a game does not depend upon:

(a) the seriousness (or lack of it) of a situation,
(b) the attitudes of the participants,
(c) the nature of the acts, or
(d) the nature of the outcomes.

Rather, it depends upon:

(a) whether certain choices of actions and certain outcomes can be unambiguously defined,
(b) whether the consequences of joint choices can be precisely specified, and
(c) whether the choosers have distinct preferences among the outcomes.

The word *game* has come to mean a great many things to a great many people, ranging along a continuum from "life is a game" to the concept of a very specific, highly delineated entity. In order to insure, therefore, that workshop participants were proceeding from a common conceptual base, initial discussions were directed both toward differentiating between the concepts of *play* and *game* and examining the relationship of *role-playing* to both.

In attempting to isolate those attributes peculiar to each, play and game were differentiated and compared along several dimensions. Play was felt to be a free, spontaneous activity which cannot be prescribed and in which there is no predictable outcome: problems, goals, and rules may change as play progresses. Both games and play contain an element of non-reality, a stepping out of oneself into another social system, and role-playing can appear in both. In addition both can be problem-solving for an individual. The difference here lies in the fact that in a game situation, prescribed roles and rules follow from predetermined goals and enable the player to reach these designated end-points, whatever they may be. Play is more spontaneous in the sense that both the goals and rules may be changed as one moves through the play situation.

Thus, in a game situation there are certain rules and roles that participants agree upon which condition what is going to happen: Players may vary the roles and the rules but there is always an awareness that something explicit is expected, and one knows whether or not he is conforming to or changing this situation. "That is not playing the game" is a colloquialism which implies that one is not really conforming to the rules of the game but is competing within the framework of a similar but nevertheless different structure. Play, on the other hand, proceeds without anticipation of what the other person is going to do, and many things are both allowable and possible.

A further distinction was drawn between the attitudes associated with playing and those associated with gaming. The gaming attitude is typically in dead earnest: Something of value is at stake and the objective is to win. On the other hand, it was suggested that the attitude of playing is less dedicated to the proposition that someone must come out ahead. However, if one looks at the game situation, it could be found that a person's attitude as he comes into it was that of playing or gaming; and similarly, one could come into the play situation with either of the two attitudes. But participation in play or game activity would tend to shape attitudes in the appropriate direction.

The playground situation was discussed at length because in this setting it becomes evident that a type of continuum exists between games and play. Rules can be implied, they are not always expressed; and this accounts for a shading in and out from one situation into the other. This is particularly evident in the kinds of spontaneous games that emerge on a playground: Kids decide they are going to engage in some activity and rules get "wired in." They might get wired in the sense of an implied set of rules, or the children may actually talk it over and be somewhat more explicit in their definition of these rules. Rules and games can, and frequently do, arise out of a relatively unstructured situation.

Since role-playing may exist in both play and games, a portion of the discussion centered upon this element and upon the distinction between it and the concept of game. Role-playing was defined as the act of *knowing* that one is taking on the role of somebody else. When young children assume the character of someone else, they actually believe that they are this other person: This would be dramatic play. Role-playing, however, is more sophisticated and entails an actual realization of deliberately taking the part of another.

Three primary differentiations between role-playing and games emerged in the discussion. The first involved the question of repetitiveness. Unlike the game which can be played again and again and a certain average achieved, there is difficulty in getting repetitiveness in role-playing because there is no specified terminal point. Thus, someone will stop playing a role because he is tired, but this is not inherent in what is going on. Secondly, it was pointed out that it is not possible either to win or to cheat at role-playing, yet the possibility of cheating (in the sense of deviating from the game's prescribed rules) is always present in a game situation. And thirdly, there is no necessary conflict of interest in role-playing. While there may be an initial conflict about being placed in a particular role (e.g., being the baby when children are playing house), once lodged into a role, there may be no competition.

In the course of the workshop discussion, the element of winning and losing emerged as one of the most frequently cited criteria by which to distinguish between play and games. Only in a game situation does a clear win-lose condition emerge. As soon as play becomes a matter of winning and losing, it becomes another communication mode. Several other elements were also felt to be necessary concomitants to a game situation: There must be specified terminal conditions; a predictable outcome; repetitiveness; a predictable sequence; a conflict of interest.

The above distinctions and the following summary of the differences between play and games served as operational definitions upon which the proceedings of the remainder of the workshop were based: When one talks about play, one has in mind a general

sort of activity which differentiates it from other kinds of activity—
an activity in which one can imagine, can have fun, can do many
things, can increase one's skill. But in talking about a game, one
is talking about a specific problem-solving situation: This doesn't
necessarily involve a social group. For example, chess has a prescribed beginning and an end. There is a definite goal and a sequence of rules upon which all participants are agreed. These rules
may be explicit or implicit: Sometimes it is necessary to penalize
players before there is general agreement, but there must be some
agreement among the participants that they will play a game according to a certain set of rules. Without this set of rules, the game
does not exist.

II. Need for Developmental Sequence of Games

The concept of and need for a developmental sequence of games
emerged as another major focal point of the workshop. Discussions
in this area developed partially in response to observations that
there is a dearth of empirically-tested game sequences which can
be used for specific age groups and partially from considering a
question about the point at which the child is able to make a transition from play to games in terms of ego-development.

While there are a number of available books containing lists of
games for various age groups, several workshop participants suggested that there is no empirical evidence that such games are proposed or evaluated in terms of the skills—social, cognitive, and
motor—that are prerequisite to meaningful participation in a game.
For example, it was pointed out that many first graders cannot play
tag: it is frequently recommended that they play tag, but many of
them cannot. The question then arises as to what there is about
being a first grader that makes tagging—i.e., running away when
someone wants to touch you instead of standing there and becoming *it*—developmentally incompatible with his repertoire of behavior and skills. At what point does a child mentally perceive that
running away is better than just standing there and being tagged?

Confronted by such questions, it was widely acknowledged by
workshop participants that increased empirical efforts should be
directed toward a formulation of the functional prerequisites of
gaming behavior: those social, perceptual, and motor skills and

the level of cognitive development which are necessary for meaningful entry into a particular game. In short, it has become increasingly necessary to specify what repertoire of behavior children must have in order to be able to play games in the first place.

In light of the above recommendation, the problem which presents itself is *how* to develop a curriculum of games that will somehow be compatible with a person's physiological development and cognitive abilities: a curriculum which would begin at zero and proceed to some nth degree of development. If one can even conceive of such a progression, how does one develop such a curriculum that starts from the beginning? In response to this question, several situations were described in which one could begin to ferret out some of the functional prerequisites of gaming behavior and in which the natural inclination towards a developmental sequence of gaming on the part of children could be observed.

Experience with children in a camp setting seems to provide valuable opportunities for observing the types of games which children make up for themselves. It was suggested that if children are given materials, they will devise games which are appropriate to their particular needs; to their frontier at that particular developmental level. From the discussions on the types of games that children devise, the concept of the *safety-valve* feature of a game emerged. This feature involves that facet of a game which constitutes a socially accepted home-base: a place where one can run and be *free* without having to say "I'm tired, or I'm afraid, or I don't want to participate." Cheating, or changing the rules, is a very primitive attempt at instituting a safety-valve feature in a game's structure. As game-playing ability progresses, however, the concept of boundaries, limits, and a structured resolution of conflict becomes more important than a "way out," although the necessity remains for a game to incorporate socially acceptable means of escaping these boundaries without repercussions in some way or another.

Professional observations of emotionally disturbed children in game situations are especially valuable in attempting to isolate developmental factors, since by establishing *why* such children are incapable for performing in a game situation, those skills requisite to gaming behavior become evident. For example, a developmental progression from motor-play techniques to cognitive areas becomes apparent when one attempts to teach disturbed children how to play. Beginning with motor play techniques seems to facilitate a transition into the cognitive areas, a fact lending support to Piaget's sensory-motor scheme of cognitive functions.

It was suggested further that the inability of emotionally disturbed and retarded children to play games is the same kind of problem that comes up in their inability to learn and their inability to have appropriate and meaningful social interactions. Picking up and expanding upon this observation, it was proposed that there is a common thread—a series of tasks—which one has to know in order to play games and in order to learn. Thus, learning and games are not two separated entities. They are both very much influenced by cognition, perception, and affect, and both require the ability to discern differences in alternatives of behavior, to make a decision, to resolve conflict, to establish social mutuality, to follow directions and orientation, to handle freedom and to handle change.

Another aspect of developmental sequence has to do not with a sequence within the game process *per se* but in the utilization of games as one of the potentials for getting through what Erickson has called critical periods of development: for example, in facilitating the transition from words signifying objects to words signifying relationships or actions, or in helping to develop motor skills that typically emerge during these developmental periods. Using the game of jacks as illustrative of this process, one can see that it not only aids in developing particular hand-skills which are very real at—for example—the second grade level, but that it also involves working with the intellectual concepts of sets and groups. Other games such as matching cards containing various geometric shapes and different colors exist for children who are passing from pre-logical concrete thought processes to more abstract thinking.

The idea of developmental sequences or developmental readiness in game playing is reinforced when one attempts to play games with emotionally impoverished children who for some reason or other have missed out on some vital developmental experiences. In such adult-child interactions, a need exists for coming down to the level at which the child now stands and for providing the necessary motivation or fundamentals which will enable him to participate at the level at which he should be functioning. Several workshop participants related experiences with this type of child in which external rewards were utilized as incentive for game playing and for achieving skills which would result from game participation. It was suggested that it is meaningless to expect an ego-deprived child to place value on winning *per se,* because he is so accustomed to failing. Thus, external rewards which are concrete and have meaning for the children on their level, particularly food, can provide an incentive for getting involved in the first place. Eventually, of course, it should be learned that one plays not only for the reward but also for what one is doing in the process of playing; but several participants seemed to feel that at the primitive states, external rewards are frequently useful incentives.

It was suggested that experienced and sophisticated users of games might constitute a select group who are using such external devices at appropriate times but who are also aware when to terminate their usage. However, it was felt useful to bear in mind that a great many other people use these external reinforcement techniques with little sophistication and as a consequence may be fostering results and attitudes which are not desirable. Perhaps rewarding a child with food is in actuality simply an act of satisfying a primary need of closeness or of providing these children with a *lap.* If a procedure were followed whereby these needs were satisfied before playing a game, extrinsic rewards would be less likely to remain associated with the game process in a disfunctional manner. Therefore, there would seem to be a delicate balance between utilizing extrinsic rewards as a catalyst when the repertoire of a player is limited and leaning upon them as a crutch so that the kind of activity going on need not be arranged so that it is intrinsically rewarding.

Many observations were made about the inadvisability of tying the learning process to the feeding process. It was pointed out that this is what typically happens in the school situation, not with food but with its equivalent in terms of social reinforcements (grades, advancement, etc.). Children who learn to expect the external reward, work just *to be told* they are right, not *to feel* they are right or *to think* that they are right. Thus, one does not find individuals who are learning because they enjoy the process of learning, but who are learning simply for the reward. Several independent streams (ego-psychological, Skinnerian S-R, Piaget) have been converging on the importance of gratifying not only physical needs but also cognitive needs as well, needs which are beginning to be felt to be not simply secondary reinforcements but rather to be more fundamental.

Several persons felt that there are a large number of intrinsic motivations contained in the gaming process: If one can hit upon the right type of game appropriate for the particular developmental level of the learner, one can effectively utilize these intrinsic gratifications as the needed incentives. For example, infants will learn movements that will lead to a rattle being set off, and they will learn the sequence just for the gratification of being able to provide themselves with a systematic sequence of stimuli. Autistic children can learn to manipulate typewriters with no extrinsic gratification.

It was suggested that if a problem is posed that is just beyond what a learner currently understands so that he is aroused to a state of curiosity, external rewards are not needed. In many situations, there may be an important relationship between the extent to which the learner perceives himself as being competent in dealing with a particular problem and the extent to which he can actually cope with it. Building a skill may significantly reduce anxieties. For example, if in arithmetic, children work on problems which are appropriate at whatever stage they happen to be, they are more likely to be able to solve them and to perceive themselves as being able to solve them: and this perception will be intrinsically reinforcing.

There are now a number of games that are so structured that a player is likely to receive the kind of positive reinforcement described above. In chess, for example, a player making a move is resolving the problem posed by his opponent's previous move and simultaneously posing a new problem for his opponent. If it is possible to arrange the situation so that all the players in such a game are at about the same level of skill in game rules and understanding the subject-matter content being dealt with in the game, the result will likely be that problems of the appropriate level of difficulty are posed: they will be difficult enough so that interest will be sustained and yet in most instances solvable so that players can perceive themselves as functioning well. In this sense, there is a similarity between computer-assisted instruction and games. In games, however, it is another person, rather than a computer, that constructs the next problem for a learner.

Setting up tournament competition in certain arithmetic games furnishes a good example of the dynamics involved in this process. Working with a group of ninety students, an equilibrium will be established by playing in three-player sets, bumping winners up and losers down so that eventually, those persons playing in each set are of about the same level of understanding. Thus, an incentive for constructing problems that are as complex as players can conceive of is established since this is how one gains in the tournament situation. If every individual in a group is at just about the same level of understanding, this means that the others for whom he is posing the problems are presented with problems just at the outer edge of what they currently understand. And yet the probability is high that they will be able to deal effectively with problems that they subjectively perceive as being difficult.

III. Ego-Enhancing Possibilities of Games

During the course of the workshop, it became evident that two different types of gaming situations were being distinguished. In the first situation, children institute and play games on their own initiative. In the second, the situation is imposed on the child by an adult who is utilizing the gaming structure in an attempt to develop or reinforce some particular ego-skill or ego-need in the child. For example, by choosing the types of games which are played, an adult can gear the games to the particular skills and abilities of a child and can thereby enhance his chances for success if this is the desired outcome. It was pointed out that people in the areas of recreation or physical education take as self-evident the fact that children will learn skills through the game process. Similarly, many people feel that games can make significant contributions to the ego structure and to the emotional development of the child. This latter contention was examined extensively during the remaining discussions.

One example of an adult's manipulating the gaming situation had already been dealt with in workshop discussions: The manipulation of external rewards—of reinforcements external to the gaming situation itself—is often utilized by the adult to induce the child to participate in the game. The question which then arises is why such participation is felt to be desirable. One answer lies in the belief that there is, at least potentially, a relationship between games and the development of ego-skills. Social group work literature has begun to define particular games in terms of their ego-rehearsal possibilities: this game for socialization, this for competitiveness, this for cooperation, this for interactive purposes. Other ego skills seen as relevant to the gaming situation consist of the management of assertiveness, aggressiveness, and hostility in socially acceptable ways. It was posited that potentially one of the greatest contributions that game situations might make is in facilitating the transition from the play of pre-school years to the work required for a successful encounter with the educational institution; and it was suggested that the exact nature of this facilitation would be a fruitful area for research.

If one views games as having ego-building potentialities, one must also recognize that the utilization of games to achieve a specific purpose involves a value judgment: What are the kinds of things, the kinds of models, the kinds of ego and problem solving skills that one ought to have when he reaches maturity? By answering these questions, by choosing one game over another, one jumps right into the area of values. It was felt that although specific value systems are involved, their existence is largely a taboo topic in many considerations of the purposes of games; and it was suggested that if adults are bent on *meddling,* on utilizing games for extrinsic purposes, it is imperative that these value issues be made explicit.

A study by Maccoby and Modiani was cited in connection with the cultural values underlying various games. In teaching a Mexican game to American children, or an American game to Mexican children, it was found that modifications soon began to appear in the social structure of the game, modifications which were felt to be consistent with some of the cultural values which were inherent in the notion of games as each group saw it. The way games change in a situation such as this gives some idea of what they are providing for children, what kinds of experiences, what kinds of ego rehearsals they contain. Each culture seems to have a differential impact on children and the impact seems to be mediated in relation to the kinds of games that the children find most satisfying within that culture.

The possibility was also suggested that unless one is very sure about the type of game one is utilizing, unless one understands the dynamics of its ego-building possibilities, there is a chance that one can build in or magnify exactly the opposite of what he thinks he is accomplishing. Analogy was drawn between games and newly developed drugs: They both have side-effects. For example, it is often felt that by channelling aggression through the gaming situation, aggressive behavior can be regulated in other social settings. One workshop participant noted, however, that in her experience, the aggression stimulated in dodge-ball frequently carried over into aggressive behavior in the classroom and after school. Several others voiced the opinion that violence in a game situation reinforces violence outside of the immediate game setting, a fact which might have some connection with Karl Menninger's analysis of violence in our society—the argument that we are not only intrigued with violence, but we teach it, foster it, encourage it, and condone it in a wide variety of ways. The point to be made is that anyone involved in utilizing games with children should be aware both of the types of activity which he might be fostering both advertently and inadvertently and of the value systems within which he is operating.

The comments on the transmission of aggression and statements that learning how to participate in a game facilitates the individual's ability in decision-making are inextricably tied to the concept of transfer. The important issue involved is whether, in fact, transfer can be expected to occur between activity in a game situation and similar activities in real life. How does one look at the transferability of the skill or learning that takes place in the game setting in relation to the functioning of people in non-game life. For example, does playing Crows and Cranes, which involves moving back and forth from one group to another, really have anything to do with the ability of a child to cope with moving from one location to another? What are the elements in life and games that are sufficiently related to be conducive to the process of transfer? While several experiences with effective transfer were cited by workshop participants, especially transfer which occurred from individual therapy session to a school situation, the dynamics of the transfer process were felt to be wide open to and beckoning for empirical investigation.

TABLE 4-I
GAMES RECOMMENDED BY PARTICIPANTS

Name of Recommender	*Name of Game*	*Purpose of the Game*	*Use with what Audience*
Layman Allen	WFF'N PROOF— The Game of Modern Logic	To teach mathematical logic and develop positive attitudes towards this kind of symbol-handling activity and towards self in doing it.	6th grade through college
	ON-SETS— The Game of Set Theory	To teach set theory and confidence in dealing with it.	1st grade through junior college
	The PROPAGANDA Game	To teach some of the manipulative and emotional techniques that are used to influence public opinion.	junior and senior high school
	CONFIGURATIONS— Number Puzzles and Patterns	A solitaire game to teach some projective geometry.	junior high school through college
	EQUATIONS	To teach arithmetic and confidence in dealing with it.	1st grade through high school
C. Brush	Games	Available Henry Brush, Bus. Mgr. 1717 Hillside Road Southhampton, Penn. 18966	all age groups
Bob Freeman	*Card Series* a) red and black b) war c) crazy 8's d) go fish e) casino	As diagnostic tool to see level at which child is able to perform.	5-6 and up
	Games such as I doubt it, Red Light, Capt. May I	Help emotionally disturbed children to deal with legal "cheating."	7-12

Name of Recommender	Name of Game	Purpose of the Game	Use with what Audiences
	Sorry®	Group interaction.	7-12
	Skunk®	Teach idea of "stop while ahead."	7-12
	Others Candyland®, Cootie®, Twister®, Lotto®, etc.	Colors, numbers, left/right direction.	4+
Ralph Hartshorn	*Variations on Charades—* Kids act out someone everyone knows: worker, principle, teacher, other kids	A form of eliciting feelings about significant individuals if group is relatively nonverbal or threatened at the time.	
Takako Salvi	*Card Tricks* Not the cheating kind but the kind than can be explained by logic	Creates a reversal of the power role between patient and doctor. Develops ego strength of a sick patient who has been forced into a position of dependency by his illness.	hospitalized, physically sick children
Loyda Shears	Sticks and Chips	To teach competitive strategies.	children 3rd grade and up
Emily Snyder	Punchanella—Each child participates (hopping, jumping, etc.)	Motor skills.	
	Hokey-Pokey	Follow and gain inner controls.	
	Finger-plays—10 Little Indians, etc.	Small muscle control.	
Marilyn Sutton	Sorry	Coping and ego integrative strength tolerance for losing, etc. channel hostility and desensitize for numeral content.	5-12
	Dominos®	(Same as above.)	5/6-12
	Junior Scrabble®	(Same as above, and desensitize for symbol formation.)	8-10
	Animated Dart Games as "baseball"	Channel hostility.	3/6-12
	Throwing bean bags at figures chalked on blackboard and erasing them	Channel hostility.	3-5

CHAPTER 5

IT'S CHILD'S PLAY

Rivka R. Eifermann[1]

INTRODUCTION

R*IVKA EIFERMANN has completed a monumental study of the actual day-by-day play and game life of children in Israel. She studied both urban and rural, Arab and Jewish samples. Only a small portion of her study is included in this chapter which is devoted to establishing the variety and stability of game-types as they occurred in play groups of deprived to affluent school-age children. Her findings answer some questions and raise others. She makes two major contributions to our understanding of the durability of games. She points out the emergence of an aspiration function after the initial assimilation function has been served. Thus, she contributes to one aspect of definition of a developmental sequence. In this broad and essentially descriptive study of children-at-their-games, Eifermann highlights the ability to hold the interest of the child participants. She cites challenge as the major component leading to durability in a game. Eifermann also opens up further questions about the ludic age of a child, especially a disadvantaged one. Her work offers valuable information about the issues that teachers need to consider as they plan games for use in the classroom.*

—Editors

[1]The research described was supported in part by the P.L. 480 Education Research Program, U.S. Department of Health, Education and Welfare, Office of Education, Bureau of Research, under Contract No. OE-6-21-010.

The enthusiasm and devotion with which children freely plunge into playing is rarely matched in their adult-controlled activities. Even so, their play interests are highly selective, and the amount of time and energy they willingly devote to their various games are by no means evenly distributed. Naturally, boys will not often readily participate in *soft, girlish* games and neither boys nor girls will happily join "childish" games. Even the popularity of games freely acknowledged by children as theirs varies considerably; many of these games are played only very sporadically, others are rather steady in the playfield, still others may acquire the dimensions of full-fledged, recurring *crazes*.

What are the dynamics underlying these "natural" processes of selection among games? What causes some games to be short-lived but recurrent, others steady, still others just sporadic, or even only a one-shot affair? What social, intellectual or physical factors determine the processes of selection of games by age and sex? In an attempt to answer some of these questions, I began, some six years ago, a large scale research study on children's games in freely formed groups. The analysis of the data collected is still in process. This presentation is by way of a preliminary review of some of the problems explored.

The major aims of our research were:

    a) The establishment of a conceptual framework adequate for
        1) exhaustive description of children's games,
        2) treatment of their commonalities in different cultures and subcultures,
        3) understanding their diversities due to the variations in socialization processes;
    b) The invention of games that children would readily accept and which would increase the individual and social benefits to be drawn from them without reducing the pleasure inherent in playing them.

Neither the fact that children's games are played at every street corner, nor even the fun inherent in their study have, strangely enough, proven forces sufficiently powerful to turn this study into a popular field of research. Even the recent surge of interest in educational and simulation games, has not led researchers to examine systematically the nature of natural games, with the result that the invention of games has been rather a hit-or-miss affair.

Perhaps it is true, as some have argued, that children's games have not been intensively and extensively studied because they were not considered serious activities but rather as peripheral, external to the serious business of living, neither affecting it, nor affected by it. The almost overwhelming richness of children's play activities were undoubtedly another powerful deterring factor: because of the enormous variety in the material involved, only a very large scale study could possibly do it justice. Moreover, while it is true that children at play are not far to seek, a valid and reliable method for observing them at play has not been readily available.

Field Observations

One aim, then, was to fill in this gap to some extent. In this review, I shall try to describe how we, a group of some 150 observers, spread in various parts of Israel, went about it and to delineate some of the tentative conclusions arrived at by our smaller research group at the psychology department of the Hebrew University of Jerusalem.

Our observations were conducted in a rather large sample of grade schools (14 in a preparatory study and an additional 14 during the main stage of the research, comprising each some 7,000 pupils). In addition, supplementary observations were conducted in the streets and playgrounds of the neighborhood of one school, after school hours.

The observations were carried out once a week at school during a 10-minute recess period and after school over 2-4 hours, during a period of 14-18 months. The schools were selected so as to constitute, as far as possible, a balanced design of the following four variables: "high" and "low" level of school achievement (which correlated highly with socio-economic level; the low level children were those now fashionably labeled "disadvantaged" or even "culturally deprived," and most of these schools form part of the Israeli version of the Head-Start program), community structure (town, new immigrant small-town, village and kibbutz), culture (Jewish, Arab), and geographic location (North, Center, and South).

The records of play participants over the extensive observation period amounted to a cumulative total of over one hundred thou-

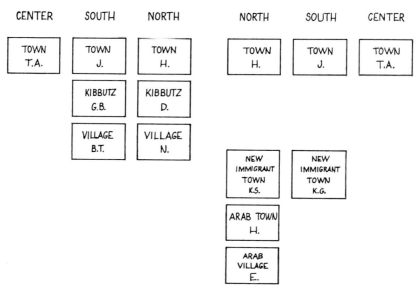

Figure 5-1. Distribution of main stage sample by socio-economic level, geographic location, community structure and culture. Reprinted from Eifermann, 1970a, by permission.

sand units.

The team of observers in each school consisted of an average of nine observers, and in addition, the top enthusiast, both able and willing to serve as local coordinator. (In streets, some 15 observers were engaged.) They were psychology students and local teachers who underwent a period of training in their research task. Furthermore, supervising contact-men from our center in Jerusalem went every week, by foot, bicycle, bus or plane, to each of the schools so as to be always present during observation, keep up the morale and interest and report back in detail. Though considerable cost and efforts were involved, this live contact proved invaluable.

The method of observation stipulated that the area observed be subdivided so that each observer covered, on the average, five

Figure 5-2. On each day of observation general information for that day was recorded (upper frame). Specific information on each play group was recorded as illustrated (lower frame). There was one frame for each play group. Reprinted frim Eifermann, 1971a, by permission of the Israel Academy of Sciences and Humanities.

The Hebrew University of Jerusalem

Department of Psychology

Games Research

Name of Observer

Amira Giora

Number of Observer	Date			School Symbol		Grades Missing		Weather				Lack of Information
	Day	Mo.	Year					Wind		Precipitation	Temperature	
1-4	5-6	7-8	9-10	11-15		16-23	24	25		26	27	28

| | | | | | | | If All × | None ① 2 Windy | None ① 2 Drizzle 3 Rain 4 Snow | Cold ① 2 Warm 3 Hot 4 Hamsin | Observer late 1 Observer absent 2 Other reason 9 |

0 1 2 4 0 9 1 2 6 5 1 1 2 0 1

8 × 80

× 1

Number of Participants by Grade

Group No.	Surface	Ethnic Group	Game Termination	Length of Game	Manner of Play	Name of Game	1	2	3	4	5	6	7	8	
1-10 11-13	16	17	18	19	20	21-25	32-33	34-35	36-37	38-39	40-41	42-43	44-45	46-47	

| dup 0 0 5 | Paved 1 Sand/soil ② Indoors 3 Stony 4 Lawn 5 Mud 6 Other surface 9 | Oriental 1 Ashkenazi 2 Both ③ | Bell 1 Internal quarrel ② External quarrel 3 New game 4 Weather 5 Teacher 6 Petered out/ended 7 Other 9 | Long 1 Short ② | Play ① Quarrel 2 Both 3 | *Rescue Tag* | | | | | | 2 | | | Boys |

| 64-65 66-67 68-69 70-71 72-73 74-75 76-77 78-79 | | | | | | | | | | | | 3 | | | Girls |

80

× 2

play groups. The variables recorded with reference to each group are shown in Figure 5-2 representing a section of the record sheet which contains a) general information for a day of observation, and b) the information on one play-group. The observers positioned themselves in the assigned sections at the beginning of the observation period so that, as nearly as possible, all incidents of formation, relevant fluctuations, changes in and termination of play activities would come to their attention. Of course, the children did not always respect our imaginary borders between sections (particularly when playing tag) and it was the task of both coordinators and contact-men to track down such groups and prevent their multiple recordings, which turned out to be surprisingly easy. In addition, the coordinators and contact-men were also trained to deal with *emergencies,* such as a quick re-division of sections during sudden crowding (as a result of a spectacular fight, for example). In the few cases in which such emergencies could not be properly coped with, the recordings of that data were excluded from our analysis.

My major worry before embarking on the field work centered around the feasibility of carrying out valid observations of the natural play scene with so many observers around who, moreover, were required to ask the children what grade they were in and what game they were up to. Indeed, at the beginning of the observation (overlapping with our training period) children were detracted from their normal activities. They would ask questions, become secretive and *perform* for our benefit. Instructions to all observers at the time were that children should be freely shown the record-sheet, with the explanation that "we want to write a book about all their games."

To my surprise and relief, the observers did not retain their novelty value for long and curiosity subsided rather quickly. After as few as four observations, the children were once again fully involved in their games and would volunteer the information required by the recorders "so as not to be disturbed." In retrospect, I think that it would indeed be amazing if children gave up *any* of their games for any length of time because of these ghosts around them.

Besides the numerical information presented in the record-sheet, there was a rubric for recording the *name of the game.* The information contained in this item was obviously insufficient for purposes of identification, since some play-activities which went by the same name were in fact completely different, whereas differently named games sometimes turned out to be identical. Nameless, *unstructured* play-activities were labeled by the observers and briefly described by them immediately following the observations. Here are the titles of a few of these descriptions, which give a flavor of the content of the activities:

"Staging a demonstration" ("low", town),
"Jumprope—without a rope" ("low", town),
"Made-up lady" ("high", town),
"Selling flowers" ("high", town),
"Building a house for snails" (village),
"Cows" (village),
"Night watch in children's quarters" (kibbutz),
"Feeding sheep" (kibbutz),
"The camel" (Arab village),
"The pyramids" (Arab village),
"Catching flies" (immigrant town),
"A wedding" (immigrant town).

Descriptions of the *structured,* formal games were independently obtained, in special interviews and demonstrations, conducted by the coordinator and contact-man. Thus, for each school, separate descriptions were obtained for every variant of each game that appeared in the play-scene (e.g. "chocolate hopscotch," "puppet hopscotch," "hospital tag," "tickle tag," "colors tag" or "redeemers tag").

Ludic Age and Educational Disadvantage

The descriptions of all structured games in each school were then compared with each other, and as a result an encyclopedia of some 2,000 (variants of) games was compiled. In addition, over 3,000 descriptions of unstructured games were collected.

Just a quick look at the material at our disposal will immediately impress us with the following two interesting facts. On the one hand, in every school games were played which were not recorded in any of the other schools. These games had sometimes, but not often, specific local features. A number of the unstructured games mentioned above were local, and so were some structured games such as a guessing game known in the Arab village as "the fig" in which, essentially, children have to guess the name of one particular kind of fig—many such names being in use in this particular sub-culture—which two of them had agreed to "carry in mind". On the other hand, on the whole, the most popular games in any one school were also those likely to appear, though not necessarily in the same order of popularity, in most other schools; moreover, in spite of the many variations, the games which have been recorded in Israel do not differ greatly from those listed in various American and British game books and which are included in the questionnaires used in the past for research purposes. Among these popular games we have such well known structured games as tag, marbles, hide and seek, prisoner's base, blindman's buff, jacks, hopscotch, soccer, jumprope and leapfrog; and such unstructured games as free wrestling, horseback carrying and imitation of adult roles (playing school, house or soldiers).

Games obviously vary considerably in the demands they make on the player's capacity for physical prowess, gross or fine physical or mental skills, on his capacity to interact with other participants, friends or foes, to perceive correctly the role and viewpoint of the others, and on his capacity to submit himself to a greater or lesser degree of mental effort or strategic thinking, his willingness to take risks and so on.

One of the problems that interested us most in our analysis was the following: Does "educational disadvantage" have a significant influence on the nature of games played at the same ages in "high" and "low" schools, or on the modes of organization of the same games, when they allow for different such modes, in short, on the *ludic age* of children? Since children enter play freely and since, moreover, the skills required in games do not completely coincide with those required in the formal school setting, this is an important and entirely open question. Here we can only take a glimpse at the partial answers our data analysis has revealed thus far.

In general, one might expect a constant decrease with age in the less structured play activities and a corresponding increase in participation in games of greater structural complexity, in particular in competitive games in which the opposing units are many-membered sub-groups.

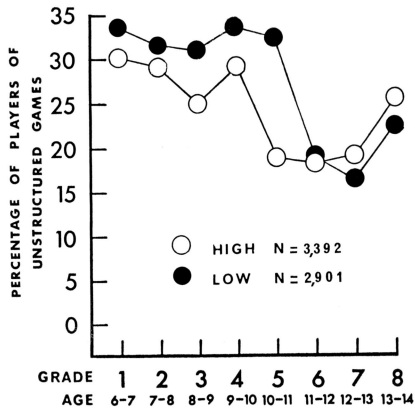

Figure 5-3. A larger percentage of young "low" children play in "unstructured" games, out of all games, than do young "high" children.

Now, if you look at Figure 5-3, which compares the data on unstructured games for one high-level and one low-level Jerusalem school, two interesting facts become apparent; first, the expected decline in unstructured playing is confirmed, in general, in both schools (though there is an interesting significant decline in this tendency in grades 7-8 in the high-level school, and in grade 8 in the low-level school, which clearly indicates that our expectations are only justified up to a certain level of development).

Second, it can be seen that "young" children in the "high" school engage more frequently in the most highly structured games, i.e. competitive games between groups. The relevant Figure 5-4 shows, for instance, that 20.5 percent of the "high" school first-

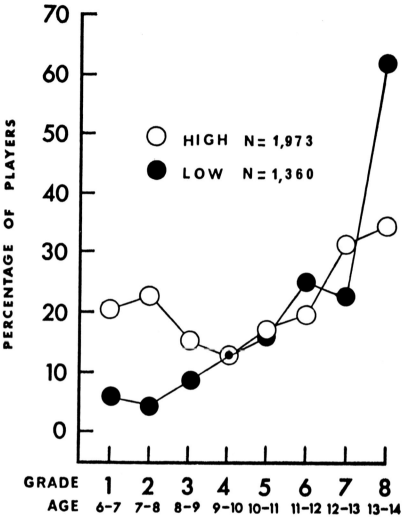

Figure 5-4. Out of all "structured" games they play, young "high" children
play more in games requiring complex organization into competing sub-groups than do "low" children in their "structured"
games.

graders play in such games, versus 6 percent in the "low" school.
This difference more or less disappears at a later age, in grades
4-7, while in grade 8 the percentage of such players is much higher
in the "low" school than in the "high" school, a phenomenon for

which I have so far no satisfactory explanation, though it makes no difference for present purposes.

Even more interesting is the fact, apparent from Table 5-I, that in the "high" school the percentage of "young" players, among all the players, of the three most popular games (which turn out to be the same in both schools, though not in the same rank order), is definitely greater than that in the "low" school.

TABLE 5-I

| | "Low" School | | | | "High" School | | |
Game	Order of preference	Percentage of all Players of Structured Games	Percentage of Players in Grades 1-4	Grades 5-8	Order of preference	Percentage of all Players of Structured Games	Percentage of Players in Grades 1-4	Grades 5-8
Tag	1	12%	77%	23%	2	9%	85%	15%
Soccer	2	7%	26%	74%	3	5%	50%	50%
Jumprope	3	6%	49%	51%	1	11%	75%	25%

When comparing games played both by "high" and "low" children, it turns out that the disadvantaged child tends to begin playing the same games at a later age.

A comparison of an additional 12 games played in both schools strengthens the impression that there is a definite tendency for "low" children to lag behind "high" children in their specific play activities.

This tendency is also apparent in a more general aspect of our findings, namely, the age at which play participation reaches its peak. Figure 5-5 summarizes this finding separately over all seven "high" and all seven "low" schools. It is also consistently in evidence in a more detailed analysis of the schools, regardless of whether they are rural or urban, Northern, Central or Southern in location. The figure demonstrates clearly that play reaches its peak of popularity already in the 2nd grade in the "high" schools but only in the 4th grade in the "low" schools. Other indicators of the same tendency are, for example, that more "low" players participate in games which last only up to five minutes (see Fig. 5-6). (It should be noted that "low" children were found to quarrel less than "high" children, so that "quarrel" cannot serve as an explanation.)

All children, at all school ages, prefer to play in relatively small groups (in fact, groups of two are dominant at all age levels), but, as Figure 5-7 clearly illustrates, the small-sized groups are still more popular with "low" children.

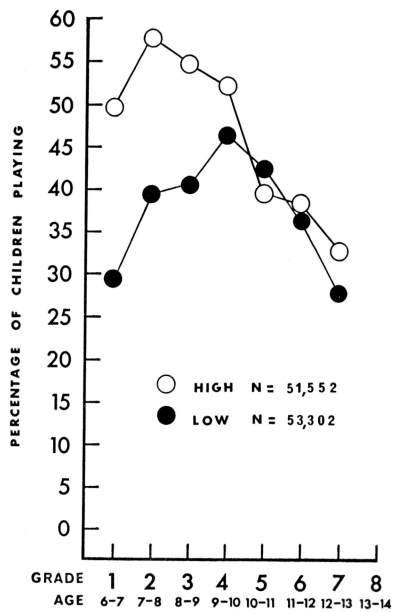

Figure 5-5. Among "high" children, the percentage of play participants in the second grade out of all children in that grade is higher than in any other grade. The peak of play participation is reached only in the fourth grade, among "low" children.

These findings bring to mind the question initially presented, which we can now restate as follows: Is the gap in play activities of "high" and "low" children indicative of a slower rate of development of "disadvantaged" children? Do these children acquire at a later age the physical, social and mental capacities required to

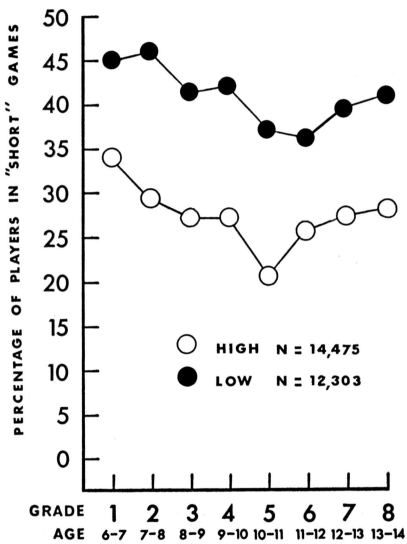

Figure 5-6. More of the "low" than the "high" players engage in play for periods of five consecutive minutes or less.

play certain games (tag, soccer, etc.), play without interruption for a longer time, and play in relatively large groups? Do they, for

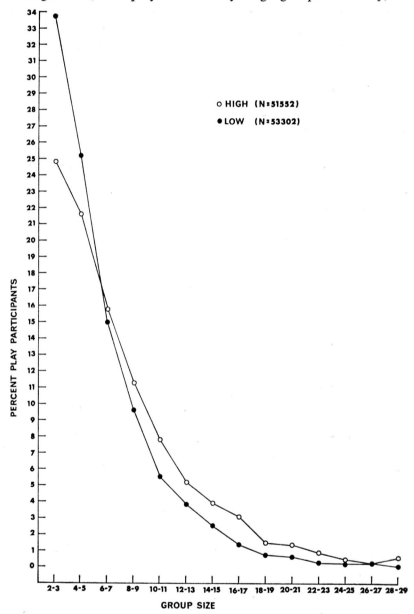

Figure 5-7. More of the "low" than the "high" players tend to play in small-sized groups.

the same reason, reach the peak of interest in play at a later age? In other words, is their *ludic age* less than that of other children of the same chronological age? Or are these findings indicative of a lack of interest rather than of incapacity? Jean Piaget describes playing unstructured games as being primarily an exercise, for pleasure, of newly acquired, already mastered skills—"assimilation."

It seems to me, however, that this conception has its grave restrictions in explaining children's games. The little block-builder will often expand his castle in all directions to the very limits of his capacities (as a matter of fact, even the adult's "assimilative," idle doodling, will typically change into an effort at drawing). Tag, and still more so, games such as hopscotch, jacks or leapfrog, which increase in difficulty in successive rounds, clearly go beyond pure assimilation to a stage where the enjoyment of play lies more in the fact that new challenges are taken up, with a good chance for success in meeting the new aspiration, than in the display of an already existent and proven mastery.

Could it then be that "low" children prefer to play games in an *assimilative* rather than *aspirative* mode, whereas with "high" children the opposite is the case? Our data at its present level of analysis, does not provide for an unequivocal reply to these questions. Here are some of our relevant findings.

From Figure 5-7 (above) it is immediately evident the "low" children play altogether less, on the average, than "high" children. This might suggest a general lack of initiative on their part. However, a more detailed analysis shows that this difference no longer holds when we leave averages and look into each school separately. Strangely enough, the precise distribution among the "low" schools was such that play participation was higher in two of these schools, and lower in the remaining five schools, than in each and every one of the "high" schools.

Moreover, a brief series of recordings of lone players and non-players in all schools has revealed the following: In the upper grades of the two Arab schools (where play participation is anyhow relatively scant) many more children engage in conversation relative to their peers in Jewish schools—apparently taking over, to some extent, the social functions of play in Jewish schools (Fig. 5-8). In the kibbutz (communal settlement) schools, in

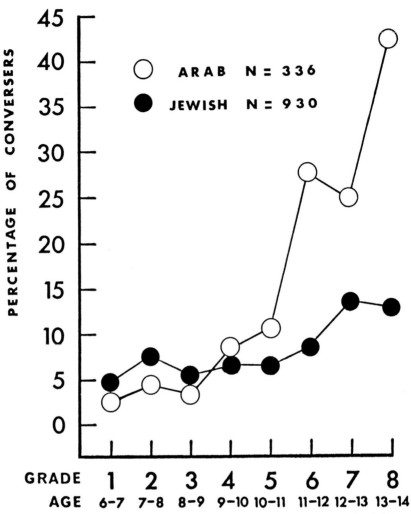

Figure 5-8. The percentage of conversers among the older Arab children is far greater than that among older Jewish children. (The percentages are out of all children.)

which group play is also rather low, there is, in comparison with the other schools, a great deal of lone playing (perhaps due to an overdose of organized, heteronomous group activities to which they are otherwise subjected, or even just to the constant presence of peers). It seems, therefore, that low participation as such in group play may be due to reasons other than unwillingness to take up challenges. Other aspects of our recordings also tend not to support an image of "low" children as more "passive" in their pursuits: thus we found that onlooking—which may be considered the most passive form of play participation—was by no means more popular with "low" than with "high" children. And even "loafing," i.e. standing or sitting around (usually associated with street-corner gangs), was just as common with "high" as with "low" children.

I tend to believe that our present inability to give a clear-cut answer to the vital question whether the lag in play activities among "disadvantaged" children is due to some lack of capacity, to lack of motivation (or, of course, to some combination of these), is now due more to the fact that we have fallen behind in theorizing than to a dearth in empirical findings. It might be that the kind of theory we need would be one in which the concepts of *challenge* and *aspiration* would take their due place beside the concepts of *assimilation,* of Piaget's vintage, and of *conflict* and *mastery* in their psychoanalytic connotations.

Classification of Games

When comparing games of different age groups, there is one obvious independent variable in terms of which these games can be profitably treated, viz. the age of the players. This is no longer true with respect to their *life span* (most so-called "seasonal games" played by children are not really seasonal at all, as will be shown below).

I have found it particularly useful to introduce the following classification of games with respect to their life span; the characterization given here applies as such only to pure (or ideal) types.[2]

    (1) *Steady Games,* which are played more or less constantly at all times, with little variation in intensity;

    (2) *Recurrent Games,* which are played only intermittently but reach great intensity during each "wave";

    (3) *Sporadic Games,* which are played only intermittently, in short waves, and never reach great intensity;

    (4) *One-Shot Games,* which have only one uninterrupted period of existence, and reach great intensity during that period.

---

[2]An abbreviated and revised version of this section appears in Eifermann, 1973b.

Four typical curves for percentage of play activity over a time
span of, say, five years would then look as depicted in Figure 5-9.

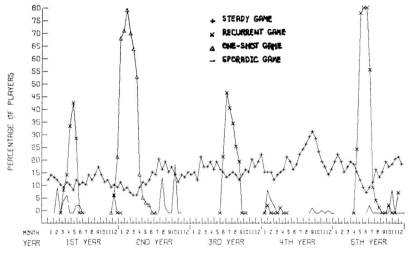

Figure 5-9. Typical curves for four game categories, over a five-year span:
a steady game, a recurrent game, a sporadic game, and a
one-shot game.

This classification, while mutually exclusive, is not meant to be
exhaustive. Real games will, of course, in general, turn out to be
various mixtures and attenuations of these ideal types. Some games
will be played only intermittently and reach great intensity on
some of their waves, but only small intensity on other waves. Other
games will have a steady look in one playground, but have a
sporadic look in another playground, at one and the same time.

A close study of this differential behavior should be revealing.
Such a study is still in progress. Here I can only present some
preliminary findings.

What is it that makes for the recurrence of games? Why do such
games as hopscotch, marbles, kites, jumprope, jacks, and tops,
seem to emerge and catch on, like wildfire, only to disappear and
then recur again? As shortly intimated above, the popular explanation to the effect that recurrence is just due to seasonality, that
such games do reappear when the right season for them arrives
and disappear when this season is over, has not been able to
survive real-life observations conducted in New Zealand, the

United Kingdom and Israel. Of the five schools we analyzed for recurrence of games, only one exhibited a close correspondence between the recurrence cycle of exactly one game and the eternal return of the seasons. The reason for recurrence must, then, be looked for not so much in external conditions but primarily in the very nature of the games concerned. Indeed, an analysis of 18 games which behaved recurrently during the observation period in the five schools analyzed for this purpose, has brought to light some revealing characteristics. For instance, it has turned out, not quite expectedly, that recurrent games tend to be either boys' games or girls' games rather than mixed games. The well-known fact that communication between children of the same sex is more intensive, so that more opportunities for imitation are created, probably contributes to the quick spreading of such games.

The Role of Challenge

The standards of excellence by which achievement in recurrent games is evaluated have, in general, a more specific and more easily determinable character than the standards in the other types of games. Recurrent games tend to be characterized by definite final outcomes, and winning, when applicable, is more frequently associated with material gain. The challenge of all-out competition and the promise of gain are, presumably, features that contribute to the great popularity of such games once they have been reintroduced. Typically, recurrent games are played sequentially by individuals whose activities are independent of each other. Consequently, these games can also be played (or, should we say, practiced) solitarily. They acquire specific skills which can often be rather quickly developed through practice, unlike, e.g. competitive running where improvement, if at all, can only be obtained slowly and painfully. But the challenges inherent in recurrent games last only for a while. Many of the very same features that make for diffusion and attractiveness at first are also causes of the games' decline: after a period of training and repeated competition between individuals, a hierarchy of players is stabilized which, naturally, will tend to reduce the challenge of playing with many of the original potential competitors, either because they are "lousy" or because they are "too good." Moreover, in the relevant

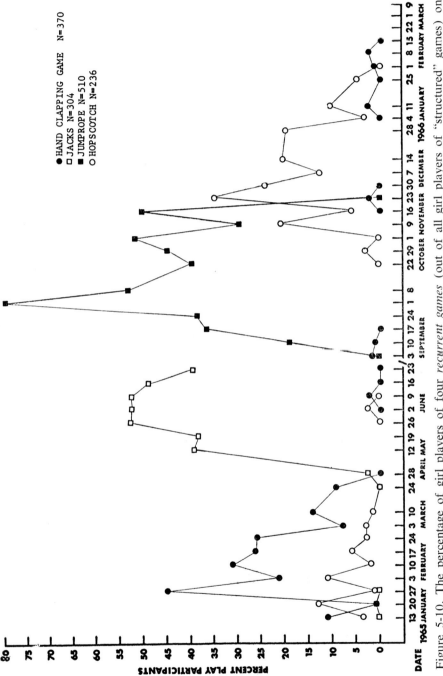

Figure 5-10. The percentage of girl players of four *recurrent games* (out of all girl players of "structured" games) on successive days of observation.

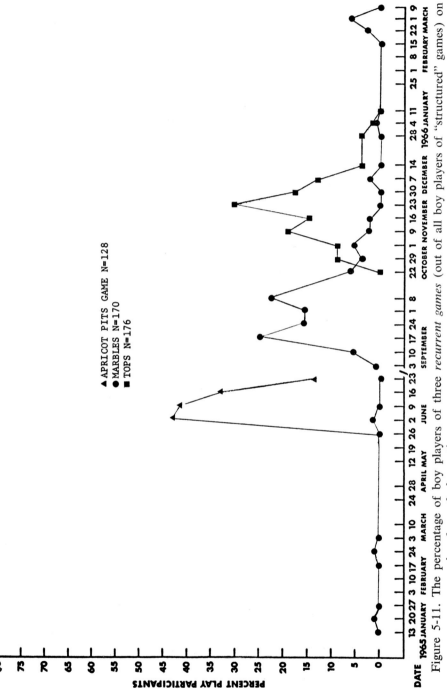

Figure 5-11. The percentage of boy players of three *recurrent games* (out of all boy players of "structured" games) on successive days of observation.

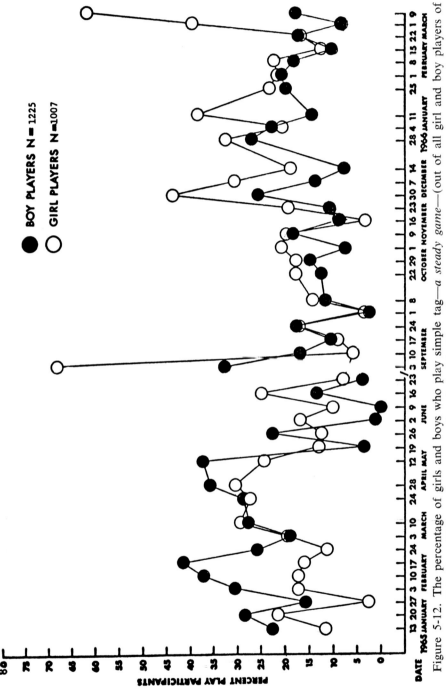

Figure 5-12. The percentage of girls and boys who play simple tag—*a steady game*—(out of all girl and boy players of "structured" games) on successive days of observation.

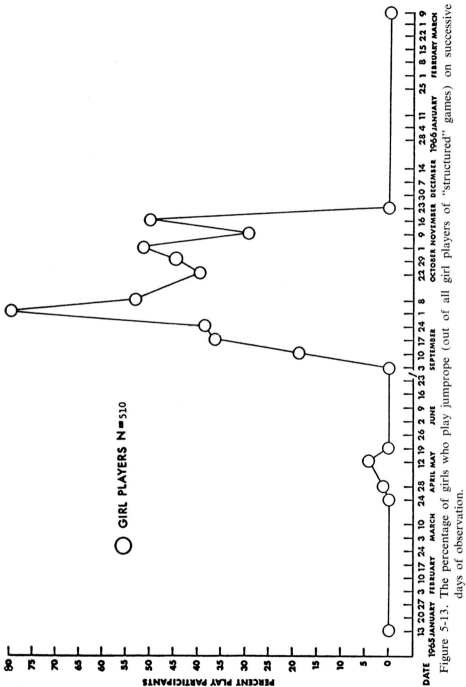

Figure 5-13. The percentage of girls who play jumprope (out of all girl players of "structured" games) on successive days of observation.

cases, many of the poorer players will now avoid playing with their obvious superiors, for fear of material loss. Thus, the game loses its potency. It may recur only after a period long enough for the hierarchy to lose its stability and for raising new hopes in further self-improvement.

The typical form of the curves depicting a recurrent game will then be a series of waves, with lines of no activity between them, with different amplitudes in different schools, and even in the same schools. As a glance at Figures 5-10 and 5-11 will show, a new wave will begin to rise and gain strength only when some other recurrent game is beyond its apex on its contemporaneous wave. A recurrent game has a still greater chance of being reaccepted when reintroduced during a period of general slackness in play.

Other relevant conditions for the appearance of a new wave, of a more secondary character, might be the personalities of the agents who intend to reintroduce the game (a "leader"), the networks of communication between children (geographic proximity or similarity in socio-economic level), and even seasonal weather (warming-up games in winter), and seasonal availability of implements (apricot pits during the apricot season). The impact of the last two factors seems to have been overestimated in the past, a misevaluation which was responsible for the very term "seasonal game." The primary factor in the recurrence should be rather looked for in the (season-independent) specific character of the challenge.

Now, look at the profile of simple tag (Fig. 5-12), in comparison with that of such a typically recurrent game as jumprope reproduced here for the convenience of the reader (Fig. 5-13). What, then, in the inherent nature of these games makes for the obvious difference? Though in tag, too, the hierarchy of physical abilities and skills (running and evading) will be rather quickly established, the game will not thereby lose its challenge, since in tag, in contradistinction to jumprope, there enters a further factor over which the players have almost complete control: The "it" has considerable freedom in determining the intensity of his engagement and the extent of his immediate risk of being unsuccessful in catching his target, by selecting either an easy or a tough "catch", while the other players can vary the initial distance from the "it", by either staying safely away from him, or getting provocatively close to him, and even teasing him otherwise. Mastery over the extent of the challenge one is ready to take upon himself in a given situation is, then, an important factor that makes for steadiness, though it need not be decisive and can be overpowered by other factors working in the opposite direction.

The situation is still different with regard to group games. Why is it that *mahanayim,* a kind of game, I believe, similar to ghost ball, is typically recurrent and the only group game of this kind observed in the five schools, while soccer (which, when played by professionals, has its definite "season") is a clearly steady game, not only when played by school children during recess but also after school hours? Again, it seems that the decisive difference lies in the possibility of making, in soccer, the challenge fit the player to a much higher degree than can be done in *mahanayim.* True enough, in soccer the "fatties" are usually assigned only defense positions and will therefore not often experience the exhilaration of kicking a goal. Nevertheless, their performance may still be crucial for the outcome of the game so that they will retain a feeling of active and responsible participation without being called upon to overexert themselves beyond ability. This is much less the case in *mahanayim.*

Theories

According to our tentative "challenge" theory of play, the explanation of the different character of the various types of games is, then, briefly as follows: a game is steady if it allows each participant to adjust the extent of the challenge to his abilities at that time, while still leaving the outcome of an individual round of such a game sufficiently undetermined. A game is recurrent, if, after the hierarchy of the players has become stabilized, the outcome of any particular round has become predictable and independent of the extent of challenge the players are ready to take upon themselves. A game is sporadic if there is little variation in the extent of the challenge it provides and little challenge to begin with altogether. One-shot games (of which the only clear-cut instance known to me is hoolahoop) are games with considerable initial challenge, but such that the mastery obtainable in them after some time is of a kind which the child has no hope of increasing even if he were to take it up again after a lapse of a year or two: That such a game will not be taken up by the next generation that has never played it before and for which it would have formed a live challenge, is probably due to the simple fact that it has gotten out of sight before the new generation was ready for the challenge.

Other theories of play seem to me not quite adequate for the treatment of the phenomena described. Two of them, however, can be expected to cover aspects of these phenomena as follows:

The "cathartic" theories of play lay heavy stress on its function in reducing anxiety by giving the child an opportunity to reduce, symbolically and on a lowered scale, conflicts which he is not able to successfully cope with in real life. The constant attraction of steady games woud then exactly lie in the fact that in them the child is able to control the level of conflict so that it both remains a meaningful substitute and retains its resolvability. The fading away of recurrent games, on the other hand, would then be due to the fact that, after the hierarchy has been established, the outcome of the substitute conflict is predetermined to such a degree as to leave insufficient leeway for the catharsis of the real conflict troubling the child.

Such theories, so it seems, are not in a position to explain the occurrence of typically sporadic games. Such games would, however, fit rather well into Piaget's theory, already mentioned, of playing as an exercise, for pleasure, of skills already mastered. These games, typically, provide little opportunity for improvement and little choice in determining the level of the challenge. The subjective challenge in these games is low altogether, so that they have been played only rarely and briefly. But Piaget's theory is, in its present form, not able to explain steady and recurrent games; as a matter of fact, it was meant to be a theory of unstructured play only, and its extension to the explanation of sporadic games is perhaps a rather unexpected bonus.

It is likely that a satisfactory overall theory of children's play will have to encompass all these theories as proper parts, though it may be hoped that this will be done not by sheer addition but rather through some kind of integration.

All this theorizing is, of course, still in its infancy. Clearly, more thinking, analyzing available data, and gathering of additional data in light of the tentative theories to be developed, will further the issue here, as elsewhere in science. It may be expected that these theories will not only serve to soothe our curiosity but will find an important application in rational Head-Start programs. It is possible, for instance, that "disadvantaged" children play to a greater extent sporadic games, finding pleasure in exhibiting whatever mastery they have over the skills required of them, than do other children. Our data are being analyzed right now with respect to this question, and we shall be able to say more about this topic shortly.

Inventing Games

The most interesting application of the future theories would, perhaps, lie in the area of inventing new games, with specific pedagogical and cultural aims in view. A better understanding of what it is that makes for the steady or recurrent nature of games would enable us to invent games "to measure", to plant them in the right place and at the right time, and achieve well-understood aims. All this need not be music of the future, but almost seems to lie around the corner. Children's play is not child's play, but a few more years of concentrated research effort should enable us to reach a degree of understanding of this universal phenomenon sufficient, among other things, for a more rational and principled attempt to combine pleasure and coping with culturally, socially and individually decisive challenges—in games which children will still consider as being truly "theirs."

REFERENCES

Eifermann, Rivka R.: Level of children's play as expressed in group size. *Brit J Ed Psychol, 40*(2):161-170, 1970a.

Eifermann, Rivka R.: Cooperativeness and egalitarianism in kibbutz children's games. *Human Relat, 6*(23):579-587, Oct. 1970b.

Eifermann, Rivka R.: *Determinants of children's game styles.* Jerusalem, The Israel Academy of Science and Humanities, 1971a.

Eifermann, Rivka R.: Social play in childhood. In Herron, R.E. and

Sutton-Smith, B. (Eds.): *Child's Play.* New York, Wiley, 1971b, pp. 270-297.

Eifermann, Rivka R.: Rules in games. In Elithorn, A. and Jones, P. (Eds.): *Artificial and Human Thinking.* Amsterdam, Elsevier, 1973, pp. 147-161.

Eifermann, Rivka R.: Free social play: a guide to directed playing. In Coopersmith, S. (Ed.): *Developing Motivation in Children,* Columbus, Ohio, Charles E. Merrill, 1974, in press.

Erikson, E.H.: *Childhood and Society,* 2nd ed. New York, Norton, 1963.

Millar, Susanna: *The Psychology of Play.* London, Pelican, 1968.

Opie, Iona and P.: *Children's Games in Street and Playground.* Oxford, The University Press, 1969.

Peller, Lillie E.: Libidinal phases, ego development, and play. *Psychoanal Study Child, IX*:178-198, 1954.

Piaget, J.: *Play, Dreams and Imitation in Childhood.* London, Routledge & Kegan Paul, 1962 (First French edition, 1951).

Roberts, J.M. and Sutton-Smith, B.: Child training and game involvement. *Ethnology, 1*:166-185, 1962.

CHAPTER 6

DEVELOPING IMAGINATIVE PLAY IN PRESCHOOL CHILDREN AS A POSSIBLE APPROACH TO FOSTERING CREATIVITY

DINA FEITELSON[1]

INTRODUCTION

A SECOND CHAPTER which fulfills the need for research in the game-play life of children has been carried out by Dina Feitelson. She concentrated on the behavior of preschool children as they engaged in some version of play. Her methodology was mainly observational and therefore descriptive at the outset, but she developed a Play Scale which allowed her to evaluate her observational data quite objectively. This scale has the added advantage of allowing any interested adult to assess the creativity of any child's preschool level in play activity. Feitelson has provided answers to two important questions in this study; 1) Is play a common activity for all children?, and 2) Can children be taught to create a play world? The first question she has answered negatively, although it has been assumed that all children played. When play activity was not observed, some sort of physical illness or other unusual condition of the culture of the child was called upon to explain its absence. The second question has been answered positively in terms of the research findings. Feitelson offers an important insight for the guidance of teachers who wish to increase creativity in play. She warns against rushing the child with massive

[1]From *Early Childhood Development and Care,* 1:181-195, 1972.

training sessions. Playfulness seemed to increase most satisfactorily when there was an interval of at least a week between sessions in which the impact of the training during the session could be "digested" by the child. Perhaps it would be well to recall that learning research findings show spaced practice superior to massed when all other conditions are held constant. We wish to call attention to the fact that the use of playfulness as an attitude and creativity as a behavioral attribute have been equated in this Introduction. We invite the potential game-using teacher to ponder the implications of such an equation. Perhaps the pressure of massed play training does not allow the child to draw back from the activity in such a way as to develop the "as if" point of view. Is this distancing *effect a necessary ingredient for the creative attitude and the playful behavior?*   —Editors

Abstract

A STUDY AIMED at investigating whether it is possible to teach young children to play imaginatively even when this type of play is not fostered in their homes was undertaken by the students of a research seminar at Hebrew University. In the first phase of the study nineteen children, ages two years six months to four years three months, in one of the poorest neighborhoods in Jerusalem were observed at different times of the day. In the second phase each child had nine play teaching sessions spaced approximately one week apart. Level of play was evaluated by dividing written records of each play teaching session into behavior units and rating every unit on a five point scale. Play on the highest level increased significantly during the final play teaching sessions.

Play has been an integral part of Western civilization for many generations.

It is beyond the scope of this paper to take our inquiry into antiquity and pursue the origin of toys, games and rhymes. Yet easily accessible evidence ranging from the beautifully wrought toys of the rich preserved in many a museum[2] to evidence of contem-

---

[2]The most extensive toy collection is probably the one at "Deutsches Spielzeugsmuseum," Sonneberg, Thuringen, East-Germany.

raries such as the paintings of Pieter Bruegel 1525-1569 (in one of which he shows eighty-four ways in which simple village children of his day passed their time in playful activities—de Meyere, 1941) clearly establishes that play in childhood was an indivisible part of everyday life in many European countries. Furthermore, toys and some playful activities have also been described in the ethnographic literature dealing with so-called primitive or pre-literate societies (Fortes, 1938; Mead, 1954).

It is not surprising therefore that at one time it was assumed that play is universal. Scholars who devoted themselves extensively to play tried to develop theories which would explain play manifestations in general, some confining their endeavors to the human realm while others also included the animal kingdom (Gross, 1899; Bally, 1966). For a time nearly every monograph on child development included a chapter on play (Woodcock, 1941; Jersield, 1946). Often play activities and interests were described as if they developed in a preordained sequence, of universal application, though in actual fact the evidence on which these statements relied had been collected only among children growing up in Western civilizations (Van Alstyne, 1932; Piaget, 1951). Moreover much of that evidence, though valuable in itself, would today scarcely be considered conclusive by modern research standards. Play in a naturalistic setting being also a somewhat elusive phenomenon, the offspring of the researchers themselves seem to have served more often than not as raw material for some if not many of their statements (Valentine, 1938; Piaget, 1951).

Thus, while descriptions of play and even theories about the developmental stages of play were relatively frequent, little progress was made towards a unanimously accepted definition of play, and a comprehensive classification of playful activities.

The term play was often used in the widest sense, and came to mean in time a wide range of very divergent activities. It is in this sense that play might well be universal and that one or another of the activities called "play" by scholars might well be found in every human society studied so far.

Yet it does seem to us that while various forms or organized games and competitive activities as well as games of chance, mime, and dance have been described in the most varied social settings, other types of playful activities might well be less widespread. For instance field work among Jews shortly after their immigration to Israel from the Kurdish mountains showed that, contrary to expectations, young children in these communities spent their time as ever present observers of adult activities, and did not engage in active play of their own (Feitelson, 1954, 1959).

Similarly Smilansky reports a lack of symbolic play among her sample of so-called culturally deprived children, most of whom were born to immigrants from Middle Eastern and North African countries (Smilansky, 1968).

Descriptions of other rural communities in the Middle East (Granqvist, 1947) and especially Ammar's excellent study of childhood in an Egyptian village (1954) all show that in these societies young children lack time, space and materials in order to engage in undisturbed active free play.

Moreover both Ammar's picture of childhood in rural Egypt as well as the LeVines' description of Gusii childhood in Kenya (LeVine and LeVine, 1963) lead one step further, in that they show that in these societies, children not only lack necessary conditions for play, but that adults in these societies actively try to prevent children from playing. Thus while some of the activities which have at one time or another been categorized as play may well be found in almost any human society, field evidence seems to show that at least one type of playful activities, namely solitary free imaginative play in early childhood, is conspicuously lacking in some societies.

We do not wish at the present stage to enter a discussion about the assumed causes of this lack, nor about how widespread the phenomenon actually is.

Instead we would like to ask, assuming that in some societies (and for our discussion it does not matter at present in how many or for what reasons) children do not have opportunities for solitary free imaginative play in early childhood, what implications would this fact have for their later development? In short, what are the attributes of free imaginative play in early childhood which these children might be missing? It might be advisable at this stage to define the meaning of free imaginative play a little more precisely.

By solitary-free-imaginative play we mean a situation in which the child has ample opportunity in terms of time, space and materials at his disposal to engage in undisturbed and uncriticized play, during the course of which he will exhibit flexibility, originality and the ability to transform. For example the little boy who uses his building blocks alternatively in order to create dwellings, shops, service stations or furniture and who moreover at one stage might start to push one of the blocks along, using it as a car, boat or even plane is engaging in free imaginative or in other words creative play. It is exactly this type of play which has been so extensively documented in research literature dealing with children who grow up in Western societies, which we feel is lacking among children in certain communities in the Middle East.

Creative seems to be the key word when one tries to elucidate the crucial qualities of this type of play. Already Wallach and Kogan's findings (1965) imply that necessary preconditions for creative output are testing (or work) situations which replicate some of the conditions mentioned above—namely absence of time-pressure and a non-critical approach to the product. Moreover the importance of a stage of free associative play with ideas as a crucial step in the act of creation is often stressed (for instance, Schon, 1967). Indeed the term "play" keeps recurring in the recent abundant literature on creativity in various connotations. If, as it seems to us, the developmental aspect of creativity has so far been badly neglected by researchers, might this not be partly due to the fact that working mainly in a certain segment of human cultures they assumed creative play in early childhood as an ever present condition without realizing that in actual fact it was a major variable.

In this connection we would like to enlarge on a statement by Wallach and Kogan (1965). They write:

> We do not mean to imply of course, that the existence of the preconditions for creativity in a child will necessarily lead to actual creative performance later in life. Such adult creativity is influenced by many factors . . .

In the same sense it would be unwise to imply that given the opportunity for free-imaginative-creative play in early childhood, every child will perform creatively in later life. But this does not absolve us from the serious question—is there no danger that the inhibition of free-imaginative-creative play in early childhood will prevent creativeness in later life? Or in other words, to what extent is free imaginative play in early childhood a necessary condition for a creative mode of reacting in later life, while of course it cannot in itself guarantee such a mode of behavior?

The implications of these assumptions are manifold and far reaching and much further work needs to be done. As a very preliminary step along the road we will have to go, a small study was undertaken by the students of a research seminar at the John Dewey School of Education at the Hebrew University of Jerusalem. The study was carried out during the academic year 1966-1967 and was terminated rather abruptly by the Six-Day War.[3]

The challenging problem posed at the outset of the project was: Is it possible to teach young children to play imaginatively and creatively, even when they have had no previous play experience?

Description of the Project

Nineteen students participated in the project which was initiated with the help of a community worker in one of the poorest neighborhoods in Jerusalem. Each student was allocated one child of pre-school age. The participating children were between the ages of 2 years and 6 months and 4 years and 3 months at the beginning of the project. Most of the parents had immigrated to Israel within the last decade, mainly from North Africa. All the families lived in two blocks of a public housing development adjoining Mandelbaum Gate, which at that time divided the two parts of Jerusalem. Many of the families allocated flats in these two blocks were multi-problem families.

The project was carried out in two phases.

Phase One: Baseline Observations

In the first phase of the project, each student observed the child allocated to him on three different occasions, twice in the morning and once in the afternoon. Each observation lasted about one hour. The student was instructed to refrain as much as possible from in-

[3] I am deeply indebted to Mrs. Ada Herzberg who worked with me on all phases of this project, as well as to the students of the seminar who gave willingly of their time and efforts.

truding on the child or his environment during these observations. A full written record of each observation was kept.

Phase Two: The Play Teaching Sessions

In the second phase of the project each student met his child for nine individual play teaching sessions, each of which lasted for one hour. These play teaching sessions were spaced one week apart, so that the second phase took about nine weeks.

During the second phase the students worked in pairs. Every student acted as play teacher to the child whom he had observed in the first phase, while another student recorded each of his play teaching sessions. The discussion of these records during Seminar meetings were aimed at developing more effective "Play Teaching" techniques.

The play teaching sessions were held either in the shelter of one of the blocks or in the particular child's home. The play materials used during the play teaching sessions were brought by the students each time they came.

Results

The first and most measurable result of the project has been in the play ability of the children themselves. The developments observed were much more fundamental than anything we had anticipated. The baseline observations tended in general to confirm prior studies. The young children studied spent their day roaming, more or less aimlessly, through the apartments of their parents or neighbors, and in the joint yard surrounding the two blocks. Only a few instances of play were recorded, and these were of very short duration. For example one child played with a ball for about three minutes in an observation which lasted one hour.

During the initial play teaching sessions the students had great difficulty in maintaining the children's interest in any one activity for more than a few minutes. Moreover it was often very hard to engage a child in contentful play, and harder still to ensure his active cooperation. For instance during most of the first play teaching session of M4[4] the student kept pushing toy cars at him while

---

[4]Individual children are identified by sex (M-for male; F-for female) and ordinal number.

emitting appropriate noises and talking about their destination and cargo. During this session she was unable to persuade M4 to push one of the cars back to her. Whenever a car reached him he would pick it up and return it to her by hand.

By the time of the last sessions the changes in the behavior of M4 and many of the other children were so radical as to be almost unbelievable. Many of the children tended to play intensively during the whole teaching sessions, and some coercion on the part of the students was necessary in order to interrupt them. More than once a child stayed in the shelter, playing on by himself during the following session.

Also the quality of the child's play tended in general to undergo basic changes. As the sessions continued, many children showed growing initiative in the use of play materials brought by the students. In a few instances we were able to discover that spontaneous play had occurred in the intervals between sessions, play which had clearly incorporated traces of activities engaged in during previous play teaching sessions of that particular child. Thus one of the students, on coming to her ninth and last session, was asked by F3 to join her and her friends in playing "shop" in the yard. The four little girls, three of whom were participating in the project, were playing without any equipment whatsoever. The eighth session of F3 with the student had been devoted to playing shop.

In order to evaluate the results of the play teaching sessions more objectively, the following instruments were devised:

1) Behavior Units

The written observational records of the nine play-teaching-sessions of each child were divided into Behavior Units (B.U.'s).[5] A B.U. was defined as the initiation of play behavior by one of the two partners of the play teaching situation and the reaction of the other to this initiative. Thus a B.U. could be initiated either by the child or by the play teacher. Both the initiative as well as the response could be by word of mouth, by gesture or by a combination of both as well as by the lack of either or both.

[5]The way in which naturalistic observational records can be divided into units which are then scored has been described by Stevenson *et al.*, 1960. We feel we have been influenced by these authors, and have been using adaptations of their method in several recent studies.

2) The Play Scale

After the observational records had been divided into Behavior Units, each B.U. was rated along a five level scale. The five levels of this scale were described in the following manner:

Level I: Teacher initiates play, child passive, withdraws or regresses.
Level II: Teacher initiates play, child shows interest (attentive, smiles).
Level III: Teacher initiates play, child takes part by word or deed.
Level IV: Teacher initiates play, child's response contributes new element.
Level V: Child initiates play or contributes original element which had not appeared before in ongoing session.

Table 6-I shows the distribution of Behavior Units on each level of the scale along the nine teaching sessions.[6]

TABLE 6-I

AMOUNT OF PLAY ON EACH OF FIVE LEVELS THROUGHOUT
NINE TEACHING SESSIONS

No. of Ses. Level	1	2	3	4	5	6	7	8	9	Total
V	7	7	4	5	5	25	7	16	33	109
IV	15	34	37	18	47	29	35	27	51	293
III	105	151	121	115	140	119	101	96	135	1083
II	42	29	17	29	29	30	39	27	16	258
I	43	24	22	31	6	10	16	15	7	174
Total	212	245	201	198	227	213	198	181	242	1917
										$p < 0.01$[7]

As we see from Table 6-I, throughout all nine sessions the largest absolute amount of play was on the third level. Most of the play activity which took place was teacher initiated, and elicited active participation by the child. In order to delineate possible developments more finely we tried to find out what percentage of all play on any one level had occurred during each of the nine sessions. Table 6-II shows the changes which occurred in the amount of play on each level, throughout the nine play-teaching sessions.

[6]Up to the outbreak of war in June 1967, only ten students had concluded all nine play teaching sessions. The following three tables are based on the work of these ten students only, comprising ninety "play-teaching sessions."

[7]Median Test, Siegel, p. 111-116.

TABLE 6-II
THE PERCENTAGE OF PLAY ON EACH LEVEL OF THE PLAY SCALE
THROUGHOUT THE NINE TEACHING SESSIONS

Level	1st Ses.	2nd Ses.	3rd Ses.	4th Ses.	5th Ses.	6th Ses.	7th Ses.	8th Ses.	9th Ses.	Total
V	6	6	2	4	4	24	6	15	33	100
IV	5	12	13	6	16	10	12	9	17	100
III	10	14	11	11	13	11	9	9	12	100
II	17	11	7	11	11	12	15	9	7	100
I	25	14	13	18	4	5	9	8	4	100

While the amount of play on the intermediate levels remained fairly constant from session to session, interesting changes took place on the two extreme levels. Of all B.U.'s of the lowest level (passivity, withdrawal regression), most occurred during the first sessions. While most B.U.'s of the highest level (the absolute number of which was rather limited; see Table 6-I) occurred during the last sessions. In order to dramatize this change Table 6-III compares the percentage of B.U.'s on the first and fifth level during the first three sessions with the percentage during the last three.

TABLE 6-III
THE PERCENTAGE OF PLAY ON LEVELS V AND I THROUGHOUT
THE FIRST AND LAST THREE TEACHING SESSIONS

Level \ Session	1 — 3	7 — 9
V	14	54
I	52	21

While the decrease in B.U.'s on the first level towards the latter sessions can be ascribed to greater familiarity of the child with the play-teacher and the play-teaching situation, it does seem that the marked increase of B.U.'s on the fifth level during the last sessions shows that the children acquired some ability to play imaginatively and creatively.

Thus the first result of the project was that in the wake of play teaching, children who had not played before were now able to initiate imaginative play.

A second result of the project was that some of the parents became sharply aware of the change in their children wrought by the project. In a few instances this new awareness resulted in buying toys, and creating some play facilities in the home.

The third result of the project was a deep personal attachment which developed between many of the students and their charges.

The students kept to the very exacting and time consuming schedule of the project, while the children awaited "their teacher" eagerly week by week, often dressing up in their Shabbath best in their honor. After the project ended, parents reported that children continued to speak of their teachers longingly, and kept asking when they would come again.

Discussion

The very marked change which occurred in the play behavior of some of the children who participated in the project, after only nine teaching sessions was rather unexpected. This change was all the more surprising because most of the students were extremely inexperienced and functioned very poorly during the first few play-teaching sessions.

We feel that a number of factors contributed greatly to the unexpected success of the project:

1) *A One to One Continuous Relation Between Child and Play-Teacher*

As time passed we felt more and more that the opportunity to have the whole undivided attention of an adult was an important ingredient for the success of a play teaching session. It is interesting to note that in this respect the presence of the observing recorder, who kept to the background, did not seem to interfere. On the other hand, we had a few opportunities to observe the disruptive influence the presence of another child or in a very few cases other members of the household (when the teaching session was in the home) had on the performance of a child during play teaching sessions.

Towards the end of the project some students found it increasingly difficult to disengage their charges from the play which had developed, when the one-hour teaching session came to an end. We had therefore records of a few instances in which a child remained in the room, at the end of his period, while the next child due for a play-teaching session was brought in. Though the first child continued to occupy himself quietly, the new child reacted in most cases to his presence and seemed startled and disturbed by it. Records of such sessions read again and again, "looks at so and so, did not pay attention but watched . . ., started but stopped and looked at . . . , etc."

Given the very small scope and preliminary nature of the study, it is very hard to hazard an opinion whether the disruptive influence of the presence of further persons can be explained simply as difficulty in concentrating[8] or whether it was due to a deeper cause like a felt threat towards a burgeoning sense of intimacy and attachment between the child and his play-teacher. But irrespective of the explanation there is no question that the presence of further persons and especially another child proved to have disruptive effects once the one to one relationship between child and play-teacher had become established.

2) *Intervals of at Least a Week and Sometimes More Between Subsequent Play-Teaching Sessions*

Spacing subsequent play-teaching sessions a week apart was an accidental outcome of rather mundane considerations like hours the shelter in which the sessions took place was available, time the students could devote to the project, etc. In retrospect it does seem that the accidentally introduced time lapse between one play-teaching session and the next actually became an important factor in the assimilation of the ideas introduced in the course of a session. Those extra days gave the child an opportunity to go over in his mind, so to speak, the new modes of behaving and reacting he had encountered during the session, while becoming accustomed to them. As at the end of each session all the things which had been produced in the course of the session were left with the child, he might in some instances even have had opportunity for further manipulation and experimentation with these modes.

It should be mentioned that in another project along similar though not identical lines, two students met their charges daily, again because of purely circumstantial factors. In both cases the play-teacher's efforts sort of boomeranged by the end of the first week. Not only did the quality and content of the play which developed remain more or less constant, so that actually each play-

---

[8]Charlotte Buhler (1928) distinguishes between perseverence and concentration and defines concentration as the ability to persevere despite the disruptive influence of an interfering stimulus.

teaching session became no more than a replica of the previous one, but the children also stopped playing and asked to be taken home after progressively shorter periods and in one instance even refused to come altogether. Once the frequency of meetings with these two children was reduced, further work progressed satisfactorily.

We assume that responding to imaginative creative play on the part of a child who has never played that way before requires of him rather fundamental adjustments. Actually our records reveal that many of the children would hesitate and cast a questioning look at their play-teacher the first times they ventured imaginative statements like, "the doll is hungry now, she wants to eat!" Only upon receiving a smiling encouragement would they dare go on. If this assumption is correct daily encounters with the play-teacher might well be too heavy a pressure or even prove threatening and more than a child is able to take.

3) *A Teaching Mode in Which the Play-Teacher Plays Along by Himself, Discarding Obvious Efforts to Engage the Child Actively*

The teaching approach which we felt was potentially most effective developed slowly by a process of trial and error. It has to be remembered that this approach was developed within the special conditions of the project here described, and for children of a very young age. So far we have not been able to compare it with other teaching approaches, and can therefore only point to some of its salient points as they were experienced, subjectively, by us.

We soon came to recognize that one of the most important factors in creating a successful play-teaching session was to have the play-teacher continue by all means a flow of active connected play. A flow which would not be interrupted by questions directed to the child in an effort to engage him actively. Our records show that such questions most often remained unanswered, a fact which seldom failed to fluster the teacher. "What do you want to play?" was thus the most fatal of beginnings for any play-teaching session. But also: "Here is a doll, what shall we name her?" or, "Look at this nice car, where is it going?" never failed to stop short any burgeoning signs of interest or rapport. Equally bad was, "What shall we do now?" after any one play situation had been brought to a satisfactory end, e.g. the doll was in bed asleep.

If, as we have assumed all along, the child has had no experience of imaginative play, there is little hope that he will be able to provide initiative in situations like this. It is only when the play already runs along, that he will be able to mobilize his resources. When for instance the play-teacher has already established that the doll will now eat, and therefore is busy in "preparing" various typical meal-elements like milk, cake, etc., a child might be able to draw on his own everyday experience and contribute a first suggestion, e.g. bread. Actually an earliest step would in most cases be just picking up something the teacher produced and holding it to the doll's mouth, maybe emitting therewhile a munching sound. How incomparably much easier such a reaction is than a verbal answer to a hypothetical question, and therefore how much easier to come by, especially at the age of 2 years and 6 months when some of the children included in the project were still not talking fluently.

IMPLICATIONS

The outcomes of the project seem to indicate quite conclusively that under certain conditions it is indeed possible to teach young children to play imaginatively even when such play has not been fostered before in their own homes.

Moreover the very nature of the response of some of the children to the teaching efforts, namely play which developed in leaps and bounds and reminded the onlooker sometimes of the unleashing of a natural force, might give credence to a feeling that a bent towards imaginative play is indeed inborn, and that in those instances where such play does not develop, one might assume that an intrusion of external forces prevented its unfolding.

Though this first result is encouraging indeed, taking matters a step further, namely trying to prove a causal relationship between the activation of imaginative play in early childhood and an acceleration in the development of creativity either at this early age or at a later stage of development, is, under present conditions, difficult and perhaps even impossible.

As yet there is little agreement on a rigorous definition of the term creativity, and even less on adequate ways of testing for this elusive phenomenon. Moreover, most of the work that has been done so far has been confined to higher age groups than the one we were dealing with. Though as a matter of fact a few of the children included in the project were tested a year after its conclusion with good results on a conventional test of creativity, we do feel that given the present stage of knowledge such findings are far from conclusive. Reporting on them in earnest would, we feel, cloud up the issue at stake.

A broad field of enquiry is opened up by the very notion that free imaginative play may be a factor in establishing a mode towards novel and original ways of approaching issues confronting one in later life. Much further work on different levels is clearly called for. Still, even the slight possibility that eventually a link between imaginative play in childhood and creativity in later life might be established would, we feel, make an intensive search for means of educational intervention urgently called for, even at this early stage of enquiry.

REFERENCES

Ammar, H.: *Growing Up in an Egyptian Village*. London, Routledge Kegan Paul, 1954.

Bally, G.: *Vom Spielraum der Freiheit*. Schwage, Basel, 1966.

Bühler, Ch.: *Kindheit und Jurgend*. Hirzel, Leipzig, 1928.

de Meyere, V.: *De Kinderspelen van Pieter Bruegel den Oude Verklaard*. Antwerpen, 1941.

Feitelson, D.: Patterns of early education in the Kurdish community. *Megamot*, 5:95-109 (in Hebrew), 1954.

Feitelson, D.: Some aspects of the social life of Kurdish Jews. *Jewish Journal of Sociology*, 1:201-216, 1959.

Fortes, M.: Social and psychological aspects of education in Taleland. Supplement to *Africa*, London, Vol. XI, No. 4, 1938.

Granqvist, H.: *Birth and Childhood Among the Arabs*. Soderstrom, Helsingfors, 1947.

Gross, K.: *Die Spiele der Tiere*. Jena, Fischer, 1899.

Jersield, A.: *Child Psychology*. New York, Prentice Hall, 1946.

LeVine, R. A. and LeVine, Barbara B.: Nyansongo: A Gusii Community in Kenya. In Whiting, B. (Ed.), *Six Cultures*. New York, Wiley, 1963.

Mead, M.: Research on primitive children. In Carmichael, L. (Ed.), *Manual of Child Psychology*, New York, Wiley, 1954.

Piaget, J.: *Play, Dreams and Imitation in Childhood*. London, Heinemann, 1951.

Schon, D. A.: *Invention and the Evolution of Ideas*. London, Social Science Paperbacks, 1967.

Siegel, S.: *Nonparametric Statistics*. New York, McGraw Hill, 1956.

Smilansky, S.: *The Effects of Socio-Dramatic Play on Disadvantaged Pre-school Children*. New York, Wiley, 1968.

Stevenson, H. C. and Stevenson, N. G.: Social interaction in an interracial nursery school. *Genet Psychol Monog, 61*:37-75, 1960.

Valentine, C. W.: A study of the beginnings and significance of play in infancy. *Br J Psychol, 8*:188-200, 285-306, 1938.

Van Alstyne, D.: *Play Behavior and Choice of Play Materials of Pre-school Children*. Chicago, Chicago University Press, 1932.

Wallach, M. A. and Kogan, N.: *Modes of Thinking in Young Children*. New York, Holt Rinehart and Winston, 1965.

Woodcock, L. P.: *Life and Ways of the Two Year Old*. New York, Dutton, 1941.

CHAPTER 7

THE GAME AS A SCHOOL OF ABSTRACTION

BRIAN SUTTON-SMITH

INTRODUCTION

IN THE INTRODUCTION for Chapter 6 we have proposed that the "as if" point of view is to be expected and enhanced in play and games. Brian Sutton-Smith proposes that the game is a school of abstraction. He has given us another example of an empirical study of children's games and play. This research deals more explicitly with the gaming rather than the playing attitude taken by participants of games. By this we mean to say that the goal "to win" is emphasized over the "fun" of the play activity. Sutton-Smith proposes that logical thinking is predicated on abstraction, and the growth of that logical thinking can be enhanced by presenting children with games that invite them to be shrewd *and to* win. *This study drew its information from preschool children in affluent circumstances rather than deprived as Feitelson's were. There was no question among them about an absence of playfulness or creativity in play. There was simply a greater or lesser ability to understand the principles of abstraction involved in number conservation. In his discussion Sutton-Smith reported his insight into the way that such games as his child-subjects played were able to induce number-conservation learning. Among Feitelson's preschool Israeli and Arab children the "as if" attitude had to be taught. Eifermann's older children from the same milieu responded to the challenge of games in which the outcome was in doubt but*

119

abandoned predetermined games as uninteresting. For the children in Sutton-Smith's study who were just beginning to try to win, the intention *to be shrewd, to pit one's wits against those of another child or children and to win seemed to help them over the difficulty that a more complex and predominantly social game presents. Feedback concerning the success of the child's intention to be shrewd seemed to be rewarding and more specifically to be a reward for learning the elements of the number conservation problem. Thus, the impact of this research stands between messages of the two previous chapters and suggests that when* play *shifts to* game *the "as if" quality becomes "focused." It is focused upon something within the game; it contributes to an abstraction of a principle; and finally, the principle and its use yields a reward that is immediately relevant to the problem before the child. The appetite for such a chain of events, while not fitting the free play pattern, will tend to maintain the activity for its own sake—a cogent and necessary part of playfulness and creativity.*

With this chapter we end the sequence devoted to game research and the insights available to teachers from such research. There has been no attempt to be exhaustive; rather the effort has been to illustrate the uses to which seemingly tangential research reports can be put. We will turn next to a careful analysis of the structure and function of games and play.

—Editors

I N *Science and The Modern World*, A. N. Whitehead makes the point that "the habit of definite and exact thought was implanted in the European mind by the long dominance of scholastic logic and scholastic divinity" (1946, p. 15). In *Studies in Cognitive Growth*, Bruner, *et. al.* contend that children who have gone to school in one country are more similar (in logical competencies) to children who have gone to school in another country, than are either to children who have not gone to school in those countries. Bruner says of the school goer: " He early shows the effect of learning to use language outside a context in which his reference is supported either by pointing or by the structure of the situation . . . School forces him to rely on linguistic encoding as a way of communicating, because by remoteness from direct action it robs him of contextual and ostensive reference as a mode of carrying meaning" (1967, p. 323).

One might say that Whitehead is talking about the university as a form of abstraction, and Bruner about the elementary school as a form of abstraction. In both cases, the separation of thought from everyday concerns and contingencies makes possible the development of those internal consistencies in thinking itself which Piaget has labelled as concrete and formal operations. From such a broadly functionalistic point of view the *ivory tower* and the *latin grammar school* may have been successful because of their unrelatedness to life, and the transfer of training they affected may have occurred in a much more fundamental way than was generally considered when such matters were moot at the turn of this century. From this point of view the apparent sterility of these grammar schools with their studies of syntax and rhetoric has to be contrasted against the surgent "paleologic" (Arieti, 1967) with which mankind has traditionally surrounded most of its concerns. Just as conversion experiences are sometimes most adequately effected by a period in the wilderness or by fasting or some other radical behavioral separation, so apparently the step from a pre-operational to an operational level of logic has been aided historically by such institutional forms of severance. It is no accident that many of the major Head Start programs which deal at an even more elementary level of logic, that is with the distinction between *as is* and *as if*, spend much of their time talking about things not seen, not heard and not touchable. In some current work of my colleague Gilbert Lazier, of the Drama Department, at Teachers College, it has been found difficult to induce just such an "as if" response set in fourteen-year-old functional illiterates. When asked to imagine that one of the statues in Central Park is about to fly off, some of the students react with profound cynicism, others wish to rush down there to see it happening. There is in both cases no recognition of the abstractive or "as if" nature of the suggestion.

Games, I would suggest, like universities, grammar schools, Head Start programs, drama classes, and we might add, art, music, poetry, etc. are schools in abstraction. Like these other institutions and processes they also involve the fundamental assumption that one cannot learn enough by direct experience, that the regularities within experience (whether those of human interaction, language or logic) require concentrated focus if the user is to master, not merely be affected by, or transmit in a partial way their formal characteristics. Such regularities usually impinge upon us deeply embedded in regularities of other orders, as well as obscured and distorted by the contingencies of momentary survival. Furthermore the regularities which guide our behavior usually arrive themselves in multi-dimensional clusters which may well defy individual analysis. One has only to think of the amazing regularities under-lying social interaction which are currently being revealed in systematic studies labelled variously as kinesics, proxemics, etc., to realize the great difficulty anyone would have in mastering the "elements" of his own interactive responses. What appears to be more typical is that one learns these relationships in packaged forms which do not require an awareness of their molecular supports. Unfortunately, such forms of holistic functioning and learning have not been extensively documented outside the domains of perception and logic. We might well assume that games are an example of a form of holistic learning through which participants acquire a wide variety of competencies which normally function in an interactional context. They abstract and present a crystalliza-tion of human relationships, particularly those that have to do with asserting power over others. In an extensive series of studies John M. Roberts and I have presented information on the func-tioning of games both cross-culturally and intra-culturally and have sought to show that they are models of power, by which we mean that they are buffered learning situations through which the child gains acquaintance and experience at the power stratagems relevant to some of the major parameters of influence within his own culture (1962, 1963, 1963, 1964, 1965, 1966, 1966). The results of these studies have been presented and assessed in a number of publications. We dealt in the main with games which were pure expressions either of physical skill, strategy or chance. It so happens, however, that most games are mixtures of these elements.

In particular, among the games of young children (six to nine years) are those which contain a high proportion of chance and a small proportion of strategy. Neither the chance nor the strategy are pure. The first doesn't contain any controlling artefact (a die, roulette wheel, etc.), nor the second any clear pattern of rational choice. Both appear in the form of a more or less well informed *guess,* a guess partly at random, and partly based on observing characteristics of the situation involved. In fact we might hazard the statement that guessing is historically and developmentally a major type of pre-operational structure, in which both magic and insight are fused into one form of power. What the child gains through his guessing, this argument would continue, is an education in "shrewdness" which is the compound virtue that seems to derive from this schooling in chance and strategy. We might speculate that such games arose historically as institutionalized forms of abstractions through which the arts of shrewdness could be practiced and learned.

A Game of Number Conservation

The present paper deals, in particular, with one game of shrewdness and seeks to show that practice at this game is as effective as direct teaching for some of the elements involved. More specifically the game involves shrewdness in the guessing of numbers, and as such is directly related to current attempts to measure and facilitate number conservation in cognitive psychology. Attempts to induce number conservation in children by using specific training procedures have not been particularly successful (Flavell, 1963). Piaget's theory which provides models for the character of logical operations such as numeration gives little guidance with respect to the acquisition of such operations.

The game of "How many eggs in my bush?" (Sutton-Smith, 1959) was chosen as requiring the processes involved in number conservation. In this game, the children take turns at guessing how many counters the other player is holding in his hand (usually between one and six). Players alternate turns and a correct guess wins the counters from the other players. The game is finished when one player has all the counters. Each player begins with ten counters. It was hypothesized that play at this game would encourage the development of number conservation, because without it the player cannot know whether he is winning and can be cheated against.

Procedure

All children were tested for number conservation using the procedure of matching a row of blocks from a pile near at hand (Flavell, 1963, p. 313). The conservation test was given before and after the game training sessions which lasted for six weeks.[1] These involved one explicit game training session per week of an hour and much more informal play by the children without the teacher. Conservers played the game eagerly from the beginning. Nonconservers had to be encouraged and instructed by the teacher on how to pay attention to the counters and in some cases on how to count, how to guess, etc., training procedures which in previous research in the literature had not been particularly effective by themselves in inducing conservation (i.e. training in counting, etc.) (Flavell, 1963, p. 377). Within six weeks all nonconservers were playing the game with considerable enjoyment. The control group was taken from the same kindergarten in the following year at the same time of year. Children in both experimental and control groups were between the ages of five years and five years and seven months, but were advanced on the average one and one-fourth years in mental age. In mental age terms, therefore, they were at an age when average children normally begin to acquire conservation.

Results

The chi square analysis of Table 7-I indicates that the experimental group with the game training changed significantly in the direction of conservation, but that the control group without the game training did not. The two exceptions in the experimental group were both extremely immature boys, one of whom was subsequently retained in the kindergarten for a further year.

[1]My appreciation to Mrs. Sheree MacDonald for carrying out the game playing phase of this study, and to Mr. Gordon Schofield, Headmaster, Maunee Valley Country Day School, for encouraging the use of the school for experimental purposes. The project received partial support from Grant MH 07994-04 from the National Institute of Mental Health.

TABLE 7-I
CHANGES IN NUMBER CONSERVATION AS A RESULT OF GAME PLAYING

Subjects	Pre Test		Post Test		P
	Con.	Non/Con.	Con.	Non/Con.	
Experimental Group, 1965	10	14	22	2	$< .01$
Control Group, 1966.	7	11	8	10	ns

Discussion

The effectiveness of this game in inducing the change is clearly of considerable pedagogic importance and parallels the use of games by others for similar pedagogic ends (Humphrey, 1966). The success of the game in inducing conservation does not, however, illuminate the psychological processes involved in number concept acquisition, though it does seem to imply that such acquisition occurs more readily when there is an interaction of influences working in its favor as typically occurs in a game.

We may perhaps theorize that when children acquire conservation there is a mutual dependency of processes as follows. On the one hand there are such operations and performances as class equivalence, seriation, counting, matching, etc., some or all of which are apparently contributory towards the development of number conservation but not sufficient to make it occur by themselves (Dodwell, 1960). On the other hand, there is the child's intention to use this information effectively in order to overcome a difficulty of which he has become aware—an intentionality which might be considered a key factor in the implicit or explicit feedback procedures successfully used in several studies of number conservation (Wallach & Sprott, 1964; Beilin, 1966). Alternatively, when a game is introduced as in the present study a variety of superordinate motives are introduced: to win the game, to acquire counters, to have fun, not to be cheated. These in turn may facilitate the acquisition of the above operations and performances, which apparently then transfer to the test of number conservation. We are thus confronted with the possibility that conservation concepts may be built into the child in an elementaristic way providing there is sufficient incentive, or in a hierarchical way as in the present case of game playing. It would make sense that if the two methods were compared, then the more rapid learning would occur in the second case where the conservation concepts had been acquired within the broader hierarchical context of the game. There is some evidence that this is the case (Humphrey, 1966). It follows that if this is the way in which children "normally" have learned such skills through enculturation, as the very existence of such a traditional game seems to imply, then we are also in a better position to understand the considerable difficulties experienced by a succession of researchers in attempting to induce conservation by more elementaristic means. Number conservation in service of the school of shrewdness comes easier than number conservation in service of the grade school teacher.

In sum, I have argued that the game is a school of abstraction. But it is a school of the holistic variety apparently evolved during cultural evolution as a way of imparting knowledge of the processes of social power. The game of "How many eggs in my bush?" has been presented as an example of number conservation, though it might have been more to the point to test for the derived learning of shrewdness rather than for number. The latter could be regarded as merely incidental to that larger end.

REFERENCES

Arieti, S.: *The Intrapsychic Self*. New York, Basic Books, 1967.
Beilin, H.: Feedback and intralogical strategies in invariant area conceptualization. *J Exp Child Psychol, 3*, 267-278, 1966.
Bruner, J.S. et al.: *Studies in Cognitive Growth*. New York, Wiley, 1967.
Dodwell, P.C.: Children's understanding of number and related concepts. *Can J Psychol, 14*, 191-205, 1960.
Flavell, J.: *The Developmental Psychology of Jean Piaget*. New York, Van Nostrand, 1963.
Humphrey, J. K.: An exploratory study of active games in learning of number concepts by first grade boys and girls. *Perceptual and Motor Skills, 23*, 341-342, 1966.
Roberts, J.M. and Sutton-Smith, B.: Child training and game involvement. *Ethnology, 1*, 166-185, 1962.
Roberts, J.M., Sutton-Smith, B. and Kendon, A.: Strategy in folktales and games. *J Soc Psychol, 61*, 185-199, 1963.
Sutton-Smith, B.: *The Games of New Zealand Children*. Berkeley, Univ. of California Press, 1959.
Sutton-Smith, B.: Novel responses to toys. *Merrill-Palmer Quarterly, 14*, 159-160, 1968.

Sutton-Smith, B. and Roberts, J.M.: Game involvement in adults. *J Soc Psychol, 60,* 15-30, 1963.

Sutton-Smith, B. and Roberts, J.M.: Rubrics of competitive behavior. *J Genet Psychol, 105,* 13-37, 1964.

Sutton-Smith, B. and Roberts, J.M.: Studies in an elementary game of strategy. *Genet Psychol Monogr, 75,* 3-42, 1967.

Wallach, L. and Sprott, R.L.: Inducing number conservation in children. *Child Dev, 35,* 1057-1071, 1964.

Whitehead, A.N.: *Science and the Modern World.* Cambridge, Cambridge Univ. Press, 1946.

CHAPTER 8

A STRUCTURAL-FUNCTIONAL ANALYSIS OF PLAY AND GAMES

PERRY GILLESPIE

INTRODUCTION

*T*HE FINAL *chapter in the theoretical portion of this volume by Perry Gillespie contains a careful analysis of play and then of games according to their structure and function. He draws a clear distinction between play and games and documents his synthesis of their meaning from the extensive literature in both fields. There is some overlap between Reardon's and Gillespie's chapters which serves to make the transition to Part Two of the volume easy. The material in this chapter is necessary to introduce the applied portion of this work.*

Gillespie points out the essentially social aspect of games. It is this aspect that he proposes yields their usefulness in teaching relationships among people, places and things. He sees games as especially useful in inducting children into the complex adult problems of decision-making. The game represents the framework of the process *by which such decisions are arrived at. Since both the framework and the process are involved he has couched his analysis in terms of the structure (framework) and function (process and its outcome) defining characteristic. Gillespie lays special emphasis on the essential characteristic of a game—namely, the requirement that something of value to the participant must be at stake to maintain the game. Further, he highlights the need to have*

128

future possession of this valued thing or event in doubt to provide all of the participants with an incentive to continue the game activity. Thus, this final chapter reiterates the insights and findings of the previous writers in summary form. We will now turn to the applications available to the classroom teacher interested in using games to enlist children in their own educational process.

—Editors

W HAT IS THE NATURE of play? What is the nature of games? What structural and functional components are typical of their organization and are they the same? First, the characteristics of play will be identified, then the characteristics of games. The two will be compared in order to identify their common elements and those peculiar to games alone.

Play

Structural Components

Play is an activity separate from behavior found in the everyday world (Huizinga, 1950, pp. 5-14). However, it bears a relationship to everyday affairs and places people in a relationship to each other, the play world and the real world. These relationships may be stated as the structural components of play.

Play stands outside of ordinary life. There is a point in time when an individual or group recognizes that they are playing rather than engaging in the activities of the real world. There is also a point at which play is terminated. Only during the period between these two points does a separate play world exist. These points constitute its *temporal* boundaries. The community of players must also acknowledge an arena of play which sets up its *physical* boundaries. This fact is accepted once a player steps from the real world into that of play. One must abide by the rules which establish the play world if it is to be maintained as a separate sphere of activity.

Play is a make believe, a second reality. Children recognize that the play world is more than just separated from the real world (Caillois, 1961, pp. 4-10). For them it has a second reality. The child pretends some object or area represents something from the real world. Within the temporal and spatial boundaries of play, the world the child creates in his imagination represents exactly what he wants it to be. For example, a child may declare: "Let's play train. I'll be the engine and you be the cars." Their world may be continually changing since the participants may modify it as often and as much as they want. It interacts with the adult world, but only to the extent that features from real life can be transformed to meet the needs and desires of the players. In this respect play performs a function rather than producing something of a material nature. Hence, it is non-task-oriented, lacking a goal, but having a purpose.

Play is rule-governed (Caillois, 1961, pp. 4-10). Only by abiding by the "rules of play" can such a world be maintained. They suspend the ordinary set of conventions regulating the actions of individuals in the everyday world. During play a new set of rules decrees what is or is not to be. Reality is transformed or cancelled out by purposefully including, excluding, or modifying features from adult life. Often the governing rules are kept secret, known only to a small select community of players. In any event, each player must accept the validity of the rules if play is to continue. Those individuals who cannot or will not abide by the rules are excluded automatically from the group by their defection.

Play is a voluntary activity. If the child were forced to participate he would not be "playing" and the activity would be robbed of its most attractive quality, that of escaping the demands and consequences of everyday life (Huizinga, 1950, pp. 5-14). For the duration of the activity, the child can suspend the conventions of the real world, pretending to do what he would like in life but cannot because of ability or social restrictions.

Play is an attitude. There is a special attitude associated with play. Play has been defined variously as being amusing, divertive, something which is not to be taken seriously. Attention is directed away from the realities of the everyday world. The child steps from ordinary life into a temporary world with its own rules and conventions which he himself determines. Players must be willing to suspend the realities of the ordinary world. They are not concerned with actions having consequences in the adult world. Each child knows he is merely pretending, that his actions can be repudiated later as having occurred in play. Such an attitude is thus derived from the non-serious, isolated, voluntary aspects of play. While operating in its sanctuary the child can alter freely or disregard the norms governing ordinary life without fear of punishment.

Play is a personal creation. It occurs spontaneously, on-the-spot, to suit the needs and desires of the individual. Since children shape features of the real world in a way acceptable to *them,* play is egocentric in nature. The selection of and shape given to the features brought into the play world are uniquely those of the individual. Because of its highly individual character, it does not have a fixed form which can be handed down from one generation of players to the next. Neither plots nor roles are codified, but are created as required. Certain plots and roles do occur repeatedly, but their choice is not predetermined (Peller, 1952, pp. 66-83). They appear as the needs or desires of the child create a demand for them. Significantly, there are no rules which state when a particular plot or role will appear, what combinations will emerge, or how they will be enacted by the child.

Play is uncertain. Neither the range nor the scope of behavior can be specified in advance (Caillois, 1961, pp. 9-10). Only the rules which maintain the play world regulate the behavior which takes place within its temporal and physical boundaries. If a child behaves such that the rules of play are violated, either he must be excluded from the activity or the play world ceases to exist. The sequence of action cannot be determined since no rules state specifically what a player is to do. In addition its outcome cannot be indicated beforehand, making it virtually impossible to declare a winner or winners, or to state criteria for winning or losing. The indeterminancy of play thus permits much freedom of action to the players, and with it a chance to exhibit personal creativity.

Play's rewards are indeterminate. The rewards are solely determined by the needs and desires which that person brings to the activity. If the child receives satisfaction in play, he is rewarded. As rewards are psychological or social in nature, they are intangible and unstateable. If a child does not receive satisfaction from playing, he is no longer engaged in play. Since the rewards gained are individually determined, no single predetermined reward or

payoff can be awarded a "winner." Because there are no criteria
for determining a winner, play for the group ends in a situation
identical with that prevailing in the beginning (Caillois, 1961,
pp. 9-10).

Functional Components

Play provides miniature life problems to be solved by the child.
Situations are created which allow him to both broaden and vary
his contact with reality in a buffered, step-by-step process. Experiences may be prolonged by means of repetition. Eventually, he
learns to cope with and solve his problems.

*Play functions to allow the assimilation of overpowering experi-
ences.* In play a child is able to assimilate piecemeal an experience
too difficult to cope with at one fell swoop (Waelder, 1933, pp.
217-218). Some individuals lack freedom to act independently
in the presence of adults or stronger playmates. During play the
child is able to alter his relationships, both with his peers and his
superiors, by means of make believe. Each encounter can be
broken down into smaller pieces which can be assimilated easily
by the child. He is able to reproduce or "replay" adult behavior
until its consequences are understood. Peek-a-Boo is an example
of early play in which the child is able to make a parent or stronger
playmate disappear and reappear at his command, thereby helping
him to learn to accept the comings and goings of his parent (Peller,
1954, p. 186).

*Play functions to provide experiences from which the child can
draw analogies to newly encountered situations.* A child in play
is able to build up a repertoire of potentially useful experiences
from which he can draw analogies to newly encountered situations (Peller, 1954, pp. 81-83). Any event which is without prece-
dent precludes drawing upon prior experience in order to deal with
it. A child, lacking the adult's life experience, can utilize play experiences. For example, a child who has never broken a leg may
act out a situation in which an imaginary companion does. The
story may derive from an actual experience which happened to
another child. In this way the child may prepare for an experience
which has not actually happened. Thus, through the medium of
play a child is able to divest an anticipated experience of its unique-
ness.

Play functions both to cancel and to transform reality. By cancelling reality, a child in play may do what he could not do in real life, such as act like a pet animal or a younger sibling (Peller, 1952, pp. 70, 77-78). He may engage in acts which are no longer appropriate to his age, sex, or position in life by simply making a verbal declaration to those around him about his subsequent role and actions. In essence, he is saying that the ordinary norms and conventions which control the behavior of a person of his age, sex, or status are modified, temporarily suspended, or cancelled for the duration of the play act. Aspects of the real world which are difficult or impossible to accept in their regular form may thereby be omitted or altered, making it possible for the child to cope with them.

Play functions to put children into active, directive roles. Often children are subject to the demands of parents, adults, or stronger playmates. They are told what they must do, how to do it, and when to do it. In the real world the ability and opportunity of the child to exercise command is severely limited. However, in play a child is able to assume an active, directive role in controlling both his actions and those of others (Waelder, 1933, p. 221). He may for example assume the role of a general directing the actions of armies (toy soldiers) against their foes.

Play provides an opportunity for the child to explore and experiment with different ways of influencing and controlling the behavior of others such as skill, strategy, or chance. He may discover and bring about different solutions to problems which he was unable to solve in real life such as how to persuade others to accept his ideas.

Games

Structural Components

The structural components of games fall into static and dynamic categories. External boundaries of games and their internal structural aspects serve to define the formal, static bounds of the game. Rules governing procedures and player interactions while the game is in progress define its functional, dynamic bounds.

Rules governing the external boundaries and those specifying the internal relationship among the parts constitute the formal, static bounds of a game. *The external boundaries of games are established by three sets of rules.* The partitioning of the game world from the real world is effected in three ways: by rules of relevance, irrelevance, and transformation. *Rules of relevance* state those features of the real world to be included or maintained in the game (Goffman, 1961, pp. 26-27). Characteristics carried over into games have an equivalent meaning both in life and in the game. For example, time has the same meaning in the context of the baseball game as it does in ordinary life. It is not scaled down. Often aspects of the one world are transferred to the other providing both realism and continuity between the two. Many items such as affect-loaded situations, clothes, roles, terms, etc., although inessential to the logical structure of the game, contain powers of suggestion which enhance its drama and setting.

Rules of irrelevance are a complementary set of rules indicating which features of the real world are to be consciously excluded from the game (Goffman, 1961, pp. 21-26). They are a purposive inattention to life's socio-cultural conventions and apply to both material and non-material features such as wealth, social position, abilities, skills and so on. In effect they equalize the players— players adopt an "affective neutrality" toward each other. Personal feelings are held in abeyance for the duration of the game. Such features excluded from the game are inessential to its operation and might detract from its more attractive qualities.

Transformation rules deal with those attributes of the real world which are to be retained, but require certain modifications before they are introduced into the game (Goffman, 1961, pp. 26-27). Certain aspects of ordinary life must be relaxed or disguised before some children are able to participate in games. A

> . . . disguise may function not so much as a way of concealing something as a way of revealing as much of it as can be tolerated in an encounter. We fence our encounters in with gates; the very means by which we hold off a part of reality can be the means by which we can bear introducing it (Goffman, 1961, pp. 77-78).

Two aspects of the real world are most often affected by rules of transformation—time and space. Both are modified to meet the special demands of the game and of the players. *Temporal rules* control the duration and pace of the game. They also determine the length of periods and the time between periods (Sutton-Smith, 1959, pp. 13-24). By altering temporal rules, units of time can be scaled to suit the abilities of the players. When the time dimensions differ from those of real life, rules tell how they differ. Furthermore, a segment of time, containing a major decision point in the game, can be repeated, allowing the testing of different decisions in order to determine their effect on the outcome of the game.

Spatial rules set the physical dimensions of the game world (Sutton-Smith, 1959, pp. 13-24). They handle the modifications made in the use of space by the players. They establish the external spatial boundaries such as a playing field or a game board, and they establish the internal boundaries as in the case of goal regions, safety zones, taboo areas, rest places, home base, etc. In addition, they determine the terrain upon which a game is to take place, e.g. on a game board or on actual ground. The abilities of the players must be taken into account. For younger children the physical dimensions of the terrain must be scaled down to match their endurance and abilities. If the spatial dimensions are not scaled down, then handicap rules are used to aid the younger child. In addition, rest periods and safety zones are often provided so that the players can catch their breath before reentering the game.

The *internal structure of games is regulated by roles, interaction, plots and goals found in a game.* Roles are given definition by their type and the power which accrues to them. The pattern of relationships and subsequent actions of the players is established by the nature of the interaction permitted, the game plot, and goals set out for each team or player to achieve while in a given role.

A basic unit in games is the role. The key actor and counter-actor roles are spelled out along with criteria for identifying them. First there must be a minimum of two *bona fide* roles. A *bona fide* role is one which permits the person or persons filling it to choose from at least two alternative moves and to receive payoffs (Rapoport, 1966, pp. 18, 21; Shubik, 1964, p. 12). Game roles and their relationships are frozen and conventional having been codified in collective rules over a period of time. As a result criteria for identifying them are known to a wide community of players. Roles are given definition by type, power, and physical and human resources.

There are three basic types of roles: (1) *group maintenance roles* which actively maintain the organization of the group and the structure of the game, (2) *task roles* which contribute to the attainment of the group or team goals, and (3) *individual roles* which contribute to the attainment of each player's personal objectives (McDavid and Harari, 1968, p. 302). Behavior for group maintenance roles is usually prescribed; i.e. a person in such a role must or ought to act in a manner detailed before the game begins. Examples of maintenance roles are game directors, analysts or messengers. Behavior for task and individual roles is either prescribed in advance or left to the person filling the role to carry out as he sees fit. In the case of enacted behavior, only those rules maintaining the game and governing procedures limit what a player is able to do.

Sources of power for roles vary both within games and from game to game. Generally, it can be ascribed to a player's ability to control what he does in a role and the type of power built into the role such as expert, legitimate, reward, and coercive.

The extent of a player's ability to control his actions and those of other players determines the amount of power contained in a particular role. It is called a *high power* role if a player can directly control both his own actions and those of other players, i.e. he can dictate who, when, where, and even how a player is to move in a game. Additional support may be derived from a greater freedom of action of special powers built into the role. If a player cannot directly control his own actions but must respond to the initiatives of players or is limited by the character of the role, it is termed a *low power* role.

A second source of power comes from the type brought to or built into a role. Typical examples are expert, legitimate, reward and coercive power (Street, 1967, pp. 11-14). *Expert power* is the willingness of other players to accept the expertise of an individual in a given area of endeavor such as law or medicine. For example, a career diplomat filling an ambassador's role would be attributed powers commensurate with his training and experience as a diplomat. *Legitimate power* is embodied in a particular job as is the case for bankers, mayors, policemen, presidents or generals. A person in such a role is able to act as that person would act in real life, e.g. a president acts as the leader of a country or a general commands an army. *Reward power* is the ability of a person filling a role to do something for or give something to another player in the game. For example, a player may ask another player to join his side in return for which he will receive a part of the team's winnings. *Coercive power* is the ability of a player filling a role to punish other players if they do not do as he wishes.

A third source of role power is derived from the physical and human resources available to the person filling the role. These include the number of players a person has to help him perform a specific task. The resource materials provided a player, such as money, capability units, trade goods, or equipment, are also sources of power. Other resources may include role-clothing, symbolic designations like "boss," "leader," or "it," or such intangible items as history, tradition, and precedence.

Those aspects of game structure which govern player interactions and procedures during game time constitute the functional, dynamic aspects of a game. *The structure of player interaction has implications for the behavior and participation of the players filling game roles.* For this reason, the nature, duration and intensity of the interaction is spelled out prior to the game. For example, is contact to be physical or non-physical?; is the interaction between living or symbolic players?; is it to be competitive, cooperative, or mixed? There are at least three basic interaction structures: one-person, two-person, and N-person (Ohm, 1966, pp. 115-116; Luce and Raiffa, 1957, pp. 3-11, 53-55).

One person games are those in which an individual competes against the environment. By definition, one-person or solitaire games cannot be accepted as social games which require two *bona fide* players to exist. They are, in fact, a special case of two-person games, with Nature, Fate, or Chance acting as the second player (and therefore, unable to decide on moves or receive payoffs). Examples are target and race games. *Hopscotch* and *Golf* are variations of the one-person game. In them individuals play against the environment and then compare their scores with one another.

Two-person (dyadic) games permit the functioning of two significant features of all groups—the ability to unite and separate

(Simmel, 1955, pp. 9-15). It takes two individuals to start a game, but it takes only the defection of a single player to end the game. Only one of the two primary functions can be carried out at one time. Because the threat of separation is ever present in the two person games, certain restrictions are imposed upon the nature of the interaction between the players. Each player is matched as closely as possible in terms of age, ability, experience, status, power and so forth. When this is not possible, handicap rules are employed to equalize the roles. Interaction can be purely cooperative with the most cooperative players receiving a higher proportional share; competitive-cooperative (mixed-interest) in which players share in the reward; coordinate in which the players seek to achieve the same goal, or purely competitive as in *Gin Rummy* when one player wins all while the other player loses all. Such competitive games pose a threat to the players thus increasing the chances of a player's defection, and with it, the end of the game. Two-person games in which units or teams replace individual players employ the same competitive structures, but the criticality of a player's defection is almost non-existent. Rarely does one team quit a game or leave the playing field. Two-person (team) games permit both between group competition and within-group cooperation to exist simultaneously as in *Football*. Such games are characteristically of mixed-interest, interdependent, and strategical.

N-person games, that is, those games with three or more players, allow both the function of union and separation to go on at the same time without fear of ending the game. The third member or player is often considered an intruder and pivotal because he is able to unite or separate with either of the other two players to form the strongest unit (Simmel, 1955, pp. 9-15). In contrast with the polarization and equalization of power in the dyadic game, the N-person game makes it possible to represent such real life features as the formation of coalitions, roles of unequal power, negotiation, the division of payments among the several winning players or teams, and the opportunity for cooperation and competition to occur simultaneously. A greater number of roles or units permits a differentiation of roles and behavior. Examples of N-person games include: business games in which companies compete while within the company employees cooperate and military games in which military units cooperate to fight against opposing forces.

Players act within a framework called a plot or scenario (Peller, 1952, pp. 66-83; 1954, pp. 192-193). The plot contains the background situation or information required for the game. It identifies the major decision-points in the game for each of the key actor and counter-actor roles and their order of appearance. The plot is therefore the framework which sets out the sequence of actions which takes place in the game. Although each decision-point and its order of appearance is predetermined, the final outcome remains in doubt until the last moves of the game have been made. Thus, the actual course of play is structured by the moves which each player makes according to the nature of his role and the information available to him about the moves of the other players.

In games, players seek a goal either as individuals or as members of a team (Coleman, pp. 8-9, 10-19). Games are therefore goal-oriented; all players strive to achieve some goal: social, psychological, or material. The *possibility of winners* is necessary as are the *rewards* associated with winning. In those games in which there appear to be no winners, the rewards are disguised in the form of intangible social or psychological rewards. Rewards of this type are embedded in the social matrix of real life. In other games, the final goal and its corresponding reward is made at the end of a series of games as occurs in *Chess, Golf* or *Tennis* tournaments. Individuals who take part in serial games may learn to expect a reward at some future point in time and not immediately at the end of each game. In this type of game, children may learn a type of behavior sometimes termed deferred gratification.

All games require planning. Players must evaluate the probability of an immediate possible outcome based upon the joint decisions of the various players at each decision point in the game. "If I do this; he will do that." The moves selected reflect a preconceived plan or strategy which anticipates how other players will respond to his choice of moves. For example, game plans are laid out in advance of a game by football teams.

Rules regulate game procedures. All games have rules or norms which govern their operation. Rules thus constitute criteria for action which are mutually perceived and agreed upon by all of the players. At least seven types of rules regulate the procedures followed in games. They are: initiation and termination; deployment and disposition; communication; arbitration; intervention; enforcement, and outcome (payoff) rules.

The activities of the game world are bounded by rules of initiation and termination which determine when a game begins and ends. It begins when the initial move is made, and is terminated when the preconditions agreed upon have been met. Two conditions generally prevail: a specified period of time must elapse and/or criteria for winning or losing must be satisfied.

Rules of deployment and disposition control who, when, where and how a player is to move in a given role. They indicate who is able to control the movements of other players. Players need to know where to score, where to rest and regroup, where they are forbidden to go.

Communication rules govern the flow of information prior to and during the game by specifying whether communication is permitted or not, direct or indirect, restricted or free and symmetrical or asymmetrical.[1] The partners may agree to divide up, transfer to one another, or save any future winnings. The type of communication net and a player's position in it influence his verbal ability to influence or control the actions of other players in the game. There are six basic patterns: no communication, circle, chain, "Y," wheel, and all channel.

Communication is *direct* if a player occupies a position in the net permitting him to communicate with every other player without going through another player. It is *restricted* if rules limit a player's ability to initiate, receive, or terminate the flow of information, or if the form, content, rate, or frequency of communication is limited in any way. It is *symmetrical* if each player can interact verbally in the same way as a player in any other position.

Rules of arbitration state what to do in situations not covered in the rules or when a dispute takes place between players that

---

[1]The seminal idea for communication rules came from Alex Bavelas, "A Mathematical Model for Group Structures," *Communication and Culture,* ed. Alfred G. Smith (New York: Holt, Rinehart, and Winston, 1966), pp. 216-222. Also see Harold J. Leavitt, "Some Effects of Certain Communication Patterns on Group Performance," *Communication and Culture,* ed. Alfred G. Smith (New York: Holt, Rinehart, and Winston, 1966), pp. 222-243.

cannot be settled within the context of the game (Coleman, pp. 7-8).

Rules of intervention make known how Nature, Fate, or Chance enter into the play of the game (Coleman, pp. 9-10). They describe how these forces are represented in the game. They also control the extent to which these forces intervene in the game. Chance cards, which indicate the occurrence of an act of nature such as fire, or the use of dice commonly represent these forces in games.

Information about penalties for breaking rules is contained in rules of enforcement (Coleman, p. 10). Three types of action can be taken based upon the nature of the infraction: (1) *restitutive action* in which play reverts back to the state just prior to the infraction, (2) *repressive action* in which a player is penalized and (3) *expulsion*. Action of the first type occurs when a procedural rule is broken as when one player moves out of turn or offsides. The second type occurs when behavior inappropriate to a role is displayed. The third type is the most serious and results when a player violates the rules maintaining the game world.

Outcome rules indicate criteria for scoring, winning and losing, and payoff. There are two kinds of scoring criteria. The first type states whether players are competing against some arbitrary figure or standard, or against their own prior score. In both cases, they are called "absolute" scoring criteria. The second type indicates that they are competing with other players on a relative score basis; for example, the player who gets the most points relative to the other players wins. The latter are called "relative" scoring criteria. Criteria for winning or losing spell out the conditions which have to be met before a winner or winners can be declared. Payoff criteria describe how or when players will receive their payoff for winning.

Functional Components

Games perform a number of functions which help to induct the child into the activities of the adult world. First, they aid in the socialization process by serving as expressive models for the various patterns of control, interaction and organization found in a culture. Second, they structure interdependent social situations in which the child can make decisions and interact with other children who exhibit different values. Third, the more stringent features of the real world can be softened or disguised so that the child can gradually become accustomed to the demands of everyday life in a buffered, step-by-step situation. Fourth, games serve to transmit knowledge that leads to a more complete understanding of the culture.

Socialization is carried out in different ways and at different levels of complexity by both games and play. Studies of games suggest that they serve as expressive models for a culture (Roberts, Arth and Bush, 1959, pp. 597-600). Play has been identified by cultural anthropologists as a universal feature of every culture, whereas games have not (Roberts and Sutton-Smith, 1962, p. 167). Yet, when games do appear in a culture they reflect the complexity and sophistication of it. There is a usual order of appearance of games in the child training inventory of a culture: "(1) training in nurturance and self-reliance with *no* games; (2) independence, responsibility and achievement training with games of physical skill and chance; and (3) obedience training and games of strategy (Roberts, Sutton-Smith, Kenden, 1963). Each type of game; skill, chance, or strategy, reflects a different pattern or style of social behavior. The individual is introduced to the various styles of behavior and soon learns to differentiate one from the other. Eventually the child is able to gain experience in using each style and learns which are most appropriate for him personally.

Since socialization is a continuous process for each child, participation in games which emphasize one or more behavioral styles is dependent upon the age, ability and experience of each individual. Roberts and Sutton-Smith, after studying games found in western cultures, reported that children move from a vicarious experience represented by folk tales and stories for the young child, through a more active social experience in games for older youth, to full scale participation in adult activities (Roberts and Sutton-Smith, 1962, p. 183).

Games provide experience in decision-making for young and old alike. Practice in dealing with such problems in a situation in which mistakes can be made without endangering the group are welcome. Decision-making can be carried out under three conditions of conflict: interest, perspective, and value.

Conflict of interest arises among individuals who have goals which they hope to achieve. If one were acting apart from the group, the attainment of one's goals would depend solely upon one's own efforts. Rarely, however, is this the case. Individuals usually operate within the context of a group. A conflict of interest develops when several persons cannot agree upon their preferences for a given outcome. The resulting range of social behavior (responses) stems from different solutions to the problem of achieving as much of one's goals as possible. In a game players may learn to estimate the consequences of their actions

> . . . taking into consideration the very important circumstances that outcomes are determined not only by one's own choices but also by the choices of others, over whom one has no control (Rapoport, 1966, p. 108; Shubik, 1964, p. 9; Luce and Raiffa, 1957, p. 1).

A conflict of perspectives, called a cognitive confrontation by Danielian, produces effects distinct from a simple conflict of interest. Instead of a conflict arising from preferences for different outcomes, it results from pitting one pattern of thought against another. Decision-making games structuring a conflict of perspective produce situations in which two or more persons (1) attempt to solve a problem of common concern, (2) offer differing solutions to the problem, (3) find that their solutions differ and (4) must then consider the other player's approach and tentative solution to the problem in order to jointly arrive at a solution satisfying to all (Hammond, 1965, p. 50).

Suppose that one approach demands that no compromise be made over any issue and another approach saw compromise as an appropriate way to arrive at a mutual decision. In a game the relative importance among several demands can be assessed and categories of negotiable and non-negotiable demands could be set up. Within each category the two approaches to decision making could be discussed and then applied. Another example presented in Danielian's Greco-American discussions "each truth was accepted as non-negotiable, but if each side *reduced* the number of its truthful demands, a compromise would then be possible" (Danielian, 1967, pp. 317-318).

A *conflict of values* produces effects differing from either a conflict of interest or perspectives. One's cultural mode of perceiving is pitted against that of another. During such an encounter an unfreezing of cultural perspectives may occur as the individual becomes emotionally engaged to the

> . . . extent that habitual, well-entrenched cultural modes of perceiv-
> ing are invoked and . . . commitment to these modes of perceiving
> is pitted against the needs of an immediately demanding and salient
> problem or situation (Danielian, 1967, p. 319).

Games function to disguise aspects of the real world. By manipulating the structural features of a game it is possible to alter and soften them so that even the most sensitive or inept child feels confident enough to engage in them. Redl found, for example, that games were one of the few means of bringing together children who suffered from hyperaggression or destructive tendencies. He observed that built-in codes of behavior associated with neighborhood games were acceptable to these children, whereas the externally imposed rules of the adult world were not. Placed in a game situation, the children themselves enforced the rules (Redl and Wineman, 1952, pp. 110-116).

Sutton-Smith reports a second example of the function of disguise. He found that emotionally disturbed or immature children obeyed game rules, although they would not abide by the rules governing adult society. Initially, these children were placed in cheating games such as *Mother May I* allowing them to function in a disguised rule-structured situation. Later as they engaged in games governed by rules more closely approximating those found in the adult world, they were introduced to games of steadfastness, the object of which was to stand fast and obey the rules (Sutton-Smith, 1955, pp. 228-229, 261-263). In them each child tried to cause the other players to make mistakes. Children who lacked physical skills engaged in Central-Person games. A Central-Person game is one in which a single person called an "It" faced a group of children called a "pack." In the case of an inept player, the "It" role is given greater control over other players thereby increasing his chances of success and concomitantly his confidence. As his skills improve, the power built into the role is gradually decreased until he can compete on equal terms with other children.

Games function to transmit knowledge on several levels of awareness and subtlety. In such games as simulations students may learn specific modes of inquiry and substantive knowledge such as facts, concepts, generalizations. In addition, students may learn to gather, analyze and act upon information. Problems can be reduced to a degree of complexity appropriate to the age, ability and experience of the players involved.

Distinctions Between Play and Games

Play and games can be compared on the basis of their functional and their structural properties. Such a comparison reveals that play and games represent distinct types of activity.

Functional Distinctions

Play serves the individual. In it he is introduced to the realities of the everyday world. Reality is fashioned by the child to meet the requirements of his personal world. He breaks down those experiences which are too much for him to accept *in toto*; he draws analogies from known past experiences to present, unknown situations. When the child encounters some totally unacceptable aspect of reality, he alters its form or cancels it out entirely. Thus through the medium of play, his contact with and acceptance of features of the real world may be increased.

During play the child makes the greatest use of the transformation and cancellation of reality. As the individual assimilates aspects of the real world he transforms them so that they fit the requirements of his personal world. In it, he may test various styles of social behavior without fear of punishment for inappropriate responses.

Only during play can the child select and enact those plots and roles which satisfy his personal needs and desires. He can be the star performer directing both his own actions and those of others, if not in fact at least in fancy. In this way, play may help prepare the individual for the day when he acts not alone, but with others.

In contrast, games serve the interest of the social group. In them children may learn to operate within the context of a group and to accept the social conventions which govern its activities. Games, therefore, aid in the socialization process serving as expressive models of social organization, control and interaction. In them children find themselves in interdependent social situations in which they face other players who perceive and think about things differently, feel about them differently and hence, behave differently. Thus, the child encounters different styles of behavior and may learn to differentiate one pattern of social behavior from another.

In games the child is exposed to as much of reality as possible. He must act as he would in real life with only the consequences of his actions temporarily set aside. No longer may the individual shape his own world.

Unlike the freedom of choice vis-à-vis role and plot allowed in play, a child cannot pick those he desires since they are already codified in the structure of a game. As a result he may or may not fill a role in which he can control the actions of his fellow players.

Structural Distinctions

Both play and games are special worlds set aside from ordinary life by rules which alter both the spatial and temporal features of the adult world. In play, the child decrees what the new "reality" will be by selecting what he will include, exclude and modify. In effect he determines the temporal, spatial and social dimensions of his play world. As a result, his world may be in a continual state of change, but always under his own control. At one moment a stick may represent a knight's lance and in the next instant it may be a soldier's rifle. In contrast with play, games present the child with a given world. Time limits are fixed and spatial boundaries set up before the start of the game. Because of this, the dimensions of the game are known to each player prior to its beginning.

Play is make-believe, i.e. a child may behave as he sees fit. His actions are neither restricted nor specified in advance. He may act as he wishes as long as he does not violate the rules governing the establishment and maintenance of the play world. Plots and roles are created on-the-spot and are an individual act of creativity characterized by fantasy as opposed to reality. The reverse may be said of games. Realism prevails. Both the plot and roles are codified, i.e. outlined in advance. Once under way, little deviation is permitted. Plots (scenarios) are used much as a script is used in a dramatic play by the actors, and roles closely approximate both the character and actions of persons found in real life.

Both play and games are rule-governed, but the nature and function of their rules differ. In play, rules are concerned primarily with establishing and maintaining the context of a make believe world. Children may choose at any time those aspects of ordinary life that are to be included, excluded, or modified. The temporal and spatial dimensions of the play world may be altered by the players as they go along. Thus at any given moment the shape and composition given to their world is determined by the players. The game world is likewise established by rules which state those aspects of the adult world to be included, excluded and modified. However, structural modifications are not permitted *unless* mutually agreed upon beforehand. Rules inform players what they can or cannot do in given roles, and how the game works. As a result the range and scope of behavior is much more restricted and formalized than it is in play. Significantly, procedural rules are known in advance of the game by all of the players.

Play is not subject to replication. It is spontaneous, personal, uncertain of character and hence, is not amenable to abstraction and codification as are games. The act of play is a one-of-a-kind affair created to meet the unique needs of an individual child at a particular time and place. The selection of plots and roles is purely an individual choice, as is their enactment by the child. One cannot predict what a child will do; how long he will do it, or if he will do it again. In contrast, as games become more widely used and better known in terms of plot, roles, interaction and goals, they become formalized and hence can be passed from one generation of players to the next. Because they have been codified with repeated use, they can be replicated in their original form as many times as desired by the players. In this way, games such as *London Bridge* have survived hundreds of years in the same basic form.

If the player is satisfied by his participation in play, he is rewarded. In play, no conditions exist which must be met in order to win and as a result there can be no winners. Since the child is not concerned with his progress relative to another player or his own prior achievements, no winners are required. As a result the need for tangible rewards is eliminated. Thus, the rewards associated with play are intangible. However, in games procedural rules indicate the conditions which have to be met before a winner can be declared. Scores are recorded and then compared with those of other players so that an individual can measure his progress relative to another player at any point in the game. Although the actual declaration of a winner is not mandatory, criteria for determining a winner must exist.

SUMMARY

The structural and functional characteristics of play and games have been analyzed and compared. In the first part of this chapter several structural and functional aspects of play were identified. Structurally play was recognized as an activity that occurs outside of ordinary life events. As such it begins and ends at definable points in time (temporal boundaries) and occurs in an acknowledged arena (physical boundaries). Although it is make-believe it constitutes a second reality. It is rule-governed in that reality is included, excluded, and/or transformed and it is a wholly voluntary activity. A special attitude of play can be defined as amusing, divertive and not to be taken seriously. In short, it is *fun*.

Play occurs spontaneously, to suit the needs and desires of the individual. As such it is a personal creation in which the rewards are indeterminate from the outsider's point of view. The rewards are subjective: determined by the individual's satisfaction with his activity. On this account the range, scope and course of play activity is uncertain. It is altered at the momentary behest of the person and is bounded only by his needs. Due to this state of affairs the person is free to exhibit personal creativity in his play activity.

The functional components of play offer some insights into the motivations that cause play to begin and end. Play allows the individual to assimilate overpowering experiences. By "replaying" the sequence of events which have or may be expected to overwhelm a person, he can divide the experience into smaller pieces, reproduce it with a different role for himself and practice roles and behaviors that could change his own outcome for similar, subsequent experiences. Thus, play functions to cancel and/or transform his past and alter his future reality. Play offers the child an opportunity to take active, directive roles which they cannot take in the real world. This function of play allows the person to explore and experiment with different ways of coping with the behavior of others. Also, the child or adult can try out different solutions to real life problems in a situation where the outcomes do not count as they do in real life.

In the second part of this chapter the structural and functional characteristics of games have been analyzed. The structural components of games fell into static and dynamic categories. That is, within the concept of structure there are formal, static aspects which serve to define the parts of the game situation. There also are rules governing game procedure and player interaction during the progress of the game. These are the dynamically functional aspects of game structure.

The static structural components of games, first, consist of boundary rules. There are three: rules of relevance specifying which real world aspects are to be included in the game, rules of irrelevance specifying which aspects of the real world are to be excluded and rules of transformation specifying which real world aspects are to be included on an altered basis.

A second class of static structural components consists of rules governing internal structure. Such rules specify the roles, inter-action, plots and goals set up by the game. Three kinds of roles are defined: group maintenance, task, and individual. Roles are characterized as having high and low power, and they derive their power from different role aspects. Thus, power may come from expertness, from assigned status, or from role behavior such as giving rewards or metering out punishment.

When a structural component has implications for the behavioral participation of players during the game it is a functional, dynamic aspect of the game. One such component is the number of players. Since games are essentially social they require two *bona fide* players to exist. Thus, one-person games are a special case in which nature is an opponent. One-person games may be made social events by comparing scores obtained against their common opponent. When the number of participants increases, interaction patterns take on some characteristics dictated solely by the number of players.

Plots or scenarios that imply demands on style in role behavior are dynamic structural aspects of games. These are often clearly irrelevant for the basic structure of the game yet they exert an influence on *how* the game is played. On the other hand, rules which dictate the goals individuals may seek and how payoff is attained directly influence cooperative or competitive styles of play and strategy at decision points.

Rules of game procedure constitute a dynamic aspect of game structure. They set the norms which govern conduct of the game-in-operation. Seven types of procedural rules are described: initiation and termination, deployment and disposition, communication, arbitration, intervention, enforcement and outcome (payoff). Each kind of rule offers a variety of choices, each of which contributes to the character of the game as a whole. Any changes in the rules alters the game character to some extent.

The functions of games have been described as they relate to the child's social development. Some, of course, apply to adult use of games as well. Four functions are identified. First, there is socialization for the complex social and cultural setting. Second, there is coping with ongoing decision making in situations where individuals are interdependent and have varied sources of conflict. Third, there is the transformation of the harsh and stringent demands of the real world in a way that permits their moderation and reduction to manageable proportions. Finally, there is the communication of factual knowledge and an opportunity to practice its application within the game setting.

When play and games are compared one aspect of the two activities is highlighted. Play serves the individual and games serve the interest of the social group. In playing, the individual sets up, changes and terminates his activity as his needs and interests dictate, and play does not exist unless he is in full accord with his activity. Greater and freer use is made of transformation and cancellation in play than in games. Thus, past or anticipated real life situations can be dealt with in defensive or creative fashion.

Games, by contrast, provide ordered and modulated social encounters in which the participant must abide by the rules during a period of time. Interdependence of roles under the rules of procedure allows the child to encounter different styles of behavior and learn to differentiate one pattern of social behavior from another. Freedom of choice is allowed within the limits of the roles. Under some but obviously not all game conditions a participant may be said to be *playing* a game. This state of affairs would exist only when a playful attitude existed. This attitude demands that the participant become involved in the game voluntarily *and* without seriousness. It is the non-serious, "as if" quality that marks the crucial difference between playful and non-playful participation.

Structurally, play and games are similar in that they alter, modify or exclude spatial and temporal aspects of the real world. The difference between them lies in the fact that, for play, changes may be made during its course, while in games, rules agreed upon beforehand limit these changes. Similarly the plots and role prescriptions are changeable during play and are prescribed beforehand in games. The net result of these differences is to make play not subject to replication. Games can be repeated as long as desired and taken up by new participants virtually unchanged.

A major difference between play and games lies in the nature of the rewards participation brings. If a player is satisfied with his play he is rewarded. In a game, there are goals to be attained and payoffs to be won. The kinds of goals set and the manner of designating and paying a winner or winners reaches back into the conduct of the game to influence strategy and choices at each decision point.

In conclusion, play and games have some similarities and many differences in structure. In function, the individual quality of play stands out as does the social quality of games. *Both activities may occur at the same time when a playful attitude is held by a player during a game.*

REFERENCES

Caillois, Roger: *Man, Play, and Games.* New York, The Free Press of Glencoe, 1961.

Coleman, James S.: *Simulation Games and Social Theory.* Baltimore, The Johns Hopkins, University, N.D.

Danielian, Jack: "Live Simulation of Affect-laden Cultural Cognitions." *The Journal of Conflict Resolution,* XI, September, 1967.

Goffman, Erving: *Encounters.* Indianapolis, Bobbs-Merrill, 1961.

Hammond, Kenneth: "New Directions in Research on Conflict Resolution." *Journal of Social Issues,* XXI, July, 1965.

Huizinga, John: *Homo Ludens.* Boston, The Beacon Press, 1950.

Luce, R. Duncan and Raiffa, Howard: *Games and Decisions.* New York, John Wiley, 1957.

McDavid, John W. and Harari, Herbert: *Social Psychology: Individuals, Groups, Societies.* New York, Harper and Row, 1968.

Ohm, Robert E.: "Gamed Instructional Simulation: An Exploratory Model." *Educational Administration Quarterly,* October, 1966.

Peller, L.E.: "Models of Children's Play," *Ment Hyg, XXXVI,* 1952.

Peller, L.E.: "Libidinal Phases, Ego Development and Play." *Psychoanal Study Child, IX,* 1954.

Rapoport, Anatol: *Two-Person Game Theory: The Essential Ideas.* Ann Arbor, The University of Michigan Press, 1966.

Redl, Fritz and Wineman, David: *Controls From Within.* New York, The Free Press, 1952.

Roberts, John M., Arth, Malcolm J. and Bush, Robert R.: "Games in Culture." *American Anthropologist, LXI,* 1959.

Roberts, John M. and Sutton-Smith, Brian: "Child Training and Game Involvement." *Ethnology, I,* 1962.

Roberts, John M., Sutton-Smith, Brian and Kenden, Adam: "Strategy in Games and Folk Tales." *J Soc Psychol, LXI,* 1963.

Shubik, Martin S.: *Game Theory and Related Approaches to Social Behavior.* New York, John Wiley, 1964.

Simmel, Georg: "The Significance of Numbers for Social Life." In Hare, A.P., Borgatta, E.P. and Bales, R.F.: *Small Groups.* New York, Alfred E. Knopf, 1955.

Street, Warren R.: "Coalitions in the Triad: Factors of Reward Value and Power Scaleing" (unpublished Ph.D. dissertation, Psychology Department, Claremont Graduate School, 1967).

Sutton-Smith, Brian: "The Psychology of Children's Games." *National Education,* New Zealand, *XXXVII,* 1955.

Sutton-Smith, Brian: "Formal Analysis of Game Meaning." *Western Folklore, XVIII,* 1959.

Waelder, Robert: "The Psychoanalytic Theory of Play." *Psychoanal Q, II,* 1933.

─────PART TWO─────

INTRODUCTION TO PART TWO

In Part Two of this volume the emphasis is on practical appli-cations of games to teaching, socialization and clinical tasks. While the school is not always the setting for the author's tryouts the games have been used by someone somewhere with some success. If the reader elects to use the game of any one author and it does not work out as expected (better, worse or just different) there is someone to turn to for counsel. If the user wishes to communicate the details of how the children changed and hazard a guess as to how and why it happened each author will be happy to hear about it. This is a burgeoning field and alert viewing is needed to under-stand the many ways that children can change when and if they learn through games.

The plan of Part Two calls for three sections; 1) classroom teaching of academic subject matter, 2) socialization and clinical applications and 3) instruction in how to devise a new game or revise an old one. Assigning any author's work to a section is likely to be an arbitrary decision due to the overlapping of the three notions in several of the chapters.

CHAPTER 9

GAMES

R<small>ICHARD</small> M<small>OON</small>

INTRODUCTION

R<small>ICHARD</small> MOON'S chapter begins the section devoted to teaching academic subject matter. He has provided a straight-forward statement about a seemingly simple, ancient game which involves transportation strategy. In Eifermann's terms this is an extremely durable game. It allows people who range widely in age and training to meet as equals (almost). Beware of anyone who can "look ahead" regardless of their inexperience or youth. For-midable opponents come in all "sizes and shapes."

This game has been used to start Part Two because it has sur-vived a long time and to the casual observer, it would seem an un-likely candidate for classroom use. Armbruster, in Chapter 10, will analyze Kalah, and demonstrate its usefulness. It can be presented here as an example of a game-form available in the public domain that any teacher can modify to utilize academic materials. The message we wish to convey in Chapters 9 and 10 is that no game-form is so ancient nor its rules so sacred that it is not capable of serving a classroom purpose for an innovative teacher.

—Editors

INTRODUCTION

O<small>NE OF THE COMMON CHARACTERISTICS</small> of games which last for a long time and have widespread popularity is that of having very

155

simple and easily learned rules. But just being easy to play and learn is not enough for a game to have persisted for many years; it must have other attributes. It turns out that the really long lived games have a social quality to them. For example, the size and elegance of the household chess set is a clue to the social standing of the owner. Many ornate and grand sets are used as decorator items in the homes of today.

It is not surprising, then, that the oldest known game, KALAH, is seen in styles as simple as fourteen holes scooped in the dirt of a playground and as ornate as inlaid rare woods and even carved marble boards costing hundreds of dollars. The simplest playing pieces are just pebbles about the size of a pea. Beans or seeds are often used as playing pieces. These simple pieces would not do for the royal houses of India or the Chieftains of Africa who used semi-precious and precious stones. One Maharajah is known to have used rubies and star sapphires.

Another common thread which seems to run through games of long persistance and wide acceptance is that of far reaching strategies available to the players in spite of simple rules. The oriental game of GO, while being simple to play, has tactics and strategies which are so numerous that one may study for a lifetime on the variations and styles of play. KALAH has this quality to it. A KALAH player may spend many long minutes between plays trying to choose the best of many available moves, only to find himself badly beaten by an opponent who was able to see "just one move ahead." KALAH can be taught to first-grade children and yet, such are the qualities of the game, very sophisticated gamesters find the game completely absorbing.

KALAH is so popular in African countries that the Smithsonian Institute has referred to it as the "African national game." It is known by many names throughout the Polynesian and Melanesian areas of the world. Although it is known by many names in these and other parts of the world, it can always be recognized by the shape of the board on which it is played. The board has two rows of hollow depressions and two larger holes, the storage pits, at the ends.

The play is simple, a player chooses a pit on his side of the board and empties it by distributing the stones on a counter-clockwise direction around the board. If the last stone falls in certain places, he either gets an extra turn or he harvests, whereupon he puts the stones harvested in his storage area.

The game is available and is distributed by Products of the Behavioral Sciences Company (the company which originated Instant Insanity).

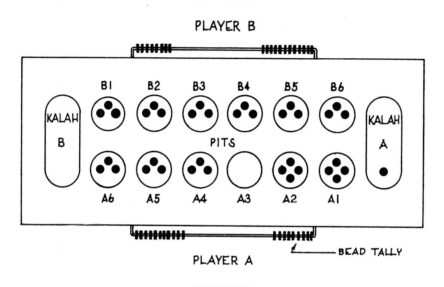

Figure   9-1.

Rules for Playing Kalah

To Begin Play

The two players sit on opposite sides of the board. Deposit three playing pieces in each of the twelve round pits.

Purpose

Purpose of the game is to accumulate as many playing pieces as possible in the large oval KALAH to each player's right.

How To Play

Each player in turn picks up all the pieces in any one of his *own* six pits and puts them one by one in each pit around to his right.

If there are enough playing pieces to go beyond your KALAH they are distributed in your opponent's pits (except skip his KALAH). They now belong to him.

If the player's last playing piece lands in his own KALAH, he gets another turn. (See illustration on page 157. Player A has emptied Pit A3. His last playing piece landed in his KALAH.)

If the last playing piece lands in an empty pit on his *own side,* he captures all of his opponent's playing pieces in the opposite pit and puts them in his own KALAH together with his capturing piece. (See illustration—Player A would empty pit A6 to capture playing pieces opposite A3 and deposits them and the capturing playing piece in A's KALAH where they remain until the end of the game.)

A capture ends the move.

To Keep Score

The round is over when all six pits on one side are empty. The other player adds the remaining pieces in his pits to his KALAH. The score is determined by who has the most pieces. (Example: Each player starts with 18 pieces. At end of round Player A has 5 extra pieces, he has won by five.) Use the convenient bead score tally on each side of the board to keep score. The first player to reach 40 points ends the game. Note: KALAH becomes more and more challenging by starting with 4, 5, or up to 6 playing pieces in each pit.

An Alternate Way of Explaining the Rules for Kalah[1]

DEFINITION OF SPACES OR AREAS ON THE BOARD. Your farm: All the pits on your side of the board (6). Your storehouse (also called your Kalah) or Silo: The elongated pit at the right hand end of your farm.

BASIC MOVE: Rule #1—Empty the entire contents of any pit on your farm. Then, starting with the adjacent pit on the right, place the beans (or stones) one-at-a-time around the board counterclockwise until you run out of beans (or stones). When you come to it, play into your own storehouse (Kalah), but you must always skip your opponent's storehouse.

1Added by Franz Armbruster of *©1971 Products of The Behavioral Sciences

EXTRA PLAY RULE: Rule #2—If, while playing according to rule #1, you cause the last bean to drop into your own storehouse, you get an extra turn. You can continue to get extra turns as long as you continue to play in this manner.

HARVEST MOVE: Rule #3—If, while playing under rules 1 & 2 (above), you cause the final bean to drop into an empty pit on your own farm, and there is some number of beans in the pit immediately opposite (across the board), *then* you must *Harvest*.

DEFINITION: HARVEST—Take the entire contents of the pit immediately opposite the pit played into and include the one bean which was in that pit and transfer them all to your storehouse. (No extra turn is permitted on a harvest).

END OF GAME: The game ends when it is one player's turn and that player cannot play.

SCORING: Count the total number of beans in the storehouse, add the total number of beans left on the farm (if any) and compute the difference. The difference is the score. The player with the most is the winner. Play to forty points. Start with three stones in each pit to learn the rules, then progress up to four, then five and finally six stones in each pit to start.

This is an attempt to clarify the rules which are packed with the game and it is *not* a different game. This sheet is another way of saying the same thing that is said on the other instruction sheet!

CHAPTER 10

LEARNING ABACUS ARITHMETIC THROUGH THE USE OF A GAME

Franz Armbruster

INTRODUCTION

*F*RANZ ARMBRUSTER *has happily combined a series of math-ematical games to arrive at a stated goal; teaching number theory. His chapter incorporates within it two examples of a single game-form. His starting point is the ancient game of* Kalah. *At first glance this game seems trivial, but this impression is misleading. It is a very durable game. Players continue to remain in doubt about the outcome of this game and the process of playing remains a challenge after many repetitions. Armbruster noted that the form of the game called upon the players to count and that movement was from left to right. Such directional movement characterizes much of our educational material.*

Armbruster's initial argument for changing Kalah *into* Arvesta *constitutes an illustration of the solution to many teacher's dilem-mas as they begin to use games in their classrooms: how to modify an existing game to make it appropriate for the task they wish it to perform. He judged that* Kalah *presented "manipulative" diffi-culties to children in first grade and below, and he followed two courses of action to make manipulation easier. He separated the cups, making it possible to reduce or increase the number of cups (or players) at will. Then, he introduced ways of learning about number concepts above one. The "playfulness" in Armbruster's*

160

approach to the use of game materials is well illustrated by his choice of the materials. He pointed out that the stones "make a nice sounding plink-plink-plink . . ." In a private communication Armbruster suggested that a child who breaks an Arvesta cup can still play, using a paper cup. This would go on until he replaced the cup. Then, his play would again yield the pleasing plink-plink-plink.

Chapter 10 contains an example of Armbruster's "Do and Say" game script. By using this method of presenting a game the teacher undertakes a kind of analysis which will allow him or her to modify the game situation when and where it seems appropriate. Ambiguity in one's current presentation can be identified by use of the script and appropriate points in the game-form can be identified for later shifts in emphasis as the game-form is modified to serve other teaching purposes.

—Editors

I F YOU HAVE TWELVE little cups about the size of oriental tea cups I can show you how to teach a game to young children which will help them learn some basic mathematics and at the same time have fun doing it. And, if you learn this game yourself and practice the teaching routines described, I promise you a very satisfying teaching experience. The logic of the argument goes something like this:

1. Number theory is easier to understand if you can do calculations on an abacus.
2. Understanding and using the abacus is easier if you use a Kalah board to invent your own abacus and learn to calculate on it. (The Kalah board is good in any number base; the abacus of the classic type can be used only in base ten.)
3. Inventing and using an abacus is easier and more meaningful if you first learn to play the ancient game of Kalah. (The Kalah board may have actually been the forerunner of more recent abaci.)
4. Children in the age range of 6-10 sometimes have difficulty playing Kalah—not because of any cognitive problems with the rules, but because of manipulative problems with the materials.
5. It is easier to play Kalah if you have first learned to play Arvesta.
6. Very young children *can* learn to play Arvesta because the manipulative requirements are less.

NOW, THEREFORE, if you can teach young children to play Arvesta, then you have begun a sequence of learning which will facilitate the understanding of mathematical number theory.

Arvesta Materials

The game which was invented for the specific purpose of teaching abacus arithmetic is called Arvesta. That's pig-latin for "harvest." It is designed around an agricultural model, partly because I don't approve of games designed around war or combat models and partly because it is an outgrowth of Kalah, an ancient game which uses seeds or beans as playing pieces.

I use earthy materials such as pottery or crockery cups for the pits, but you can of course use any handy container which you happen to have on hand. Paper cups are adequate, even holes dug in the dirt of a playground will work. Some teachers have used egg cartons, but please *don't* use egg cartons, they spoil the nice tactile and auditory quality which I think is important. The ideal combination is small rounded pebbles and heavy crockery cups (the kind we call custard cups). These have a nice sounding plink-plink-plink when the game is being played. The sound somehow seems to add something to the enjoyment of the game for the youngsters who play it.[1]

Abacus and Soroban

As early as 1963 I became interested in teaching the use of the abacus as an adjunct to the teaching of number theory. I had been taught nothing about the abacus in my own schooling, although I had more than the average exposure to mathematics as part of my education. I bought a book and began with a Chinese abacus to do simple operations with small numbers. It soon became evident to me that this was indeed a valuable teaching tool, and I wondered why it was not used more in occidental schools. I am still wondering!

As I learned more about how to use the abacus to do simple calculations, it became obvious to me that the Japanese bead cal-

---

[1]The reader may want to turn to p. 170 at this point and read how the game of Arvesta is taught. The text will continue on the assumption that the reader is familiar with the general method of play.

culator, soroban, was a superior instrument for my purposes.[2]

At any rate I set about the task of teaching the soroban. The idea was to avoid the use of pencil and paper but to still be able to show and use the ideas of number and operation and their equivalent numeral and operation sign.

The soroban seems to be well suited to pointing up the difference between the cardinal and ordinal number systems. I have not yet had anyone make the assumption that the number representations on the soroban are anything other than cardinal numbers.[3] It is now important to reason through the steps to making the soroban a teaching device.

IF IT IS GIVEN that a knowledge of how to do simple operations on the soroban aids in the understanding of arithmetic AND IT IS FURTHER GIVEN that few occidental teachers are familiar with the operation of the soroban (let alone know how to teach it); HOW DO YOU GO ABOUT teaching something which uses the *soroban* as a precursor? I chose a game to assist me.

Kalah Aids Teaching of Soroban

I had learned to play Kalah as a recreation and my family also enjoyed it. Kalah is a modernized version of an ancient game played in almost all parts of the world except the English speaking and western European countries. The ancient game is know to anthropologists as Mancala.

Kalah had the required characteristics. It is played without symbols and so required no reading or special language ability. It is played with small stones or seeds which could simulate the beads on an abacus. It is played on a long narrow board with two rows of pits or depressions carved in it parallel to the long axis of the board. Its layout resembles the layout of an abacus. In fact one

---

[2]Abaci (*ah*-buh-kai) are found in several different types. The oldest Chinese versions are recognized by their having two beads above the bar and five beads below the bar; a more recent Japanese version with one bead above and five below; and the most recent (and fastest) type has four below and one above. For readers of this chapter it is recommended that one of the modern four-and-one styles be obtained. The reasons will become evident in the chapter.

[3]This difference is easily demonstrated to the learner. Hold out a group of objects (coins for example) and say: a cardinal number is the answer to the question "How many?" and an ordinal number is the answer to the question "Which one?"

author suggests that the Kalah board was the forerunner of the abacus.[4]

Mr. William Champion of Holbrook, Massachusetts (founder of the Kalah Game Company) has written that he had good results teaching youngsters to play Kalah and that "Kalah not only induces children to like arithmetic, it also makes them think." In affirmation of this, Mr. John Haggerty, a seventh grade teacher in the Holbrook School District says "small children learn to count without using their fingers; to distinguish multiples; to assess special arrays in a physical order of objects as well as to acquire other mathematical concepts in a natural way while playing an interesting and absorbing game."

Now, Champion and Haggerty had used the game for its own sake, just wanting to have fun and practice in some aspects of arithmetic and "to make them think." I had in mind introducing Kalah and then taking the elements of the game and actually reconstructing an ancient calculator from the fun objects they had used in the gaming situation. I also sought to teach a much younger group of learners than they had attempted to work with.

I had developed a teaching strategy for the abacus, but it (the strategy) seemed to be lacking something. It could be taught, since I had taught several youngsters to express numbers on the abacus and also translate the bead patterns into their numerical equivalents. But the youngsters did not try to teach these skills to other youngsters, and they did not seem to be enjoying the process. What was needed was a "thing" which could provide some continuity through the *affective* domain. There was also the problem of my teaching strategy requiring a one to one correspondence between teacher and learner. This was inadequate.

AT THIS TIME in my career I was exposed to another element which has had such a profound effect on my attitudes about teaching that it must be mentioned at this point. That is the idea of *behavioral objective.* The expressing of instructional objectives as *descriptions of the desired behavior* to be expected from the learner

---

[4]H.J.R. Muvray says "It may be significant that the earliest boards all occur in the neighborhood of building operation. Could the board have been used for the calculation of wages to be payed to workmen, and the board be originally a primitive kind of abacus?"

is such a powerful strategic teaching tool that it still surprises me how few educators are practicing its principles. Let me illustrate:

An Instructional Objective, Terminal Variety

"AT THE CONCLUSION OF THE TEACHING SEQUENCE, THE LEARNER WILL BE ABLE TO DO ADDITION AND SUBTRACTION OPERATIONS ON A SOROBAN AT LEAST AS FAST AND AS ACCURATELY AS HE CAN DO THE SAME OPERATIONS USING PENCIL AND PAPER. THE NUMERALS INVOLVED WILL BE NO GREATER THAN THREE DIGIT NUMERALS, AND (FOR THE SUBTRACTION OPERATIONS) NO NEGATIVE RESULTS WILL BE REQUIRED."

When this terminal instructional objective had been partially achieved, I took the Kalah board, and using it as a substitute for the abacus in the teaching sequence that I had used before, tried to accomplish the same objective. *It worked,* not perfectly, but a lot better than I had ever achieved using the actual soroban. And of course, there was the additional value of the game idea which could sustain the interest from one student to another. One student *can and will* teach another to play Kalah. I now feel confident that, using the method described, I can teach any youngster of fifth grade or higher to do any addition or subtraction operation on the Kalah board which he is able to do with pencil and paper and that includes these operations in *any number base.*

I believe that playing the game in its conventional fashion as a competitive exercise will strengthen these skills.[5]

Inventing an Abacus

Here's the strategy for using the Kalah board as a teaching aid:

1. Place the board between yourself and the learner, crosswise.
2. Tell the learner to start counting.
3. As he calls out each number, you place the stones in the appropriate pits so as to represent the number called out (See Fig. 10-1).
4. Ask the student periodically if he's "discovered the code yet?" Tell him he can call out any number up to three digits he wishes.
5. When he thinks he has discovered the method, he will say something

---

[5]Rules for playing Kalah are reprinted in the preceding chapter of this volume.

Student sits here

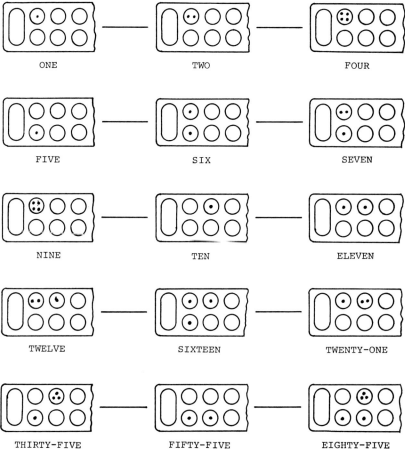

Figure 10-1. This shows the pattern of the numerals.

like "I get it!" When this happens, give him the stones and *you* call
out the following numbers: ZERO, ONE, FOUR, FIVE, SEVEN,
NINE, TWO, SIX.

6. If he gets these right, give him these numbers: TEN, ELEVEN,
   TWELVE, SIXTEEN, TWENTY-ONE, THIRTY-FIVE, FIFTY-
   FIVE, EIGHTY-EIGHT.

7. If he gets these right, give him as many three digit numbers you feel are necessary to prove that he can place the stones for any number up to 999.[6]

Okay, up to this point we have learned to perform like this:
(This is one of the interim behavioral objectives.)

GIVEN A NUMBER OF NO MORE THAN THREE DIGITS, THE LEARNER WILL BE ABLE TO PLACE THE BEADS ON THE BOARD PROPERLY WITH NO ERRORS IN THE QUANTITY OR LOCATION OF BEADS PLACED.

Please notice that in this objective the student is handling the beads, and the instructor is calling the numbers.

And the next interim objective is:

WHEN SHOWN A BEAD PATTERN ON THE BOARD, THE STUDENT WILL BE ABLE TO CALL OUT ITS NUMERIC EQUIVALENT.

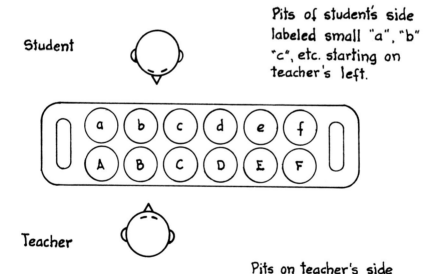

Figure 10-2. Playing Kalah.

---

[6]As you look at the chart, don't forget that *you* are going to have to learn the abacus upside down in order for it to come right for the student. I have learned it myself this way and I can assure you that it is no handicap; in fact, it has taken on some of the aspects of a status symbol for me! Practice on another adult before you begin with your children so you can become comfortable with the technique.

Notice that in this objective *you* place the beads, and the student identifies the pattern. Now you might think that just accomplishing the first objective would lead to an understanding of the code we use to show numbers on the abacus, but please don't assume your student understands the concept until you have put him through *this* sequence as well (See Fig. 10-2).

Place stones as follows, the student should respond as indicated.

1. Put one stone in "a," one in "b" and one in "c" (a-1, b-1, c-1).
2. The student should say "one hundred eleven."
3. Put one in "A," one in "B" (A-1, B-1).
4. The student: "fifty-five."
5. A-1, a-2, b-3, C-1. "five hundred thirty-seven"
6. a-4, B-1, b-4, c-3. "three hundred ninety-four"
7. Continue this practice method until you are convinced that the student can call out any three digit bead pattern.

These two lessons combine to achieve *this* general instructional goal:

THE STUDENT WILL UNDERSTAND THE METHOD USED TO REPRESENT COMMON BASE TEN NUMERALS ON THE ABACUS.

From Third Grade Down

I believe this objective is sufficient for bright second graders and all third grade children. I also believe that these children are fully capable of the *cognitive* requirements. All that remained at this point was to see how a young child can be taught to play the recreation game. I began teaching younger and younger children until I saw where their difficulties arose. One of the first difficulties was that they could not master the act of picking up the stones from the pits on the board. They would reach into one of the pits, try to pick out all of the stones with their hand palm down and drop and scatter several of the stones. This frustrates the player and his opponent. Arguments as to where a certain stone fell or where a certain stone came from developed. I determined that this was the first obstacle to overcome.

A wholesale house in San Francisco provided the solution in the form of heavy oriental tea cups. With these the youngsters would pick up the cup, hold his hand palm up and dump the entire contents into it. This worked much better. And if some stones *were* inadvertently dropped, they went to the floor and not into an adjacent pit as in Kalah. Small manipulative errors did not disturb the play of the game.

Another difficulty which I saw when younger children played Kalah (on the board) was the board was rigidly constrained to twelve pits and the "Kalahs" (storage pits). I thought that it would be easier to introduce the game if I used fewer cups, perhaps as few as three for each player. I also noticed that practice in gross motor movements left-to-right and across the body center-line was a useful byproduct. It is clear to the reader, now, how I came to invent Arvesta. Related counter-clockwise circular movement is also in the Arvesta game, but this is not so on the Kalah board.[7]

CONCLUSION

This chapter is an attempt to condense certain experiences spanning the last ten years of my life into a few pages of expository text. In that time period I have been able to design and test a strategy for teaching some fundamental ideas of mathematics to very young children.

My target student population has included mentally retarded and perceptually handicapped children as well as the culturally deprived and minority group learner—in the kindergarten to third grade levels.

IF I HAVE communicated effectively, the reader—after having practiced a bit—will be able to teach the game of Arvesta to kindergarten and first grade children. And, after teaching Arvesta, you will then be able to teach the game Kalah and then progress through a series of experiences which will lead ultimately to the teaching of simple multiplication and addition operations on the abacus, or its Japanese equivalent—soroban.

I wish to reiterate now what I said at the beginning of this piece: If the reader will practice the sequences as described and if results obtained are similar to those which I achieved, a great deal will have been learned about the teaching of arithmetic to young children and a great deal of satisfaction will result.

---

[7]At this point it is recommended that the reader turn to the appendix and actually practice the playing of Arvesta using the sequence provided.

Game Directions for First to Fifth Grades

First Grade "Arvesta"

How to teach the game.

Note: These instructions are written like a motion picture script. You are the actor. Your spoken lines are written in the left-hand column and your gestures and actions are in the right-hand column. Please don't improvise until you have played it through at least twice. This sequence of instructions has been tested and is known to work. So say the words exactly as they are written. Do the gestures exactly the way they are described. If the instructions for speech are in line with those for the action, then you do them simultaneously. If the speech is above the action, then say the speech first. If the other way around, then do the action and *then* make the speech.

Materials: 12 cups and three dozen small stones.
The sequence begins with the action

SAY	*DO*
	Place ten cups on the floor about two feet in front of you. Sit on the floor.
"I'm about to teach a game called ARVESTA. It is played with cups and these little stones.	Gesture toward the cups.
	Pour about ten stones on the floor.
Now, we need two players. Will you two be the players?	Point to two players.
You sit here.	Gesture for one of the players to sit at your left knee, near the cups.
And you sit here.	Gesture for the other player to sit on your right. (The cups should be between.)
Now, will you two please arrange the cups in a circle.	DON'T TOUCH THE CUPS, LET THEM DO IT THEM-SELVES. Gesture in a circle

(after a circle is formed) Very good, now make it about this big. Now, spread it apart a little bit right here."	with your hands if you must, but don't touch the cups. Hold your hands to show a circle about the size of an automobile steering wheel. Indicate the split in the circle so the cups are a half circle in front of each player.

At this point you should have a circle of cups in front of you which, if it were a clock face, has a space at 12:00, a cup at 1:00, one at 2:00, one at three, one at four and one at five o'clock and another space at six o'clock. These cups should be in front of the right-hand player who sits directly behind the three o'clock position. There should be cups at the seven, eight, nine, ten and eleven o'clock positions. The player at your left should be directly behind the nine o'clock position (See Fig. 10-3).

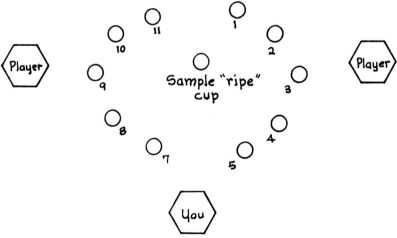

Figure 10-3.

"This is going to be your farm.	Facing the player on the left, and with fingers outspread, move your left hand over the cups in the seven through eleven o'clock positions.

And this is your farm.

Here's how you make a
play in the game. When you
take your turn it's called
'sowing'—like sowing
seeds.
Now you—

Empty that cup into your
hand.
Put the cup back where it
was.
Now, put one stone in here.
One in here, and the last one
in here.

Now, where did you sew the
last stone?

Right.
Now we'll practice one over
here. We'll get ready.

Okay, you start here.
Pick up this cup, empty it,
and put it back.
Sow one here.
And one here.
One here and one here.
Where will you sow the last

Do the same for the player on
the right. Use the right
hand and indicate cups at
the one through five o'clock
positions.
Pick up three stones and hold
them in your right fist, then
drop them all at once into the
cup at position 1 (cup 1).

Point to the player on your
right.
Point to cup 1. Wait until he
empties it into his hand.
Wait until this is done.

Point to cup 11.
Point to cup 10.
Point to cup 9.

Always wait for each direction
to be completed before
continuing.
Address the question to the
player on your right. He
should indicate cup 9.

Point to the player on your
left. Take four stones and
drop them in cup 10. Cup 10
should now have five stones.
Point to cup 10.

Point to cup 9.
Point to cup 8.
Point to cups 7 and 6.
Player should drop the last

one?
Right, very good.

You have both practiced how
to take your turn.
Remember that it was just
practice, when we're really
playing the game, you can
start with any cup on your
own farm. I just used these
two turns to show you how to
do it.

Here are the important parts
of the move:
(1). Empty the cup
carefully.
(2). Put one stone in
each cup around the
circle this way.
(3). Check the last cup.
You will find out why
later.

Let's practice that a little
bit, and take turns playing
. . . but remember we're just
practicing the sowing part."

stone in cup 5.

To both players.

Hold up one finger and then
pantomime picking up a cup
and dumping it into your
left hand.
Pretend to be dropping stones
around the circle in a
counter-clockwise direction.

Put stones in several cups.
Don't put more than five
stones in any one cup.

Allow at least three correct practice turns for each player.
Watch to be sure that they select a cup of their own farm to begin
with. If they do it properly, immediately *reinforce* the player with
a comment, "Good," "Right," or "Yes." Watch to make sure they
start by emptying the cup completely and placing it back in its
correct position. Again, *reinforce each step* individually and
promptly at the beginning. Watch to make sure they put the first
stone in the cup immediately to the right of the one they emptied
and then one stone in each of the cups going around in a counter-

clockwise direction. Reinforce each dropping of a stone with a nod, a gesture or other approval. DON'T TOUCH THE STONES, THE CUPS, OR THE PLAYERS.[8]

COMMON ERRORS

The most common mistakes at this point are:

1. Starting on the wrong side of the circle.
2. Not emptying the cup completely.
3. Not putting the cup back in the circle.
4. Not starting in the right cup.
5. Skipping a cup when sowing.
6. Not looking in the final cup sown.

After each player has had several practice turns without making a mistake, proceed to the next part of the procedure,

LEARNING HOW TO SCORE

"Now you are going to learn how to score in the game of 'Arvesta.' Scoring is called 'harvesting.' Watch closely and I'll show you how to harvest.

To both players.

Place one of the two remaining cups in the center of the circle.

I'm going to make this cup 'ripe.'

Drop two stones in the cup.

If a cup has this many in it, it is 'ripe.'

Hold up two fingers.

I'll leave that one there as a reminder of what ripe means.

Point to the cup in the center.

Now we're going to practice some more.

Redistribute stones as follows:

two stones in cups 2, 3,

---

[8]If a player makes a mistake, do something like this: "Let's start that play over, pick the one you want to start with, but remember it has to be on your own side of the circle. (Point.) Pick it up and empty it into your hand. (pantomime). Now put the first one here. (Point.) One here (point), and one here (point), and check the last one here (point). Turn to the other player and say, Now it is your turn . . ."

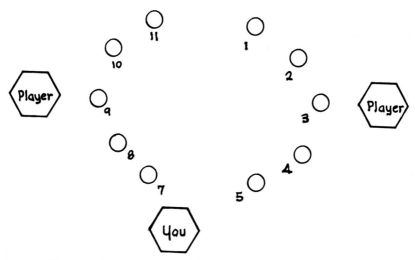

Figure 10-4. Position for start of "harvest" practice.

	5, 7, 9, & 10
	one stone in cups 1, 4,
	8, & 11

Which cup would you start with to make the last cup ripe?	Address the question to the player on your left. If he answers or points to 10, he is correct. If he doesn't know you say—
Try this one. Start your play here.	Point to cup 10. (Fig. 10-4) Wait for the player to sow stones into cups 9 and 8.
Right, which is the last cup sown? Is it ripe?	He should answer "yes."
Right. You get to harvest them. Pick up the cup, empty it in front of you.	
Then put the cup back where it was.	
Now it's your turn. Let's see if you can harvest."	To the player on your right. The player should play from cup 2 and harvest from cup 11.

At this point, each player should have some practice at havesting. Put varying amounts of stones in the cups and let the players take turns sowing and harvesting when possible. Make sure that each player gets at least three chances to harvest correctly during the course of this practice.

As in the previous practice, DON'T TOUCH THE CUPS, STONES, OR PLAYERS. Let them do it for themselves. Watch carefully and reinforce verbally for each correct play and each correct choice.

Common mistakes at this point are:

1. Sowing correctly, making the last cup ripe and failing to collect the harvest.
2. Skipping a cup when sowing. (so the last one comes out ripe).
3. Sowing two stones in one cup (so the last one comes out ripe).
4. Sowing clear around to the opponents farm and not harvesting when possible.

After each player has had several correct harvests, stop the practice.

"That's enough practice. Now
we're going to play the game.

Empty the cups (except the sample one in the middle). Put the stones in the center of the circle.

We'll start by
putting this many stones in
each cup.

(hold up three fingers)

When this is done, begin play.

You go first.

Point to *youngest player.*
Allow the players to play
and continue playing until
one of them no longer has any
farm.
stones in his cups on his

The game is over when one
side is empty.
And *you* get to harvest all of
these.

Point to the player who has
stones remaining and gesture

to the stones in the cups.
He should dump them in
front of him.

Now, let's see who won.

Put this many of your stones
in each of your cups and
see if you have more or less
than when you began."

Hold up three fingers.

Both players put back the
stones that they have harvested.
The winner will have his cups
filled and have one or more
extra stones. The loser will
not be able to refill his
cups.

IT IS SUGGESTED that very young children do not go farther than
this. They either won or lost. As they get more advanced, you can
let them keep a tally of how many stones they won by. This
completes the lesson for First Grade "Arvesta."

When each player has won a given number of First Grade
games, perhaps ten, you may introduce the additional instructions
for Second Grade "Arvesta."

Second Grade "Arvesta"

For Second Grade "Arvesta," the basic method of play is the
same: the players take turns, they sow, and if possible harvest. The
principle change is the condition under which a harvest may take
place. In this variation, the sample cup in the center of the circle
contains three stones. The cup is then "rich." The other change is
in the number of stones placed in each cup at the beginning. Each
cup now contains four stones. After a suitable number of wins at
this level a player may learn the next game in the sequence—
Third Grade "Arvesta."

Third Grade "Arvesta"

To begin with, it is suggested that any player who learns Third

Grade "Arvesta" be promoted to the rank of "Teacher" of First Grade "Arvesta." Suitable badges can be awarded.

In third grade, we change the conditions for harvest, the beginning quantity of stones, and the number of cups.

Summary of the rules are:

1. Six stones in each cup to begin play.
2. Both ripe (2) and rich (3) are conditions for harvest.
3. Twelve cups are used—six in each farm.

Fourth Grade "Arvesta"

Fourth grade is very similar to the preceding games.
Summary of the rules are:

1. Three players may play (use four cups to each farm).
2. Six stones in each cup.
3. Harvesting is permitted on ripe (2), rich (3), or bounty (5).

Fifth Grade "Arvesta"

Summary of the rules are:

1. Up to four players may play (divide the 12 cups evenly).
2. Six stones per cup are given to each player and he may arrange them any way he wishes to begin play.
3. Harvesting is permitted on ripe (2), rich (3), or bounty (5).
4. When a player has his turn, he may elect to sow his stones in either a counter-clockwise or clockwise direction. He may sow stones in different directions each turn if he chooses.

Any player who achieves ten wins at the game of Fifth Grade "Arvesta" is entitled to wear the title "Professor of Arvesta" and should be honored with appropriate ceremony!

CHAPTER 11

CHILD LEARNING THROUGH ACTIVE GAMES

JAMES H. HUMPHREY

INTRODUCTION

*J*AMES HUMPHREY *speaks as a physical education teacher who can translate the activity of young people into an avenue for their fuller education. He was careful to point out the importance of activity in his conceptualization; he noted the general value of activity in teaching children and the special relevance of activity in educating boys. In arguing for the use of active games as educational tools he was careful to present evidence for their advantages obtained from field situations where objective evaluation methods were applied. In the main, Humphrey's game-forms are familiar playground games.*

Throughout this chapter there is evidence that practice sits lightly on a student when it is part of a game. Humphrey has, thus, underscored the fact that the child's motivation to participate in his own education may be tapped when games are the teaching tools. Although this is a likely state of affairs it clearly hinges on what the author calls "facilitative factors," muscle learning and effective rewards. Both of these ideas have been used as components of motivation. They play particularly important roles when games are used to alter the way the task of learning is perceived by the learner.

For Humphrey's work there is a rich library of prepared game materials which can be obtained with a minimum of delay. He is interested in the effectiveness of his materials as used by a variety of people in a variety of situations.

—*Editors*

INTRODUCTION

THE IMPORTANT role of play and games in cognition and learning has been recognized for centuries. In fact, the idea of the playing of games as a desirable learning medium has been traced to the ancient Egyptians. Through the ages some of the most profound thinkers in history have expounded positively in terms of the value of play as a way of learning. Such pronouncements extend over several centuries from Plato's suggestion that ". . . in teaching children; train them by a kind of game and you will be able to see more clearly the natural bent of each," to a modern twentieth century statement by L. P. Jacks that "The discovery of the educational possibilities of the play side of life may be counted one of the greatest discoveries of the present day."

Statements such as the above, along with numerous others, have been based essentially upon hypothetical postulation. In modern times there has been a revival of the "play way" of learning among educators and psychologists. In this age of scientific inquiry and research an effort is being made to build an objective foundation under what has long been held only as a theoretical assumption. It is the purpose of this chapter to analyze and discuss theoretical implications along with research conducted by the writer over the last decade in the area of active games as a medium for child learning.

Throughout the chapter the term "active games" will imply *active interaction of children in cooperative and/or competitive situations.* When we speak of active games as a learning medium we refer to things that children do *actively* in a game situation in order to learn.

The Theory of Learning Through Active Games

The active game approach to learning is concerned with how children can develop skills and concepts in such subject areas as reading, mathematics and science while actively engaged in game situations. It is based in part on the theory that children—being predominantly movement oriented—will learn better when what we might arbitrarily call "academic learning" takes place through pleasurable physical activity, that is when the *motor* component operates at a maximal level in skill and concept development in school subject areas essentially oriented to *verbal* learning. This is *not* to say that "motor" and "verbal" learning are two mutually exclusive kinds of learning, although it has been suggested that at the two extremes the dichotomy appears justifiable. It is recognized that in verbal learning which involves almost complete abstract symbolic manipulations there may be, among others, such motor components as tension, subvocal speech and physiological changes in metabolism which operate at a minimal level. It is also recognized that in active games where the learning is predominantly motor in nature, verbal learning is evident, although perhaps at a minimal level. For example, in teaching an active game there is a certain amount of verbalization in developing a kinesthetic concept of the particular game that is being taught. The approach is also based on the theory that *motivation,* particularly as it relates to *interest,* plays a large part in child learning.

The procedure of learning through this medium involves the selection of an active game which is taught to the children and used as a learning activity for the development of a skill or concept in a specific subject area. An attempt is made to arrange an active learning situation so that a fundamental intellectual skill or concept is being developed in the course of participating in the active game. The active games are selected on the basis of the degree of inherency of a skill or concept in a given school subject area.

Examples of Active Game Learning Situations

The following representative examples of active game learning situations include one from each of the elementary school subject areas of science, mathematics and reading. The first example is concerned with science at the fourth grade level. The concept to be developed is: *Electricity travels along a pathway and needs a complete circuit over which to travel.* The active game to develop the concept is *Straddle Ball Relay.* The children stand one behind the other in relay files. All are in a stride position with feet far enough apart so that a ball can be rolled between the legs of the players. The first person in each file holds a rubber playground ball. At a signal the person in front of each file starts the activity by attempting to roll the ball between the legs of all the children of his file. The team that gets the ball to the last member of the file first in the manner described scores a point. The last player goes to the head of his file and this procedure is continued with a point scored each time for the team that gets the ball back to the last player first. After every player has had an opportunity to roll the ball back the team which has scored the most points is declared the winner.

An application of this would be as follows: The first player at the head of each file becomes the electric switch which opens and shuts the circuit. The ball is the electric current. As the ball rolls between the children's legs it moves right through if all legs are in proper lineup. When a leg is not in the proper stride, the path of the ball is impeded and the ball rolls out. The game has to be stopped until the ball is recovered and the correction made in the position of the leg. The circuit (that is the child's leg) has to be repaired before the flow of electricity (which is the roll of the ball) can be resumed.

The second example involves mathematics at the third grade level. The concept to be developed is: *Dividing to find how many groups there are in a larger group.* The activity to develop the concept is the game, *Get Together.* In this game the players take places around the activity area in a scattered formation. The teacher calls any number by which the total number of players is not exactly divisible. All players try to form groups of the number called. Each small group joins hands in a circle. The one or ones left out may have points scored against them. The low score wins the game. The numbers called at third grade level usually should be 2, 3, 4, 5, or 10 since these are the numbers with which they learn to divide. This game is useful for reinforcing the idea of groups or sets and that groups are of like things (in this case children). It can give the children the idea that there may be a *remainder* when dividing into groups.

The final example involves an active game learning situation which is designed to help children learn a skill which may be important in reading. It concerns the phonics skill, *auditory perception of long and short vowels.* The activity used to develop this skill is an adaptation of the game, *Steal the Bacon.* Two teams face each other about fifteen feet apart. An object (the bacon) is placed in the middle of the space between the two lines. The members of both teams are given like vowels—some with a short sound and some containing a long vowel sound. The teacher calls a word with a short vowel, such as *flash, fact* or *trap,* or a word containing a long vowel such as *rode, shade* or *wave.* The two children on each team who have the correct vowel sound run out and try to grab the object and return it to their line. If the player does so his team scores two points and if he is tagged by his opponent in the process, the opposing team scores one point. For example, if the teacher calls the word "cave" the child with the long ā on one team and the child with the long ā on the other team would try to retrieve the object. The children should be identified periodically with different letters.

Ways of Studying the Effect of the Active Learning Medium

There are numerous satisfactory ways of studying how behavioral changes take place in children. In order to establish an objective foundation under the long-held theory that desirable worthwhile learning could take place through active games, certain logical sequential steps had to be taken into account. (Humphrey 1966a, pp. 135-142).

One of the first problems to be reckoned with was whether this type of learning activity could be accomplished in the regular school situation and also whether teachers who had been prepared and experienced predominantly in traditional methods would subscribe to this particular approach. For this purpose a procedure arbitrarily identified as the *Modified Case Study* was developed.

In our *case study* technique a "case" is described as *one teacher working with a particular group of children in an attempt to develop a given skill or concept through the medium of an active game.* The teacher then evaluates how well the skill or concept was developed through the active game learning medium. The criteria for evaluation are the past experiences of the teacher with other groups of children and other learning media. Referring back to the example given of the science concept inherent in *Straddle Ball Relay* we will cite an example of a teacher evaluation after using that particular case. It should be recalled that the concept in Straddle Ball Relay was: *Electricity travels along a pathway and needs a complete circuit over which to travel.* The first player (who was the electric switch) opened the circuit by passing the ball (which was the electric current) through the children's legs (the circuit). One teacher evaluated this case in the following manner:

> The children were quick to see and make the analogy themselves after seeing how the interference in the path of the ball sent it out of bounds and stopped the activity. In similar fashion any blockage of an electric circuit would break the current and stop the flow of electricity. An experiment with wired batteries and a bell was also used in connection with the development of this concept. Some children reported that they understood this better after they had played Straddle Ball Relay because they could actually "see" the electric current which in this case was the ball.

Obviously, this technique is grossly lacking in objectivity because there is only a subjective evaluation to support the hypothesis. However, as mentioned previously, in the early stages of our work this technique served our purpose because at that time we were mainly concerned with having teachers experiment with the approach and to find out their reactions to it. As might be expected, in the large majority of cases teacher reaction was very positive.

The next consideration was whether or not children could *actually* learn through the active game medium. Although for centuries empirical evidence had placed the hypothesis in a positive light, there still remained the need for some objective evidence to support the hypothesis. In order to determine if learning could actually take place through active games the *Single Group Experiment Procedure* was employed. This technique has been applied in the following manner:

1. A group of children is pretested on a specified number of skills or concepts in a given curriculum area.
2. Active games are selected which are suitable to the grade level of the children, and in which the skills or concepts are inherent—one for each activity. (Several such examples were given previously in the areas of reading, mathematics and science.)

3. These active games are taught to the children over a specified period of time and used as learning activities to develop the skills or concepts.
4. The children are tested again after the specified period of time and the results of the second test are compared with the results of the first test.

All of our studies involving this technique in which the subjects were their own controls have shown significant differences between pre- and post-test scores at a high level of confidence. Hence, it appeared reasonable to conclude that learning could actually take place through the active game medium.

The next and obviously the most important step, was to determine how the active game medium compared with other more traditional learning media. For this purpose the *Parallel Group Experimental Procedure* was employed and used in the following manner:

1. A group of children is pretested on a number of skills or concepts in a given curriculum area.
2. On the basis of the pre-test scores, children are equated into two groups.
3. One group is designated as the active game group (experimental group) and an attempt is made to develop the skills or concepts through the active game medium. The other group is designated as the traditional group (control group) and an attempt is made to develop the skills or concepts through one or more traditional media. Both groups are taught by the same teacher over a specified period of time.
4. Both groups are tested again after the specified teaching period. Comparisons are made of the first and second test scores of each group and the second test scores of both groups.

Along with the above standard procedure, a number of variations of this technique have been employed. In these parallel group studies the experiment is usually carried on over a period of ten days. There are ordinarily eight and sometimes ten skills or concepts involved. The ten-day period allows for two days of testing and eight days of teaching. Reliability for the objective tests has ordinarily been obtained by using a test-retest with similar groups of children. All of our experiments have been done in the actual school situation. We would like to carry them out over longer periods of time but it has been impractical to do so because it usually involves some interruption in the regular school program. It should perhaps be mentioned at this point that in order to study the effectiveness of the active game learning medium for boys as compared to girls a variation of the single group experimental procedure was used. This involved parallel groups of boys and girls within the total single group.

In some of our studies it was practically impossible to design a completely objective technique. In these cases *Naturalistic Observation* was employed with teachers observing the behavior of children and recording data on especially prepared checklists for the final analysis.

Some Representative Findings

The results reported here are representative examples of studies that we have conducted in the use of active games as a learning medium. They have been classified into the academic areas of *reading, mathematics* and *science*.

Reading

The theory that there is a degree of relationship between active play and reading is not new. For example, well over two centuries ago Fénelon is reputed to have said that he had seen certain children who learned to read while playing (Johnson, 1907). A representative statement of more modern times and in a more specific vein suggests that with children "the kinesthetic sense—the sense of *feel* they get through their muscles—seems to be highly developed and it helps some children remember words they would take much longer to learn by looking at or sounding out." (Beaumont and Franklin, 1955).

Our research with active games and reading has been concerned essentially with the extent to which children can develop, practice and maintain reading skills and other language arts skills through the active game learning medium.

In a study which involved the parallel group experimental procedure, 20 third grade children were divided into two groups on the basis of pre-test scores of ten language understandings (Humphrey, 1965). One group was taught by means of active games; the other was taught through traditional language workbooks. Both groups had the same teacher. Comparisons were made of the pre- and post-test scores of the language workbook group and the active game group and of the post-test scores of both groups. While learning took place in both groups there was more significant gain in the active game group.

In a study designed to evaluate the effectiveness of active games as a means of *reinforcing* reading skills with fourth grade children, the parallel experimental procedure was employed (Humphrey, 1967b). The purpose of this study was to determine how well certain reading skills could be reinforced by the active game medium as compared with some of the traditional ways of reinforcing these skills.

Seventy-three fourth grade children were pretested on eight reading skills. Thirty of these children were divided into two groups on a matched-pair basis. One group of 15 was designated as the active game group and the other group of 15 as the traditional group. Each reading skill was introduced and presented verbally to the two groups together. The groups were then separated and with one group the reading skills were reinforced through active games. With the other group the reading skills were reinforced by such traditional media as a language workbook, dictionary and prepared ditto sheets. Both groups were taught by the same teacher. The types of reading skills used in the study were: structural and semantic analysis, phonics, word recognition and vocabulary development. In 14 of the 15 matched pairs the child in the active game group scored higher on the post-test than did his counterpart in the traditional group. Statistical analysis showed that gains made by the active game group indicated that they learned significantly more than the traditional group.

The final experiment reported here which is concerned with reading and active games involves a detailed study of the reactions of six- to eight-year-old children when independent reading material is oriented to active game experiences. This experiment utilized the technique of *Naturalistic Observation* and was initiated on the premise of relating reading content for six- to eight-year-old children to their natural urge to participate in active games (Humphrey and Moore, 1960).

Ten active games were written with a story setting, with the original manuscripts being very carefully prepared. Care was given to the reading values and the literary merits of each story. Attention was focused upon: (1) particular reading skills; (2) concept development; (3) vocabulary load, that is, in terms of the number, repetition and difficulty of words; and (4) length, phrasing and number of sentences per story.

After the manuscripts were prepared the *New Spache Readability Formula for Grades I-III* was applied to judge the reading difficulty of the material. After this formula was applied to the material, 30 teachers in rural, suburban and city school systems working with 54 reading groups of children used and evaluated the stories in actual classroom situations. The reading groups varied in: (1) number, from 3 to 33; (2) chronological age, from 5 years 9 months to 9 years 8 months; (3) intelligence quotient, from 52 to 136; and (4) grade placement from first grade through third grade. The children represented to a reasonable extent a cross section of an average population with respect to ethnic background, socioeconomic level and the like. In all, 503 children read from one to three stories for a total of 1,007 different readings.

On report sheets especially designed for the purpose the teachers were asked to record observable evidence of certain comprehension skills being practiced by the reading groups. The teachers were requested to make their evaluations on a comparative basis with other materials that had been read by the children. Comprehension skills practiced by the total of 54 groups of children as observed by teachers were recorded as follows:

Comprehension Skill	Percent of Groups Practicing Skill
Following directions	91
Noting and using sequence of ideas	76
Selecting main idea	76
Getting facts	67
Organizing ideas	46
Building meaningful vocabulary	41
Gaining independence in word mastery	35

The observations of the teachers indicated that the active game stories gave the children opportunities to practice and maintain skills necessary for intelligent reading. While enriching and extending their experiences the children improved their general ability to read independently and *on their own.*

In another dimension of this study teachers were asked to rate the degree of *interest* of the children in the reading on an arbitrary 5-point scale as follows: extreme interest, considerable interest, moderate interest, some interest, or little or no interest. Again the teachers established their own criteria in rating for degree of interest. The fact that there was sustained interest in the active play reading content is shown by the result which indicated that 70 percent of the children demonstrated either "considerable" or "extreme" interest. These results become more meaningful when it is considered that many of the classroom teachers reported to the investigators that untold numbers of children sit in school and read with little or no interest. This dimension of the study tended to show that reading was an *active* rather than a *passive* process. Apparently the children had a real and genuine purpose for reading and to satisfy the natural urge to play they were *interested* and read to learn a new game.

On the basis of the findings of this study and with the limitations involved in conducting such an experiment, the following tentative conclusions appeared warranted:

1. When a child is self-motivated and interested, he reads. In this case the reading was done without the usual motivating devices such as picture clues and illustrations.
2. These stories oriented to active play were found to be extremely successful in stimulating interest in reading and at the same time improving the child's ability to read.
3. Because the material for these active game stories was scientifically selected, prepared and tested it is unique in the field of children's independent reading material. The outcomes were most satisfactory in terms of children's interest in reading content of this nature as well as motivation to read.

It should be interesting to note that the ten active game stories used in the above experiment were extended into over 130 stories comprising six books for first and second grade children and published in the United States and abroad (Humphrey and Moore, 1962, 1965).

Mathematics

The use of play and games in number experiences of children has long been recognized. In one section of his "Laws," the suggestion is made by Plato that, "teachers mix together objects adapting the rules of elementary arithmetic in play." The opportunities for such procedures as counting, computing and measuring abound in many active game experiences of the child in present day society. In certain types of games, such as tag games, children caught can be counted and compared to the number not caught. In those kinds of activities requiring scoring there are opportunities for counting, adding and subtracting. In fact, it would be difficult to identify any kind of active game situation where quantitative factors are not involved.

It has been our experience that teachers are enthusiastic about the active game approach in the development of mathematical concepts with children and have used it with various degrees of success. There has remained, however, the necessity to obtain objective evidence to support the theory that the active game learning medium is a useful adjunct to learning in the area of mathematics. Our attempts in this direction have been most encouraging as exemplified in the representative examples of our research which follow.

One study involved the Single Group Experiment Procedure with parallel groups of boys and girls within the single group (Humphrey 1966b). Thirty-five first grade children were pretested on eight mathematics concepts. Ten boys and ten girls who had the same scores as the boys were selected for the experiment. Eight active games in which the mathematics concepts were inherent were selected. The active games were taught to the 20 children and used as learning media for the development of the mathematical concepts, after which the children were retested. In every case there was a gain in the scores of each child between the first and second test. A statistical analysis indicated that there was a highly significant difference between the mean scores of the first and second tests. In computing the results for the ten boys and ten girls separately, a difference in the mean scores favored the boys.

It was concluded from the results of this study that first grade children could learn mathematics concepts through the active game medium and that the approach tended to be more favorable for boys than for girls.

The second study on active games and mathematics reported

here (Humphrey, 1968) was patterned somewhat along the lines of the one reported previously which utilized active game reading content, except that the *Parallel Group Procedure* was used rather than *Naturalistic Observation*. An attempt was made to discover the value of such reading content when it contained inherent mathematics skills and concepts. In the area of mathematics we have referred to this kind of reading content as the "mathematics motor activity story" (Humphrey, 1967a).

The purpose of the mathematics motor activity story is to put into story form a pleasurable physical activity in which one or more mathematics concepts are inherent. The development of such a story involves selecting an active game or other suitable play activity for a particular age level in which certain mathematics understandings may be inherent. A story is then composed from the activity and written to the readability level for a given grade. An example of such a story follows: The name of this story is "Find a Friend" and it is an adaptation of an active game called "Busy Bee." The readability level of this example is 1.5 which means fifth month of first grade. The mathematics concepts and learnings inherent in the story are *groups or sets of two, counting by twos and beginning concept of multiplication*.

FIND A FRIEND

In this game each child finds a friend. Stand beside your friend. You and your friend make a group of two. One child is "It." He does not stand beside a friend. He calls, "Move." All friends find a new friend. "It" tries to find a friend. The child who does not find a friend is "It." Play the game. Count the number of friends standing together. Count by two. Say two, four, six. Count all of the groups this way.

Two groups of second grade children with 21 in one group and 23 in the other group were pretested on two-number addition facts, three-number addition equations, and subtraction facts. One group of children was taught through six mathematics motor activity stories of the type illustrated above. The other group was taught by such traditional procedures as the printed number line, plastic discs, and abstract algorisms. Both groups were taught by the same teacher.

Both groups were retested with the same test four days after the mathematical processes were taught as indicated above. A statistical comparison of the pre- and post-test indicated that there was a significant gain in favor of the active game group.

At an extended interval of ten days after the post-test the same test was given. The same statistical procedures were applied to the post-test and extended interval test with essentially the same results.

In recognition of various limitations imposed by a study of this nature any conclusions should be characterized by caution. If one accepts the levels of significant differences in the test scores as evidence of learning, these second grade children could develop certain number processes better and perhaps retain them longer, through the active game learning medium than through some of the traditional procedures.

Finally, it seems pertinent to mention certain observations which would not show up in the statistical analysis. It was noted that the children in the experimental group appeared to be stimulated by the use of the active game learning medium. In fact, some of them commented, "We didn't have arithmetic today." This could mean that the learning activities were enjoyed to the extent that the children might not have been aware of the particular number skills they were using. It is worthy of comment also that several of the children in the experimental group seemed to have had little or no interest in any of their work until after they got into the experience provided by the active game learning situations.

Science

The opportunities for science experiences through active games are so numerous that it would perhaps be difficult to visualize an active game situation that is not related to science in some way. This is particularly true of physical science principles since practically all voluntary body movements are based in some way on one or more principles of physical science. For example, *equilibrium* is involved in many active games, and *motion* is the basis for almost all such activities.

Two representative examples of studies involving science and active games are reported here, both of which employed the Parallel Group Experimental Procedure. In the first study (Humphrey,

1966a, pp. 216-217) 48 fifth grade children were equated into two groups of matched pairs on the basis of pre-test scores. Both groups were taught by the same teacher. The active game group was taught through the active game medium in which science concepts were inherent. The traditional group was taught through such traditional procedures as oral presentation, visual aids, class discussions, and experimentation. After a nine-day period in which both groups were taught as indicated they were retested. A comparison of the second test scores of both groups favored the active game group.

In the second study, 23 first grade children were pretested on eight concepts involving simple machines (Prager, 1968). All 23 of the children were taught by traditional procedures by their regular classroom teacher. Immediately after each lesson the physical education teacher took 11 of the children on the basis of pre-test scores and attempted to reinforce the concepts through active games. After this procedure was followed for a two-week period, all of the children were again tested. The results of this post-test showed that the group whose learning was reinforced by the active game medium was significantly higher. In comparing each group separately as their own controls it was indicated that the groups reinforced by the active game medium gained significantly from pre- to post-test, while the other group did not improve significantly. One of the conclusions drawn from this study was that the physical education teacher might be consulted in the planning of certain science learning experiences of first grade children.

DISCUSSION

During the early school years, and at ages six to eight particularly, it is possible that learning is frequently limited by a relatively short attention span rather than only by intellectual capabilities. Moreover, some children who do not appear to think or learn well in abstract terms can more readily grasp concepts when given an opportunity to use them in an applied manner. In view of the fact that the young child lives in a "movement world" so to speak, and also that he deals better in concrete rather than abstract terms, it would seem to follow naturally that the active game learning medium is best suited for him.

The active game approach to learning appears to have what might be termed certain inherent facilitative factors which are highly compatible with child learning. Three such factors are *motivation, proprioception* and *reinforcement,* all of which are interrelated and somewhat interdependent upon each other.

Motivation

In examining motivation as a facilitative factor in learning through active games, it will be considered from the point of view of some principles that center around (1) interest, (2) knowledge of results and (3) the competitive element.

Considering *interest* as a state of being and a way of reacting to a certain situation, interest is closely related to motivation. Under most circumstances a high interest level is concomitant with active game situations simply because of the expectation of pleasure children tend to associate with such activities. The structure of a learning activity is directly related to the length of time the learning act can be tolerated by the learner without loss of interest. Active game situations by their very nature are more likely to be so structured than many of the traditional learning activities.

Regarding the principle of motivation involving *knowledge of results,* child development specialists are generally agreed that children learn better when they know the results of what they have done than when they are left in doubt about it. Active game learning experiences provide a fine opportunity for this because the child can actually "see" and "feel" himself throw a ball and tag or be tagged in a game.

With reference to the element of *competition,* it has been shown in various studies that competition and rivalry produce results in effort and speed of accomplishment. There is a natural group competitive element in many active game situations.

Proprioception

In general, proprioception is concerned with "muscle sense." The proprioceptors as sensory nerve terminals give information concerning movements and position of the body. A proprioceptive feedback mechanism is involved which in a sense regulates movement.

In view of the fact that children are so movement oriented, it appears a reasonable speculation that proprioceptive feedback from the receptors of muscles, skin and joints contributes in a facilitative manner when the active game learning medium is used to develop academic skills and concepts. Herein lies the essential difference between the *active* game learning approach and other educational games which are more or less passive in nature. The latter which involves the use of cards, dice, boards and the like, although they are motivating, are obviously lacking in the highly important aspect of proprioception.

Reinforcement

In considering the compatibility of the active game learning medium with reinforcement theory, the meaning of reinforcement needs to be taken into account. An acceptable general description of reinforcement would be that there is an increase in the efficiency of a response to a stimulus brought about by the concurrent action of another stimulus. The basis for contending that the active game learning medium is consistent with general reinforcement theory is that this medium reinforces attention to the learning task and learning behavior. It keeps children involved in the learning activity which is perhaps the major area of application for reinforcement procedures. Moreover, there is perhaps little in the way of human behavior which is not reinforced, or at least reinforcible, by feedback of some sort, and the importance of proprioceptive feedback has already been discussed in this particular connection.

In summarizing this discussion it would appear that the active game learning medium generally establishes a more effective situation for learning reinforcement for the following reasons. First, the greater motivation of the children in the active game learning situation involves accentuation of those behaviors directly pertinent to their learning activities, making these salient for the purpose of reinforcement. Second, the proprioceptive emphasis in active games involves a greater number of "responses" associated with and conditioned to learning stimuli. Finally, the gratifying aspects of the active game situations provide a generalized situation of "reinforcers."

SOME GENERALIZATIONS

In view of the fact that there are now some objective data to support a long-held theory, perhaps some generalized assumptions, along with some reasonable speculations, can be set forth with some degree of confidence. Obviously, the available data are not extensive enough to carve out a clear-cut profile with regard to learning through the active game medium. However, they are suggestive enough to give rise to some interesting generalizations which may be briefly summarized as follows:

1. In general, children tend to learn certain academic skills and concepts better through the active game medium than through many of the traditional media in such subject areas as reading and language, science and mathematics.
2. This approach, while favorable for both boys and girls, appears to be more favorable for boys.
3. It appears to be more favorable for children with normal and below normal intelligence.
4. For children with high levels of intelligence it may be possible to introduce more advanced academic skills and concepts at an earlier age through the active game learning medium.

In closing, it should be mentioned that we have discussed the active game learning medium with some of the leading neurophysiologists, learning theorists, child development specialists and others. There is pretty general agreement among specialists in the various professions and disciplines that the premise is very sound from all standpoints: philosophical, physiological and psychological.

SOURCES OF MATERIALS FOR USE

Read and Play Series, by James H. Humphrey and Virginia D. Moore, published by Garrard Publishing Company, Champaign, Illinois, 1962, and Great Britain edition by Frederick Muller, Ltd., London, England, 1965.

A series of six books comprising 130 stories for first and second grade boys and girls. The reading content is oriented to active play, and hence it involves an active rather than a passive process. Consequently, the child has a real and genuine purpose for reading.

The stories in this series are designed to give the child opportunities to practice and maintain skills necessary for intelligent reading. This is due to the fact that this approach enables the teacher to make a valid evaluation of how well comprehension skills are being practiced because the children actually engage in what they read.

Child Learning Through Elementary School Physical Education, by James H. Humphrey, published by Wm. C. Brown Company, Dubuque, Iowa, 1966.

This book is for teachers and goes into complete detail regarding the use of active games as a learning medium. Numerous examples are given and suggestions are given on how the teacher can develop these types of activities.

Teaching Children Mathematics Through Games, Rhythms and Stunts (Two long play albums with teacher's manual) created by James H. Humphrey, published by Kimbo Educational Records, Box 55, Deal, New Jersey, 1968.

The children listen to the selections on the records and then with various degrees of teacher guidance participate in the activities in order to develop the mathematics concepts. This approach removes the learning of mathematics skills and concepts from the realm of the abstract and makes them a part of the child's physical reality.

Teaching Reading Through Creative Movement (The AMAV Technique) (Two long play albums with teacher's manual) created by James H. Humphrey, Robert M. Wilson and Dorothy D. Sullivan, published by Kimbo Educational Records, Box 55, Deal, New Jersey, 1969.

Children listen to the stories on the records and then create expressive movements. The teacher is able to evaluate how well they are practicing and maintaining comprehension skills. The materials also include books for children, to be used to "read along" while listening.

REFERENCES

Beaumont, Florence and Franklin, Adele: "Who Says Johnny Can't Read?" *Parents Magazine,* June, 1955.
Humphrey, James H.: "Comparison of the Use of Active Games and Language Workbook Exercises as Learning Media in the Development

of Language Understandings with Third Grade Children," *Percept Mot Skills, 21,* 1965.

Humphrey, James H.: *Child Learning Through Elementary School Physical Education.* Wm. C. Brown, Dubuque, 1966a.

Humphrey, James H.: "The Use of the Active Game Learning Medium in the Reinforcement of Reading Skills with Fourth Grade Children," *Journal of Special Education,* Summer, 1967b.

Humphrey, James H.: "An Exploratory Study of Active Games in Learning of Number Concepts by First Grade Boys and Girls," *Percept Mot Skills, 23,* 1966b.

Humphrey, James H.: "The Mathematics Motor Activity Story," *The Arithmetic Teacher,* January, 1967a.

Humphrey, James H.: "Comparison of the Use of the Physical Education Learning Medium with Traditional Procedures in the Development of Certain Arithmetical Processes with Second Grade Children," *Research Abstracts,* American Association for Health, Physical Education and Recreation, 1968.

Humphrey, James H. and Moore, Virginia: "Improving Reading Through Physical Education," *Education* (The Reading Issue), 1962.

Humphrey, James H. and Moore, Virginia: *Read and Play Series,* Six Books for First and Second Grade Children, Champaign, Illinois, Garrard Publishing Company, 1962. Selected for publication in Great Britain by Frederick Muller, Ltd., London, 1965.

Johnson, George Ellsworth: *Education by Plays and Games,* Ginn, Boston, 1907, p. 31.

Prager, Iris: "The Use of Physical Education Activities in the Reinforcement of Learning of Selected First Grade Science Concepts," Unpublished Master of Arts Thesis, University of Maryland, College Park, Maryland, 1968.

CHAPTER 12

ASSEMBLY LINE[1]

Dennis Dobbs, Robert F. Hill and Carol Guyton Goodell

INTRODUCTION

*D*ENNIS DOBBS, ROBERT HILL, and CAROL GOODELL
*have prepared a game that is predicated on a situation found in
the industrial life of the country. It simulates the processes of the
assembly line. In that sense it does not have a familiar game-form;
rather it depends for its game quality on the unfamiliarity of the
players with the process that is simulated. The outcome is in doubt
only so long as naive (or unskilled) players participate. In this
respect it resembles* Tic-Tac-Toe. *We hasten to say, however, that
this characteristic does not disqualify (make either ineligible or
trivial) either* Tic-Tac-Toe *or* Assembly Line *as games and useful
teaching tools. The value of* Assembly Line *lies in the complexity
of the game processes and the control that the students have over
these processes, once they understand how they work. Faults in the
system that they themselves set up will be played out before them,
and the discussion of how and why the play went awry will highlight the alternatives in planning on the one hand and remedies
on the other.*

*Since this is a game that is based on existing situations in real
life, the innovative teacher only needs to analyze any situation or*

[1]Reprinted from *Real World Learning; Educational Simulation Games* by Dennis C.
Dobbs, Carol G. Goodell, & Robert F. Hill. Assembly Line Game: All Rights Reserved.
©Real World Learning, Inc., copyright 1969.

199

process he or she wishes to bring into the classroom to follow the lead of the authors.

This team of game-innovators has approached social, historical, geographical and economic teaching problems as they expanded their game teaching tools. They are interested in any teacher's problem as they seek to use games. They welcome inquiries.

—Editors

Assembly Line is a simulation game. It provides a concrete experience with the real world of work and modern technology. The purpose of the game is to provide the learner with a dramatic and dynamic activity, one where he can readily obtain information about mass production methods. More specifically, it is an activity where he can become acquainted with the actual operation of an assembly line.

ASSEMBLY LINE provides first-hand experience with the varying attitudes and feelings that are so often a part of being employed in our highly mechanized society.

ASSEMBLY LINE leads to an understanding of how assembly line methods have made possible such current advantages as our increased productivity and our reduced rate-per-item in the total cost of production.

ASSEMBLY LINE, in addition, demonstrates one of the major cultural changes stemming from the Industrial Revolution; that change was a major departure from the previous hand operations in the manufacturing process.

ASSEMBLY LINE displays some of the modern consequences of specialization, including such common concepts as division of labor and the use of interchangeable parts.

ASSEMBLY LINE players will soon gain insight into the social consequences that lead to such things as (1) the creation of new jobs, (2) the disappearance of old jobs, and (3) man's sharp increase in his use of natural resources.

ASSEMBLY LINE provides players with the simulated opportunity to undergo many assembly line working conditions. These include (1) lack of contact with (and therefore lack of pride in) the final product; (2) boredom that often results from repetitive tasks; (3) demands to speed up or slow down production; and

(4) pressures and responsibilities in man's "work-a-day world".

Figure 12-1. Chris Ingle, Illustrator.

GAME AT-A-GLANCE

Goals

1. Introduce concept of mass production in industry.
2. Gain information about the operation of an assembly line.

3. Experience some of the feelings of workers on an assembly line.
4. Utilize related social and academic skills.
5. Use problem solving skills.

Concepts

Mass production
Competition
Division of labor
Job specialization
Market demand
Capital investment
Interchangeable parts
Gross income / Net income
Collective bargaining
Market projections

Materials

1. Tables and chairs or desks with legs on outer corners to permit conveyor to pass on the floor beneath.
2. One to two foot wide roll of butcher paper for conveyor belt. (Improvise)
3. Scissors and paste or glue.
4. Tag board for car templates to be used with colored construction paper, *or* dittos and white construction paper.
5. Pencils for tracing templates on colored construction paper, *or* crayons for "painting" cars on dittoed white construction paper. Do not paint G (glueing) surfaces.

Directions

1. Transfer car diagram to a ditto *or* trace parts on tag board paper to be used as tracing templates.
2. Arrange desks or tables in a long row with seating for workers on each side.
3. Set up roll of butcher paper as a conveyor belt. Paper is taped together after being looped over and under the line of tables or desks.
4. Demonstrate to players the assembly of one car. (Optional)
5. Designate player roles and places.
6. Distribute materials and tools and start production.

Roles

ASSEMBLY LINE can be adapted for groups from 8 to 60 in size.
Billers (0-2)

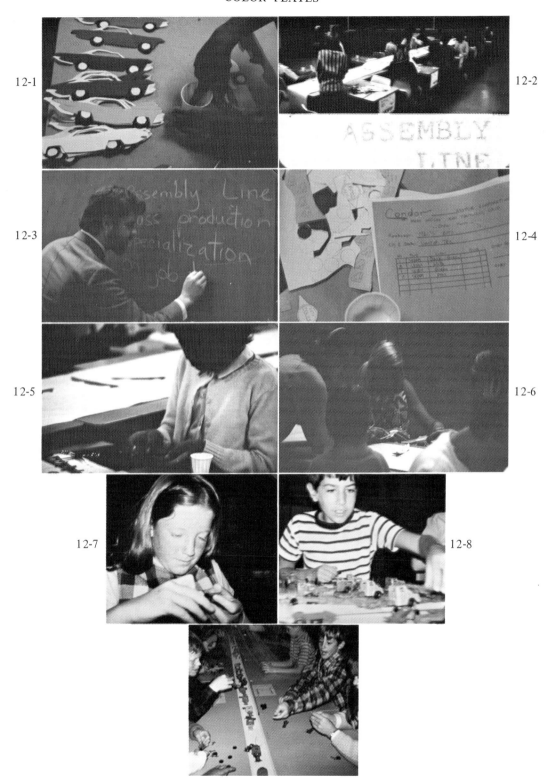

12-1
12-2
12-3
12-4
12-5
12-6
12-7
12-8
12-9

Tracers (4-8) (Template)
   or
Rough cutters (0-2) (Ditto)
Fine cutters (3-12+)
Gluers (2-10+)
Inspectors (0-2)
Line Mechanic (1)
Line Supervisors (1-3)
Accountants (1-2)

Optional Players

Efficiency Engineers
Foreman
Auto Dealers
Customers
Design Engineers
Managers
Union Representatives
Salesmen
Maintenance Crew

Time

45 minutes to 75 minutes
(depending on time taken for discussion)

HOW TO BEGIN AND WHAT TO EXPECT

Setting Up

Let's assume that you are ready to try ASSEMBLY LINE for the first time. You can (1) transfer the outlines of automobile parts to a ditto and run off about fifty copies on white construction paper, or you can (2) tear out the pattern page (p. 207, 8) and tape it to tag board to cut out and use as templates. A practical sequence of operations is shown in the illustration of the conveyer belt set-up (p. 204). Students may experiment with other arrangements in order to achieve a more efficient operation.

Efficiency Engineers

Before playing ASSEMBLY LINE, the leader should have three or four children set up the conveyer belt. In their role as *Efficiency Engineers* they should arrange the assembly sequence in order to maximize efficiency. These tasks should be done by the children.

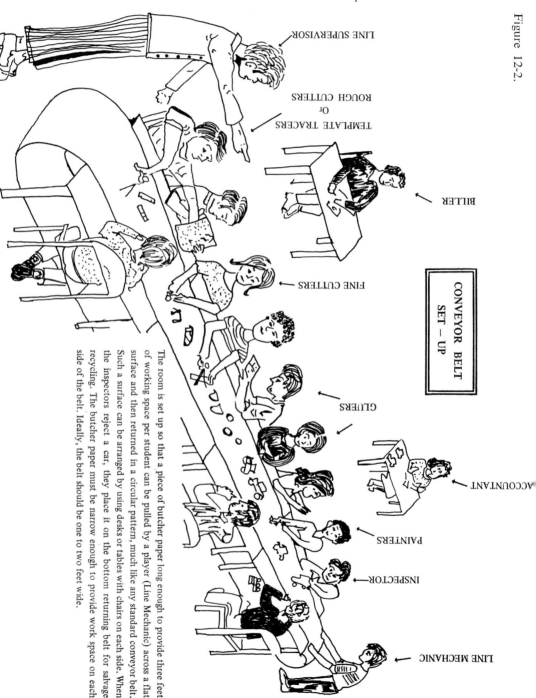

CONVEYOR BELT
SET – UP

LINE SUPERVISOR

TEMPLATE TRACERS
or
ROUGH CUTTERS

BILLER

FINE CUTTERS

GLUERS

ACCOUNTANT

PAINTERS

INSPECTOR

LINE MECHANIC

The room is set up so that a piece of butcher paper long enough to provide three feet of working space per student can be pulled by a player (Line Mechanic) across a flat surface and then returned in a circular pattern, much like any standard conveyor belt. Such a surface can be arranged by using desks or tables with chairs on each side. When the inspectors reject a car, they place it on the bottom returning belt for salvage recycling. The butcher paper must be narrow enough to provide work space on each side of the belt. Ideally, the belt should be one to two feet wide.

Figure 12-2.

They should have the opportunity to make and correct their own errors, for problem solving is the central learning experience of the game.

Demonstration

When it is time to play ASSEMBLY LINE, the leader may wish to begin by demonstrating how to put together one car before the students begin production. Ideally, the children who set up the conveyor belt and assembly line layout can provide "on-the-job" training for others.

Foreman

Students who are able to do their task well may be promoted to *Foreman*. They direct the workers and carry out the instructions of the *Line Supervisors*. *Foremen* also see to it that defective autos are correctly reassembled or salvaged.

Supervisors

Supervisors handle problems that arise and order materials when supplies are low. They also make decisions about changes in the sequence of assembly tasks.

Maintenance Crew

The *Maintenance Crew* sees to it that the work area is kept clean.

Inspectors

Inspectors can be placed at several points along the belt and at the end of the line.

Safety

At this point, the teacher may wish to discuss safety considerations, particularly when using scissors, and relate this to the safe use of real tools on a real assembly line.

Order Blanks

Allow the students to have a chance to play with ASSEMBLY LINE and become acquainted with how it works (approximately

10 minutes). They are now ready to receive their first *Order Blank*. The teacher may make these out in advance, or they can be made out by the *Biller*.

Management Procedures

The *Order Blank* is turned over to a *Line Supervisor* who in turn sees to it that the *Foremen* complete the order. At the end of the assembly line the *Inspector* compares the final product with the order and signs the blank if the auto passes inspection.

Workers' Duties

The first few *Workers* along the belt rough-cut the sheets of parts along the dotted lines, and place them on the belt. The next several *Workers* cut each part out along the solid lines, and return them to the belt. If the parts are reproduced on white paper, the next step is to have them "painted" by *Workers* using crayons, taking care not to color areas to be glued. The *Foreman* must know what colors have been specified on the *Order Blank* so he can pass this information along to the *Workers*. The next *Workers* on the line paste parts together. Near the end of the line, the remaining *Workers* add decals and accessories as ordered.

Discussion

After ASSEMBLY LINE has been in operation a while, students may ask to try working at another job. It may be appropriate to discuss the possibility of becoming bored while doing the same thing eight hours a day, five days a week. Solutions such as assembly teams are currently under consideration.

Problem Solving

All will not go smoothly during the experience, nor should it, for this would cut off problem-solving opportunities for the learner. For instance, if there seems to be a snag in the sequence of operations, the leader can (1) let it go on until a solution is devised by leaders among the children; or he can (2) intervene and ask the children to describe the problem and proceed to a discussion as to what the alternative solutions might be. Later, research or a field trip could reveal how real assembly line operations deal with such problems.

What Is a Good Simulation?

Part of what makes a good simulation good is that it makes very clear that there are few absolutely right or absolutely wrong decisions in life, that there are often priorities to be established, compromises to be considered, decisions to be made, and consequences with which to deal.

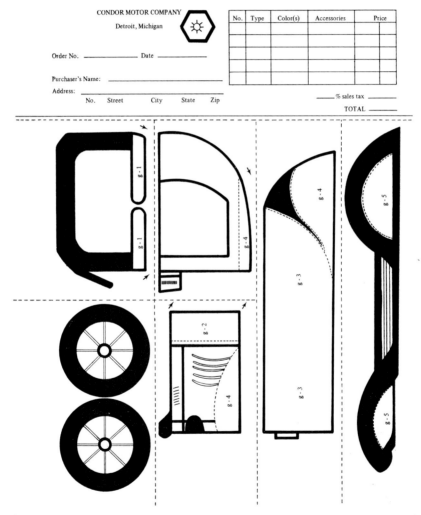

Figure 12-3.

Figure 12-4.

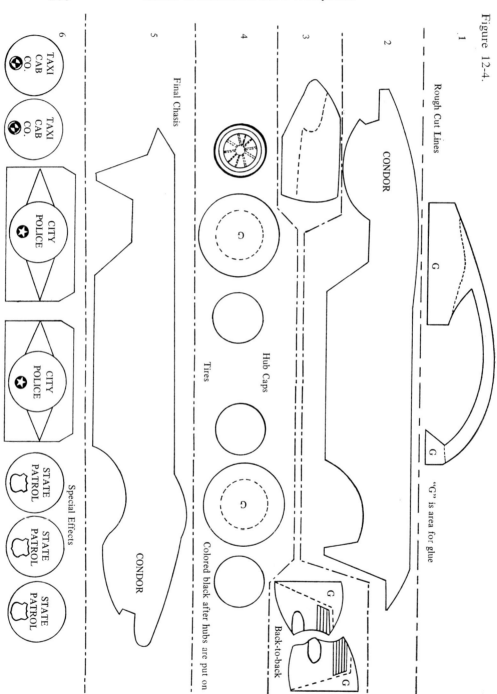

Rough Cut Lines

1

2

CONDOR

3

4

5

6

"G" is area for glue

G

G

G

G

G

Back-to-back

TAXI CAB CO.

TAXI CAB CO.

CITY POLICE

CITY POLICE

STATE PATROL

STATE PATROL

STATE PATROL

Final Chasis

CONDOR

Special Effects

Tires

Hub Caps

Colored black after hubs are put on

Production

1. Do some people have harder jobs than others?
2. Is there a more efficient way of increasing the number of cars produced?
3. Does anyone get behind? What can be done about this?
4. What are some other factors hindering productivity?
5. Are there high enough standards of quality in the cars being produced?
6. What are the special problems of workers on the assembly line?
7. How can management improve working conditions?
8. How can costs be cut?

Sociological

1. How are differences between labor and management settled?
2. What must a worker do in order to be promoted?
3. What is an Equal Opportunity Employer?
4. Could physically or mentally handicapped people work on an assembly line?
5. What should be done about the worker who "just can't do it right?"
6. What are society's responsibilities toward people who can't hold a job?
7. What responsibilities does an individual have in doing what is necessary to make a living?

Psychological

1. How are people affected by monotonous tasks?
2. How can a worker be helped to feel that what he does is important?
3. Does a worker's attitude toward his job affect the nature of his work? How?
4. What accounts for many people being "clock watchers" while on the job?
5. Would some people receive a good deal of satisfaction from assembly line work? Who? In what way?
6. When you are older would you want to work on a real assembly line? Why?

Economic

1. How are income, expenses, and profit determined?
2. Why might a manufacturing company use an assembly line operation?
3. How does demand affect the likely profits of a manufacturing company?
4. What are some of the consequences of a large company having to shut down operation?

5. What are some reasons for workers going on strike?
6. How does mass production affect our supply of natural resources?
7. What happens if a product is defective and is returned?

Variations and Extensions

ASSEMBLY LINE has been used successfully by both elementary and secondary students. In classes for educationally handicapped and mentally retarded children, teachers have used ASSEMBLY LINE to emphasize social skills such as cooperation, as well as working on academic skills involved in sorting by color and sequencing of operations. It has also been used in a vocational training program for a continuation high school in an inner city project.

1. Extensions

It is possible to have students organize on paper some of the auxiliary companies that are needed to supply products and materials for the assembly line which lead them to find out where rubber, steel, and glass come from, how much they cost and how they are transported to the manufacturer. They might go as far as to study physical geography to determine the best routes for moving raw materials and manufacturing parts to the automobile factory.

Two teachers took the basic format and designed a game called "Manufacturing" for eighth graders. It involved two competing auto manufacturers. The winners were the company that made the most profit, and the individual worker in each company who accumulated the greatest wealth in relation to his initial salary. Rules for setting up each company were established by the teachers who also ran a bank and a supply store. Each company used its capital to buy tools and materials from the suppliers. Students assumed company management and labor roles. In addition, they became consumers as they were required to buy at least one automobile during the game from student owned automobile dealerships. The teachers acted as judges of the quality of the work done by using templates cut to fit predetermined specifications. Workers could change jobs by proving to the directors of the employment office that they were qualified to handle the new job. Among other expenses, the manufacturers had to pay the cost of any changes that were made in the initial design of their automobile. The students spent ninety minutes a day for five days on this game, each day representing one year.

2. 3-Dimensional

ASSEMBLY LINE was first designed to be done with outlines of cars to be cut out and pasted together. Since then, small plastic trucks and trailers with twenty-seven parts for older children and large, simple, seven piece trucks for primary and educationally handicapped children have been used.

The three-dimensional snap-together model is a more accurate representation of an assembly line, and it is highly motivating because the layout is colorful and the toys look like real trucks. However, it is much more expensive.

The disassembled trucks and trailers are stored in a large box which is emptied on a table at the beginning of the game. The children, on their own initiative or at the teacher's direction, are to inventory the parts. Some mechanically minded children will soon have at least one model put together. These students can then be utilized as instructors to help the rest set up an efficient line. Sometimes students who achieve least well in the traditional classroom set up come through as the real leaders in this sort of situation. This reversal of the usual academic pecking order, if only for an hour, is important to the self concepts of all the children involved. They become aware of the need in a complex society to have many different kinds of talent and they see the application of a variety of talents in a real world learning situation.

Once the line is going, it operates much the same as the paste and cut line, but production tends to be much faster. A group of about twenty middle grade children can assemble forty trailers and trucks from an unsorted box to finished, inspected products in less than thirty minutes, including time off for discussions. In order to keep the line going, a crew of dismantlers can go to work supplying the workers with more raw materials. This is also necessary in order to reduce the cost of the materials for the simulation and to compensate for the almost certain loss of parts as the game is used and reused.

3. *Accounting Worksheet*

CONDOR MOTOR COMPANY
DETROIT, MICHIGAN
ACCOUNTANT'S COMPUTATION SHEET

Date: _____

GROSS INCOME:

Car Type	Number Sold		Selling Price		Income	
Sedans	_____	X	$2,100.00	=	$_____	(1)
Convertibles	_____	X	$2,300.00	=	$_____	(2)
Special Makes	_____	X	$2,500.00	=	$_____	(3)
				+	=========	

(Add lines 1, 2, & 3) Total Gross Income: $_____ (4)

TAXES

Enter Total Gross Income $_____ (Same as line (4)

Multiply by Tax Rate of X _____ .20 (%)

$_____ (Taxes owed)

Enter Taxes Owed on line (5) and subtract from line (4) $_____ (5)

—
=========

Adjusted Income: $_____ (6)

Material Costs:

Enter number of pieces: # _____ X $_____   = $_____ (7)

Enter cost per piece of material: Multiply

If prices vary, add together and enter on line (7)

Labor Costs:

Enter number of employees: # _____ X # _____ Time = _____ (8)

Enter number of minutes of production:

Enter Time (line (8)): _____ X $28.00   Labor Costs = $_____ (9)

Overhead Costs:

Enter Total Gross Income (line (4) $_____ X .20% = $_____ (10)

+
=========

Add lines (7), (9), & (10).   Total Expenses = $_____ (11)

Profit or Loss:

Enter Adjusted Income (Same as line (6)): $_____

Enter Total Expenses (Same as line (11)): $_____

Subtract line (11) from line (6)

=========

$_____ $_____ (12)

PROFIT OR LOSS

Arithmetic computations are used in inventory controls, and cost determination, including price of raw materials, wages, and overhead expenses such as plant operation and use of utilities. Students may wish to pursue the problem of determining income and expenses by writing a letter to an auto manufacturer.

4. Visual Instructions

Students who do not read may be given a completed model to follow rather than a written order blank.

5. Discovery

Instead of choosing supervisors and foremen, the teacher can allow the students a chance to discover the need for leadership and organization as they experience the chaos of trying to do without. They will probably notice a change in the amount of noise as they become organized. They may also find the need to set-up effective ways for people to communicate with one another about such things as order specifications, lack of materials and poor workmanship.

6. Competing Companies

If the leader wishes to make ASSEMBLY LINE a game with win criteria, competing lines may be set up. In order to emphasize the contrast between an assembly line and handwork operations, a competing custom auto manufacturer can also be established.

7. Car Design

As an art project, have the children design next year's "new" model for a replay of the game. Students could enter their designs in a "Car of the Future" contest.

8. Producing Useful Things

Have the group use the assembly line procedure to mass produce holiday place mats or other favors for patients in a nearby hospital. They could also make decorations or greeting cards for various holidays. Other groups may wish to use this game as a format through which to produce something to sell. The group might wish to make simple bird houses, decorated pencil holders, etc.

9. Challenge

What would the Condor Company's net profit be, assuming the following projections for the future are correct:
Labor force decreased by 8% due to mechanization.

Raw materials increased 7% (inflation factor)
Average salary increased 6% due to new union contract
Cars sold for $100 more per vehicle
Number of sedans sold increased by 15%
Number of convertibles increased by 12%
Number of special makes increased by 14%
Taxes changed to 21%
Other expenses declined by 1%

Obviously, months of research could emanate from this one simulation if all avenues of exploration were followed in depth. While such a complete unit would rarely be pursued, it does offer a wide variety of research topics into which students could delve according to their individual interests.

EVALUATION

A major problem in any simulation is how to evaluate what academic progress children have made as a result of their participation in it. The following suggestions by David Rawnsley, Assistant Director of Research of the San Mateo, Calif., County PACE Center can help the teacher develop performance objectives and related test questions for the purpose of evaluating achievement.

Let us suppose that we're talking about using a simulation as a part of a learning activity or teaching unit which would extend over a few weeks. There are at least three possible uses of a simulation in such a unit. The simulation would have a different set of performance objectives for each of these uses.

ASSEMBLY LINE could be used as a beginning experience in a social studies unit having to do with mass production. The instructional objective would be to assure that each student has a set of referents to which further learning can be referred to or developed from. This simulation would have the advantage of providing a commonality of reference for all the students.

Since the instructional objective is basically one of providing experience upon which to base learning, it is an extremely difficult, if not impossible, task to develop adequate performance objectives. An outcome objective for using the simulation as an experience might read somewhat like:

—During the remainder of the learning activity, each student will use the simulation as an example in discussions, papers, or projects. He will make such reference a specified number of times.

The simulation might be used perhaps somewhere in the middle of the learning activity in order to reach the instructional objective of developing a specific concept. Let's take the instructional objective to develop the concept of efficiency in relation to production. Performance objectives could read as follows:

—After participating in the simulation and discussion of it, the student will identify and relate to specific aspects of the simulation a specified number of factors which affect the quantity or quality of production.

The same objective could be written with the last phrase being:

—a specified number of factors which affect the amount of money the company makes.

Another form of basically the same objective might be:

—The student will identify a specified number of factors which affect the amount of money the company makes and relates these factors to the assembly line by naming an operation which exemplifies the factors or the person doing the operation.

Another type of performance objective could be:

—The student will make a written description of the assembly line which will, without instruction to do so, include reference to parts of the operation connected with the concept being taught.

The simulation could be used as an instruction tool in the teaching of abstractions. The instructional objective might be to teach the meaning of the word "efficiency" and to develop the ability to use this abstraction. Performance objectives could be written as follows:

—The student will, with a specified degree of accuracy, identify from a list of operations present in ASSEMBLY LINE, those which directly affect efficiency.
—Given a set of interrelated operations which can be arranged so as to achieve some goal, the student will arrange the operations so that the goal can be reached with the least effort.

A simulation like ASSEMBLY LINE can be an instructional tool to reach a wide range of objectives. In order for these goals to become performance objectives, the teacher must have a specific instructional objective in mind in using the tool, and should manipulate the use of the simulation in such a way as to emphasize the experience, concept, or information he wants to teach. There are many ways this can be done in ASSEMBLY LINE. For example, the teacher can vary the speed of the conveyor, the size or timing of orders, the presence or absence of certain job categories, etc. At some ages or levels of achievement, it is possible to have different performance objectives for each individual in the game. For example, one student might be working on an objective related to efficiency, while another might be working on an objective having to do with labor relations. Merely by playing the game, a teacher cannot expect his students to reach all the performance objectives which could be written. The simulation format must be arranged to serve the objectives for which it is being used.

CHAPTER 13

THE SIMULATION OF A COMPUTER-ASSISTED INSTRUCTION PROGRAM FOR TEACHING A NON-SIMULATION GAME: MEEMI—EQUATIONS AUTO-MATE IMP (INSTRUCTIONAL MATH PLAY) KIT #1

LAYMAN E. ALLEN AND JOAN K. ROSS

INTRODUCTION

*L*AYMAN ALLEN *and Joan Ross have devised two extensions to the game of* EQUATIONS. *Allen has utilized the concept of mathematical balance in constructing games that bear a variety of academic content (for example, ON-WORDS and ON-SETS). The game quality in such cases depends on the complexity of problems that one player constructs for the others. The game is more durable when it is set in a metagame matrix that matches equally proficient players at each level of competence. When EQUATIONS is set in such a metagame it can become an Olympian struggle. In fact, during the past eight years there has been a National Academic Games Olympics in which students from many different states have participated. These Games have been held in Florida, Louisiana, Michigan, Ohio, and Pennsylvania. Schools interested in participating in future Games may secure information about them by writing to Robert W. Allen, Director; National Academic Olympics Project; Box 214; Newhall, California.*

The two games presented in Chapter 13 are additions to EQUA-TIONS to facilitate introduction of the basic game to beginners and to permit extension of the basic game to more sophisticated mathematical ideas for more experienced players. With EQUATIONS AUTO-MATE IMP KITS, Allen and Ross have arranged for a single individual to play by himself. In a series of look-up tables the other player is represented and his choices are indicated. Furthermore, the learning player's mistakes are explained and corrected. In effect, this variation transforms the basic structure of EQUA-TIONS into a teaching machine which retains the drama and uncertainty of plays of the actual games between two or more players.

ADVENTUROUS EQUATIONS calls for several players and is similar to Dealer's Choice in POKER. Each player can change the rules at the beginning of play as well as play the game. This change is an open invitation for the players to take part in the rule-making function and to experience control over the rule structure. Under the rules governing orderly change, both individual and group controls are exercised. The rules for change permit certain kinds of individual advantage, thus teaching that taking relevant and legitimate advantage is allowed. At the same time irrelevant advantages are banned as illegitimate. It is the teacher's role to define relevant and legitimate changes. Since players will think of rules that the authors do not mention, this teacher function becomes a valuable dynamic tool in the mathematical and social education of the players. Be prepared for both delightful and sticky innovations. The authors will be interested in the innovations and your decisions. They are ready to serve as a court of appeal when needed.

The senior author is a prolific game inventor who has concentrated on ways to practice academic content dynamically. He is interested in other game-inventor's products and will gladly advise and encourage them.

—Editors

T HE VALUE OF GAMES is being increasingly recognized by educators who are seeking ways to tailor the classroom situation to fit the needs and abilities of individual pupils.[1] Games are particularly appropriate for such individualized teaching of mathematics and several effective ones have been developed. One of these is EQUATIONS. The EQUATIONS kit (WFF 'N PROOF series) is actually a set of games. The simplest involves only the operations of addition and subtraction on the numbers 0, 1, 2 and 3. The most advanced of the basic games involves the other six digits and uses the operations of multiplication, division, exponentiation, and root extraction also. It is not the purpose of the game to teach arithmetic facts (although knowledge of such facts is improved and is relevant for playing well). The main purposes of the game are two-fold. One is mathematical: to develop the player's insight into the relations between the arithmetic operations. The other is psychological: to increase the probability that a player will view himself as competent at rigorous symbol-handling activities and thus will develop a favorable attitude toward such activities.

The chief bottleneck preventing rapid introduction into the

---

[1]Research into the use of games for education is currently going on at the University of California, Johns Hopkins University, Cornell, Nova University, and the University of Michigan (among others). Many independent research groups are also studying instructional games. Included are Abt Associates, Science Research Associates, and Western Behavioral Sciences Institute.

Some publications which discuss games as learning devices are Coleman, James S.: *The Adolescent Society*. New York, Free Press, 1961 (see especially Chapter 11); Sutton-Smith, Brian: "The Psychology of Children's Games," *National Education* New Zealand, 1955, 37, 228; Allen, Layman E., Allen, Robert W. and Miller, James C.: "Programmed Games and the Learning of Problem-Solving Skills: The WFF 'N PROOF Example," *The Journal of Educational Research*, 60, 1, September, 1966, 22-25; Zieler, Richard: *Games for School Use*. 845 Fox Meadow Road, Yorktown Heights, New York: Center for Educational Services Research, Board of Cooperative Educational Services, First Supervisory District, Westchester County, New York; *American Behavioral Scientist*, 10, 2, October, 1966. Part I; *American Behavioral Scientist*, 10, 3, November, 1966. Part II.

The two issues of *American Behavioral Scientist* consisted entirely of articles on Simulation Games and Learning Behavior. It is important to note that EQUATIONS is *not* a simulation game. The players do not simulate doing mathematics, but actually do it. Thus, although the *American Behavioral Scientist* articles are useful, the conclusions expressed by Cleo Cherryholmes in his article do not apply to EQUATIONS.

A bibliography on educational games is included in *American Behavioral Scientist*, November, 1966.

Two recent general discussions of instructional games are given in "Games in the Classroom," A Scholastic Teacher Report, a reprint of articles from *The Scholastic Teacher* of November 9, 1967, which also includes a very useful list of pedagogical games; and "Games in the Classroom" by Elliot Carlson from *The Saturday Review of Literature*, April 16, 1967.

classroom of intellectually sophisticated instructional games like those in the WFF 'N PROOF series[2] has been the lack of effective techniques for quickly training teachers to appreciate the full richness of learning situations organized around such games. Furthermore, we believe that until a substantial number of teachers get tuned in on the value of such games to stimulate learning, the benefits reaped will be meager and fragmentary relative to the potentialities. We simply cannot by-pass the most significant resource available in a learning situation—namely, the teacher—and expect to get the same results that the enthusiastic assistance of that teacher would have elicited. There has never yet been designed a set of materials that are "teacher-proof," and in our view it is highly unlikely that there ever will be.

But help to the teacher, there certainly can be. We believe that the solitaire version of EQUATIONS exemplified in MEEMI—EQUATIONS AUTO-MATE IMP KIT #1 set forth below is an illustration of the kind of help that will facilitate and direct a teacher's efforts at moving his/her class along to the deeper mathematical implications in EQUATIONS and the other WFF 'N PROOF-type games. This variation allows the teacher to suggest EQUATIONS to individual students as enrichment. As is suggested by the ancient Chinese proverb:

I hear . . . and I forget.
I see . . . and I remember.
I do . . . and I understand.

Doing is better than talking about, so let's get at it! Both instructions for using EQUATIONS—AUTO-MATE IMP KIT rules and the new official rules for playing EQUATIONS are presented below. Experienced players should glance at the changes in the play made by rules R8, R9, R10, and R11. Newcomers should read through the rules below before undertaking EQUATIONS—AUTO-MATE IMP KIT.

---

[2]The particular games we have in mind are: WFF 'N PROOF—The Game of Modern Logic (by Layman E. Allen); EQUATIONS—The Game of Creative Mathematics (Layman E. Allen); and ON-SETS—The Game of Set Theory (by Layman E. Allen, Peter Kugel, and Martin Owens).

Description of Basic EQUATIONS

In playing Basic EQUATIONS the first player rolls the cubes out on the table. The resulting symbols facing upward on the cubes are the Resources for that play of the game. The first player decides whether or not to set a Goal. If he does set a Goal, then the players take turns moving cubes into the Forbidden, Permitted, or Required sections of the playing mat. Play ends when there is a challenge, when a player asserts that a Solution can be built with one more cube from the Resources, or when a player says "No Goal."

Number of Players: Two or More

EQUATIONS may be played by as many players as can gather around a table and see the cubes. Three-player games are recommended for classroom use.

Level of Play

EQUATIONS may be played at many levels of difficulty. The level is determined by: (a) the number of cubes used, (b) the color of cubes used, and (c) the extent to which the players understand the ideas used in the game. A good beginning game for second graders uses just the twelve red cubes. What cubes are used thereafter depends upon the abilities and progress of the players. Sixth graders can learn to play well with all four colors of cubes. After players are familiar with all levels of Basic EQUATIONS, there is an advanced form of the game called Adventurous EQUATIONS that introduces the possibility of increased levels of difficulty through new game rules.

Game Levels

Game Level	Approximate Age Level	Number of Cubes to Use			
		Red	Blue	Green	Black
1	6	12			
2	.	8	8		
3	.	6	6	6	
4	11 & up	5	5	5	5

Figure 13-1.

What Symbols on Cubes Represent

The + on the red cubes and the black cubes indicates the addition operation. The — on the blue and green cubes indicates subtraction. These signs are not used to indicate either the positive or negative property of a number; they represent operations on pairs of numbers, but not properties of single numbers.

The * on the green cubes indicates the exponentiation operation (that is, "to the power of"). Thus, in Basic EQUATIONS $\boxed{3}\ \boxed{*}\ \boxed{2}$ is interpreted as "three to the second power" (or 3^2). Similarly, $\boxed{2}\ \boxed{*}\ \boxed{3}$ is interpreted as "two to the third power" (or 2^3).

The $\sqrt{}$ on the black cubes indicates "root of." It must be preceded by some cube or cubes indicating a number to indicate which root is being extracted. Thus, in Basic EQUATIONS $\boxed{2}\ \boxed{\sqrt{}}\ \boxed{9}$ is interpreted as "the square root of 9" (or 3). Similarly, $\boxed{3}\ \boxed{\sqrt{}}\ \boxed{8}$ is interpreted as "the third root of 8" (or 2), and $\boxed{1}\ \boxed{\div}\ \boxed{2}\ \boxed{\sqrt{}}\ \boxed{3}$ is interpreted as "the one-half root of 3."

Aim in Playing

To win by correctly challenging or by being incorrectly challenged.

In EQUATIONS you can win either (a) by correctly challenging a Flub that another player has made or (b) by being incorrectly challenged by another player. An important feature of EQUATIONS is that you can win by challenging at any time (if somebody has Flubbed).You do not have to wait until it is your turn to play to make a challenge. Consequently, because in a three-player game two players are competing to challenge first, the play is more exciting than in a two-player game, where such competition is absent.

Start of Play

The players decide which cubes and how many to use. The player chosen to go first rolls the cubes out on the table. The resulting symbols facing upward on the cubes are the Resources for that play of the game. The first player must decide whether to set a Goal or to say "No Goal."

Play

After a Goal has been set, the players take turns moving Resource cubes from the table to the Forbidden, Permitted, or Required sections of the playing mat.

End of Play

Play ends when there is a challenge, when a player asserts that a Solution can be built with one more cube from the Resources, or when a player says "No Goal."

Summary of Play

When it is the first player's turn to play, he does one of the following:

(a) declares "No Goal", or

(b) sets a Goal.

After the first play when it is a player's turn, he does one of the following:

(a) declares that a Solution is possible with just one more cube from the Resources, or

(b) challenges the previous move as being a Flub, or

(c) moves a cube from the Resources to either Forbidden, Permitted, or Required.

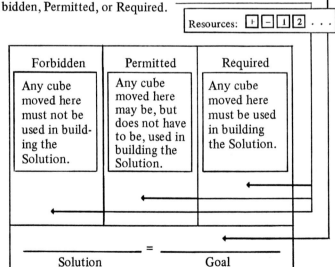

Figure 13-2.

Rules of Basic EQUATIONS[3]

R1. Goal Rule

On your shake, you must either say "No Goal" or set a Goal by moving one to five cubes from the Resources to the Goal section of the playing mat. The Goal must express a number. You indicate that the Goal is complete by saying "Goal."

Comments

(1) The Goal is the right side of an equation. After you have rolled the cubes, the symbols that appear on their upward faces are the Resources for that play of the game. When it is possible to set a Goal for which a Solution (the left side of the equation) can be built from the remaining Resources, then in order to avoid Flubbing you must set such a Goal and you must not say "No Goal." For example, if no numerals appear as Resources, you may say "No Goal" without Flubbing; but if any two identical numerals appear as Resources, you must set a Goal.

(2) The Goal must be a string of cubes that expresses a number. At most five cubes may be used in the Goal. The operation signs, $+$, $-$, $\times$, $\div$, $*$, and $\sqrt{}$ may be used in the Goal. Multiple-digit numbers, as well as single-digit numbers, may be used in the Goal. Some examples of permissible Goals are 1, 1+2, 12, and 123−4. Expressions such as $+$ and 5− are not permissible Goals because they do not express numbers. The expression −23 is not a permissible Goal in Basic EQUATIONS because the minus sign is inappropriately used.

(3) If you use two operation signs in the Goal, the insertion of parentheses may be shown by the grouping of the cubes. Thus, $\boxed{2}\boxed{-}\ \boxed{1}\boxed{+}\boxed{3}$ may be used to indicate (2−1) + 3, while $\boxed{2}\boxed{-}\ \boxed{1}\boxed{+}\boxed{3}$ may be used to indicate 2 − (1+ 3). If the Goal-Setter fails to group the cubes to show how the parentheses are to be inserted, then expressions that satisfy either grouping are acceptable Solutions as the left side of the equation.

---

[3]Three other games in the WFF 'N PROOF series have essentially the same game rules as EQUATIONS. They are ON-SETS (about set theory), ON-WORDS (about word structures), and the PROOF games of WFF 'N PROOF (about mathematical logic). Because of this similarity, once you have learned to play EQUATIONS you will also be well down the road toward learning these other games.

(4) The Goal is not changed after it has been set in Basic EQUATIONS.

R2. *Move Rule*

After the Goal has been set, play progresses in a clockwise direction. When it is your turn to play, you must either challenge, assert (without challenging) that a Solution can be built with one more cube from Resources, or make one of the following moves:

(A) move a cube from Resources to the Forbidden section,
   or
(B) move a cube from Resources to the Permitted section,
   or
(C) move a cube from Resources to the Required section.

When it is your turn, you are not permitted to pass.

Comment

By their moves, the players shape the Solution. Cubes are never moved after they have been placed on the playing mat.

R3. *Bonus Rule*

On your turn to play you may take a bonus move before making a regular move (before setting a Goal or moving a cube to the Forbidden, Permitted, or Required sections). A bonus move consists of saying "Bonus" and moving one cube from Resources to the Forbidden section. If you do not say "Bonus" before moving the cube to the Forbidden section, the move does not count as a bonus move but as a regular move to Forbidden.

Comment

The Bonus Rule has the effect of allowing a mover to move two cubes to the playing mat, but one of them *must* go into the Forbidden section. Both of them *may* go into Forbidden.

R4. *Solution Rule*

The Solution (or left side of the equation) must be equal to the Goal, and in attempting to build a Solution

(A) you must not use any of the cubes in the Forbidden section;
(B) you may use as many of the cubes in the Permitted section as you like;

(C) you must use all of the cubes in the Required section;

(D) you may always use at least one cube from Resources; you may use at most one cube from Resources when there has been an A-claim challenge or a C-claim challenge that stems from a previous A-claim violation (see the Flubbing Rule, Rule 5, below), and you may use as many Resources as you like when there has been a P-claim challenge, a C-claim challenge that stems from a previous P-claim violation, or a No-Goal challenge (note that on a No-Goal challenge you must set a Goal as well as build a solution);

(E) you may use only one-digit numerals (multiple-digit numerals, however, are permitted in the Goal);

(F) you may insert parentheses wherever you want to put them (to show in which order the operations are to be performed);

(G) you may use the plus and minus signs on the cubes (+ and −) to denote only the operations of *addition* and *subtraction*; you must not use them to denote the *positive* or *negative* properties of numbers (this usage also applies to setting the Goal); and

(H) if you use the radical sign ($\sqrt{}$), it must always be preceded by an expression to denote its index (this usage also applies to setting the Goal).

Comment

Since several Resource cubes may show the same symbol, it is possible to have a $\boxed{2}$ in Forbidden which *must not* be used in the Solution at the same time that there is a $\boxed{2}$ in Required which *must* be used.

R5. Flubbing Rule

If you do either of the following, you have Flubbed:

(A) you declare "No Goal" when, in fact, you could have set a Goal for which there was a Solution;

(B) by your move you violate one of the following C-A-P claims:

C I cannot Correctly challenge on this turn.

A If possible, I am Avoiding by this move allowing a Solution to be built with at most one more cube from Resources.

P It is still Possible for the remaining Resources to be so played that a Solution can be built.

Comments

(1) The P-claim means that you Flub if you make a move that destroys all possibilities for building a Solution.

(2) The A-claim means that you Flub if you make a move that

permits a Solution to be built with just one more cube from Resources when you could have made a move that both avoided doing so and at the same time fulfilled the P-claim. Of course, when only two cubes are left in Resources, you may have to move one of them into the Permitted or the Required section and permit a Solution to be built with just one more cube from the Resources, because Forbidding either cube violates the P-claim. This is not an A-claim violation because in such circumstances it is not possible to avoid allowing a Solution to be built with just one more cube from the Resources without violating the P-claim.

(3) The C-claim means that once a Flub is made, every subsequent move is a Flub because every subsequent mover could have Correctly challenged. Since only the most recent Flub may be challenged, the C-claim makes it possible to win by laying a trap: make a deliberate Flub, and as soon as the next player moves, challenge him for failing to challenge you.

R6. Challenge Rule

Whether or not it is your turn, you may at any time challenge the other player who has just completed a move or has just said "No Goal." You do so by saying "Challenge" and specifying which kind of Flub you think the Mover has made. The move of setting a Goal is completed when the Mover says "Goal." The move of a cube to Forbidden, Permitted, or Required is completed when the cube touches the mat. Prior Flubs are insulated by later ones; therefore, you cannot challenge any player except the one who has just completed his play.

Comments

(1) A challenge cannot be retracted once a player has said "Challenge."

(2) To determine priority in those rare cases where two players say "Challenge" simultaneously, a coin should be placed in the center of the table when the cubes are first rolled. The first of the simultaneously-challenging players to pick up the coin shall be the Challenger; the other player shall be the Third Party.

R7. Burden-of-Proof Rule

After a challenge, the burden of proof is cast upon the player who, in the particular situation, is claiming that a Solution can be built. The burden of proof is sustained by writing a Solution on a sheet of paper.

Comments

(1) A Solution must, of course, satisfy the conditions imposed by the Solution rule and the previous plays of the cubes into the Forbidden, Permitted, or Required sections.

(2) Sometimes the burden of proof will be upon the Challenger —namely, when the Challenger alleges that there has been a Flub by virtue of a false No-Goal declaration, an A-claim violation, or a C-claim violation that stems from a previous A-claim violation. On the other hand, sometimes the burden will be upon the Mover —namely, when the Challenger alleges that there has been a Flub by virtue of a P-claim violation or a C-claim violation that stems from a previous P-claim violation.

(3) When a Challenger has alleged an A-claim violation or a C-claim violation that stems from a previous A-claim violation, he also has the burden of proving that there was an alternative move that

    (a) did not allow a Solution to be built with at most one more cube from the Resources, and

    (b) did not violate the P-claim.

(4) If there has been a challenge of a No-Goal declaration, the burden of proof is upon the Challenger, who, from the Resources, must not only build a Solution but also set a Goal.

R8. Correctness Rule

After a challenge, a player is Correct if and only if

    (A) he has the burden of proving the existence of a Solution and he sustains it (by writing one), or

    (B) he does not have the burden of proving the existence of a Solution (somebody else has the burden), and nobody sustains that burden of proof.

R9. Challenge-Scoring Rule

If there has been a challenge, then

    (A) the Third Party (T) must join either the Challenger (C) or the Mover (M), and

(B) if the player that T joins has the burden of proving the existence of a Solution, then T must sustain the same burden of proof by independently writing a Solution, and

(C) if T is Correct, then T scores 1 point if he has joined C and 2 if he has joined M, and

(D) C scores 2 if C is Correct, and

(E) M scores 2 if M is Correct, and

(F) if anyone is Incorrect, then he scores 0.

Comments

(1) If the game involves four or more players, then all of the players other than the Mover and the Challenger are Third Parties.

(2) The effect of this scoring rule is usually (although not always) that one of the two players involved in a challenge scores 2 and the other 0. In some circumstances they both may wind up with 0. T can score 2 when he joins M. However, T can score at most 1 by joining C. This places a premium upon being the first player to challenge another's Flub.

R10. Non-Challenge-Scoring Rule

If there has not been a challenge, then

(A) if a player has asserted that a Solution can be built with one more cube from Resources, but that there is no Flub, then

(1) each player who writes a Solution within the specified time limit (usually from one to two minutes) scores 1, and

(2) if the player who has asserted that a Solution can be built cannot build one, he scores −1, and

(3) all other players score 0, and

(B) if the first player has said that No Goal can be set, then each player scores 1.

Comment

The situation described in (A) will generally arise when (1) there is only one cube left in Resources or (2) the only equations that can be built from the Resources are trivial ones of the form $X = X$. In the latter case, nobody should challenge such a trivial Goal unless he sees another non-trivial Goal (that is, one that is possible but has no one-cube twin in Resources). There is no Flub by an A-claim violation unless such a non-trivial Goal is possible. When deciding whether to challenge in this situation, players should remember that the Goal-Setter can place a cube in Forbidden as a bonus play before setting the Goal.

R11. Stalling Rule

At any time any other player can call "stall" on the player who is
(A) deciding whether to set a Goal or to declare "No Goal", or
(B) deciding whether to move a cube, to challenge, or to assert that a Solution can be built with one more cube from the Resources, or
(C) deciding whom to join after a challenge, or
(D) trying to build a Solution.

The stalling player then has some specified time (usually one to two minutes) to complete what he is doing. If he fails to meet the deadline, he loses one point, and another limited time period begins. If he fails to meet the second deadline, he loses another point; and so on.

Sample Game of Basic EQUATIONS

Ann, Buzz, and Chris are about to begin a game of EQUATIONS. They are using the twelve red cubes. Ann shakes them out and the Resources that come up are as follows:

Resources: $+ \quad - \quad - \quad - \quad 0 \quad 0$
$1 \quad 1 \quad 1 \quad 2 \quad 2 \quad 3$

a. Ann sets a Goal of 3 by moving the 3 into the Goal section of the playing mat. She did not set 0, 1, or 2 as the Goal because

Forbidden	Permitted	Required

$$\frac{}{\text{Solution}} = \frac{3}{\text{Goal}}$$

This situation can be represented without the cubes and the playing mat as follows:

Resources: $+ \quad - \quad - \quad - \quad 0 \quad 0 \quad 1 \quad 1 \quad 1 \quad 2 \quad 2$
Permitted:
Forbidden:
Required:
Equation: $\underline{} = \underline{3}$
 Solution Goal

Figure 13-3.

she knew that if she did, Buzz or Chris would challenge her for violating the A-claim. She now has a Solution of 2 + 1 in mind. If she is challenged for violating the P-claim, she will be able to win by writing down that Solution. After Ann's play, the situation looks like this: $\boxed{+}\boxed{-}\boxed{-}\boxed{-}\boxed{0}\boxed{0}\boxed{1}\boxed{1}\boxed{1}\boxed{2}\boxed{2}$

Hereafter, such abbreviated representations will be used to show various stages in the play of a game.

b. Buzz plays next. He moves one of the 2's into the Required section. He has in mind (2 + 2) − 1 as his Solution.

c. On his play, Chris puts one of the 0's into Required. He has in mind (2 + 1) − 0 as a Solution. Ann and Buzz now have to revise their Solutions because of Chris' move. If one of them cannot think of a Solution that uses a 0, he probably will want to challenge Chris for violating the P-claim. After Chris' move the situation looks like this:

Resources: + − − − 0 1 1 2
Forbidden:
Permitted:
Required: 2 0
Equation: $\dfrac{}{\text{Solution}} = \dfrac{3}{\text{Goal}}$

d. It is now Ann's turn again. She thinks of a Solution that uses a 0, so she does not challenge. Instead, she plays a 1 in Permitted. She is thinking of (2 + 1) − 0 as a Solution.

e. On Buzz' turn he forbids a 1. He has revised his original Solution to use a 0. His new Solution is (2 + 2) − 1 − 0.

f. On Chris' turn he puts the + into Forbidden. He has in mind the Solution 2 − (0 − 1). He is hoping that either Ann or Buzz does not understand about negative numbers and will challenge him for a P-claim violation. The situation now looks like this:

Resources: − − − 0 1 2
Forbidden: 1 +
Permitted: 1
Required: 2 0
Equation: $\dfrac{}{\text{Solution}} = \dfrac{3}{\text{Goal}}$

g. Buzz challenges Chris saying that Chris has violated the P-claim. Chris has the burden of proof on this kind of challenge. Ann decides to join Chris because she also has a Solution. Chris writes down his Solution: $2 - (0 - 1)$ and Ann writes down hers: $2 - (1 - 2) - 0$. Ann and Chris each score two, and Buzz scores 0. The game just described can be summarized in the following table:

Sample Game

Resources: $+$ $-$ $-$ $-$ 0 0 1 1 1 2 2 3

Play	Player	Forbidden	Permitted	Required	Solution (in Mind of Player)	Play that eliminates Solution
a	Ann		(Goal of 3)		$2 + 1$	c
b	Buzz		2		$(2 + 2) - 1$	c
c	Chris			0	$(2 + 1) - 0$	f
d	Ann		1		$(2 + 1) - 0$	f
e	Buzz	1			$(2 + 2) - 1 - 0$	f
f	Chris	$+$			$2 - (0 - 1)$	
g	Buzz Challenges: P-claim violation.					

Ann Joins Chris

Ann's Solution: $2 - (1 - 2) - 0$

Chris' Solution: $2 - (0 - 1)$

Ann and Chris win. Buzz loses.

The letter in the elimination column indicates what subsequent play (if any) eliminates the Solution listed in the row where the letter appears. Thus, it is indicated that the Solution $2 + 1$, Ann had in mind when making Play a, was eliminated by Chris' Play c.

Types of Challenges With Examples of Each

Understanding the C-A-P claims is absolutely essential for playing EQUATIONS competently. Each time a player moves a cube to the playing mat, in effect, he makes each of the following three claims:

C   I cannot Correctly challenge on this turn.

A   If possible, I am Avoiding by this move allowing a Solution to be built with at most one more cube from Resources.

P   It is still Possible for the remaining Resources to be played so that a Solution can be built.

If any of the claims is not true with respect to the move made, then the Mover has Flubbed and is thereby vulnerable to a Correct challenge by another player.

If you consider the typical two-player game situations that are presented below and think carefully about why the most recent play made is a Flub, you will learn enough about the C-A-P claims to begin playing EQUATIONS. In each case, an EQUATIONS game is in progress, and the most recent play is a Flub—and therefore vulnerable to being challenged Correctly. The most recent move is shown by encircling the symbol just moved. The type of challenge and its result are indicated below the tabulated summary of the game situation.

a. Resources: $+ \ + \ - \ - \ - \ 0 \ 1 \ 1 \ 2 \ 3 \ 3$
   Forbidden:
   Permitted:
   Required:
   Equation: _____ $= \ \ ③$

Challenge: A-claim violation.
Burden of Proof: On Challenger; sustained.
Solution which uses only one cube from Resources: 3.
Alternative Goal which would not have been a Flub: 0.
Solution for Alternative Goal: 1 — 1.
Result: Challenger wins, and scores 2. Goal-Setter loses, and scores 0.

b. Resources: $+ \ + \ + \ 1 \ 1 \ 1 \ 2 \ 2 \ 2 \ 3 \ 3$
   Forbidden:
   Permitted:
   Required:
   Equation: _____ $= \ \ ⓪$

Challenge: P-claim violation.
Burden of Proof: On Goal-Setter; not sustained (Goal-Setter cannot build a Solution).
Result: Challenger wins, and scores 2. Goal-Setter loses, and scores 0.

c. Resources: $+ \ + \ + \ + \ + \ - \ - \ - \ - \ \div \ \div \ \div \ \div \ 2 \ 3 \ 6$
   Forbidden:
   Permitted:
   Required:
   Equation: _____ $=$ No Goal

Challenge: False No-Goal declaration.
Burden of Proof: On Challenger; sustained by showing a Goal of 3 and a solution of 6 ÷ 2.
Result: Challenger wins, and scores 2. Shaker loses, and scores 0.

d. Resources: $+$ $+$ 0   2
   Forbidden: 3   1   2
   Permitted: 1   1   —
   Required: ②
   Equation: _____   =   3

Challenge: Moving the 2 to Required violates the A-claim.
Burden of Proof: On Challenger; sustained.
Solution: $2 + 1$.

       The 2 is from Required and the 1 from Permitted. The $+$ is moved from Resources.

       Mover here apparently forgot that cubes in Permitted do not need to be used in building a Solution.

Alternative Non-Flubbing Move: Forbid a $+$.
Result: Challenger wins, and scores 2. Mover loses, and scores 0.

e. Resources: $+$ $-$ $-$
   Forbidden: 3   3   ③
   Permitted: $-$ $+$
   Required: 2   0   0
   Equation: _____   =   1

Challenge: P-claim violation.
Burden of Proof: On Mover who cannot write a Solution; not sustained.
Result: Challenger wins, and scores 2. Mover loses, and scores 0.

f. Resources: $\div$ 1 $\times$ 1 $\times$
   Forbidden: $+$ $-$ 3   ②
   Permitted: $\times$ $\div$ 2
   Required: 1   2   1
   Equation: _____   =   6

Challenge: C-claim violation stemming from previous P-claim violation. (Once the 3 was forbidden, there was no way to make 6 no matter how the remaining Resources were played.)
Burden of Proof: On Mover who cannot write a Solution; not sustained.
Result: Challenger wins, and scores 2. Mover loses, and scores 0.

g. Resources: 3   1 $\div$ $\times$
   Forbidden: $-$ $-$ $\times$ 1
   Permitted: $+$ 1   ⓪
   Required: 1 $+$ 3   0
   Equation: _____   =   2

Challenge: C-claim violation stemming from A-claim violation.
Burden of Proof: On Challenger; sustained.
Solution: With the $\times$ from Resources $(1 + 1) + (3 \times 0)$ was built.
Alternative: Forbid a $\div$ instead of allowing above Solution to be built with one more cube from the Resources.
Result: Challenger wins, and scores 2. Mover loses, and scores 0.

h. Resources: $+$ $+$ $+$ $+$ 0 0 0 1 2 2 2
   Forbidden:
   Permitted:
   Required:
   Equation: _____ $=$ ⓪_____
   Challenge: A-claim violation.
   Burden of Proof: On Challenger; not sustained.
   Solution: 0.
   Alternative: Challenger could not find a Goal which was possible and for which there was *not* a one-cube Solution. Thus, Challenger did not sustain the second half of his burden of proof for the challenge that asserted an A-claim violation.
   Result: Mover wins, and scores 2. Challenger loses, and scores 0.

i. Resources: $-$ $-$ $-$ 0 0 1 1 2 2
   Forbidden:
   Permitted:
   Required:
   Equation: _____ $=$ ③⊕①
   Challenge: P-claim violation.
   Burden of Proof: On Goal-Setter; sustained.
   Solution: $2 - (0 - 2)$.
   Result: Goal-Setter wins, and scores 2. Challenger loses, and scores 0.

j. Resources: $-$ $-$ $-$ 0 1
   Forbidden: $+$ $+$ $+$
   Permitted: ⊖
   Required: 1 2
   Equation: _____ $=$ 3_____
   Challenge: A-claim violation.
   Burden of Proof: On Challenger; not sustained.
   Solution: Move $-$ to build $1-$ -2.
       This expression is not acceptable as a Solution because the Solution Rule (Rule 4) states that $-$ must represent subtraction and *not* negative property.
   Result: Mover wins, and scores 2. Challenger loses, and scores 0.

k. Resources: 2 $\times$ $\times$ 1
   Forbidden: $\div$ $\div$ 1
   Permitted: $\times$ 3 3 ⊖
   Required: 3 3 3
   Equation: _____ $=$ 22_____
   Challenge: A-claim violation.
   Burden of Proof: On Challenger; not sustained.
   Solution: Move 1 to build $31 - (3 \times 3)$.
       This expression is not acceptable as a Solution because the

Solution Rule (Rule 4) permits only one-digit numerals in the Solution and 31 is not a one-digit numeral.

Result: Mover wins. Challenger loses.

1. Resources: $\div$

Forbidden:	—	—	3	3	2	6	$+$	$\times$
Permitted:	0	1	$+$	⑤				
Required:	$\times$	5	2	2				
Equation:						$=$	4	

Challenge: A-claim violation.

Burden of Proof: On Challenger; not sustained.

Solution: Move $\div$ to build $(2 \times 2) \times (5 \div 5)$.

Alternative Move (that would not permit a one-cube-move Solution): *None!*
Since there were only two cubes left and both were needed for any Solution it was not a Flub for Mover to Permit the 5.

Result: Mover wins. Challenger loses.

m. Resources: $\div$ $\div$ 1   4   6

Forbidden:	$\times$	5	5	⊗	
Permitted:	0	$\div$	0		
Required:	3	1			
Equation:				$=$	$10 + 2$

Challenge: P-claim violation.

Burden of Proof: On Mover; sustained.

Solution: $3 \div (1 \div 4)$.

Result: Mover wins. Challenger loses.

EQUATIONS—AUTO-MATE IMP KIT

Now that EQUATIONS rules have been set forth the additional materials used in EQUATIONS—AUTO-MATE IMP KITS are presented. These materials allow EQUATIONS to become a multibranched learning program.

Each Auto-Mate IMP Kit sets up an EQUATIONS game for you to play with our research group at the University of Michigan. In the series of kits you will have the opportunity to learn some of the tricks and strategies of EQUATIONS by playing a carefully ordered sequence of practice games. This is done in a way that resembles a computer-assisted instruction program, except that with the Auto-Mate IMP Kits you do not need access to a computer. All you need is the IMP Kit itself plus an EQUATIONS game. By playing in solitaire fashion through the IMP Kits, you will learn to be a better performer in playing EQUATIONS with your classmates and friends.

Our moves in a two-player game of EQUATIONS have been specified in the look-up tables that follow. You may come to view these tables as a mate with whom you play EQUATIONS. In any event we shall refer to them as "Mate." The IMP Kits are designed to give you an opportunity to develop some interesting strategies by testing your ideas in the course of playing EQUATIONS with Mate, and his main purpose is to alert you to such strategies. In the EQUATIONS game that each IMP Kit sets up, your moves will be as *you* choose; Mate's response will be found in the appropriate look-up table from the set of tables in each kit.

If you are familiar with the EQUATIONS game and with mathematical subscript notation, you may be able to learn how to use the IMP Kits from the brief summary that appears on pages 243 and 244. Otherwise, read on.

Ordinarily in EQUATIONS, the first player rolls out the cubes, and the resulting symbols on their upward faces are the Resources for that play of the game. From the Resource cubes, the first player then sets a Goal (the right side of the equation) on the playing mat. The cover of each IMP Kit tells you the Goal and remaining Resources for the game. It is as if Mate were the first player and had already rolled out the cubes and set a Goal. For example, the cover may look as follows:

Resources: $+$ $-$ $-$ 2 2 2 3
Goal: 0

You should arrange cubes from an EQUATIONS kit on a table so that they show the Resources listed on the game cover, and you should put a cube (or cubes) on the playing mat to show the Goal that Mate has set. In the rest of the play of the game you make the first play, then Mate takes his turn, then you, etc., until there is only one cube left in the Resources. On your turn you may do one of three things:

—you may challenge,
—you may indicate that a Solution (the left side of the equation) can be built with just one more cube from the Resources, or
—you may move a cube from the Resources to the Forbidden section (F), the Permitted section (P), or the Required section (R).

The moves of the players shape the Solution because in building a Solution *all* of the cubes played in the Required section must be used, *any* of those played in the Permitted section may (but do not have to) be used, and *none* of the cubes played in the Forbidden section can be used. The game ends when there is a challenge or when you indicate that a Solution can be built with just one more cube from the Resources.

When it is your turn to play, you have three obligations:

—*you must not move too near to a Solution* (not allow a Solution to be built with just one more cube from the Resources along with those already available in the Permitted and Required sections),

—*you must not move too far from all Solutions* (not make it impossible to build a Solution regardless of how the remaining Resources are played), and

—*you must challenge a player who has just moved too near or too far or who has just moved when he should have challenged.*

You have these three obligations because, by the rules of the game, each time a player sets a Goal or moves a cube into Forbidden, Permitted, or Required he is making the following three claims:

C Because the previous move is not a Flub, on this turn I cannot correctly Challenge it

A If possible, I am Avoiding by this move allowing a Solution to be built with just one more cube from Resources.

P It is still Possible for the remaining Resources to be so played that a Solution can be built.

These are called the CAP-claims as a device for remembering them easily. If any one of the claims is false, then that claim has been violated, the mover has flubbed, and the other player can correctly challenge and win. The challenges are abbreviated as follows:

Cc—challenge that the C-claim was violated,
Ca—challenge that the A-claim was violated,
Cp—challenge that the P-claim was violated.

A player wins either by correctly challenging the other player or by being incorrectly challenged by him.

First Round

Suppose you have set out the Resource cubes and placed the appropriate cube (or cubes) as the Goal. You will find it helpful to follow an actual example; you should set out the Resources, + − − 2 2 2 3, and put a 0 in the Goal. It is your turn to play. Let's say you decide to forbid the 3. You do so by placing the 3 cube in Forbidden (F) on the playing mat. That is a move whose row/column (r/c) name is 3/F; you could make note of it as follows:

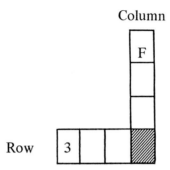

Figure 13-4.

To find out Mate's response to your first move, you should look up the r/c name of your move in the first-round look-up table. Suppose it looks like this:

Mate Play #1

1st ROUND	F	P	R
+	F−	R2	a
−	F+	F3	F3
2	F3	F3	F3
3	F2	P2	a
Ca		b	
Cp		c	

Figure 13-5.

Mate's response is found in the row determined by the cube you moved and the column determined by the section of the mat into which you played. In the example you played a 3 cube in Forbidden (F); the r/c name of your move is 3/F, and therefore you want the entry in the row labeled 3 and the column labeled F. This entry is F2 indicating that Mate's response to your first move is to forbid a 2 cube. You should now make Mate's move of a

$\boxed{2}$ cube into Forbidden so that your playing mat and Resources look as follows:

EQUATIONS Playing Mat

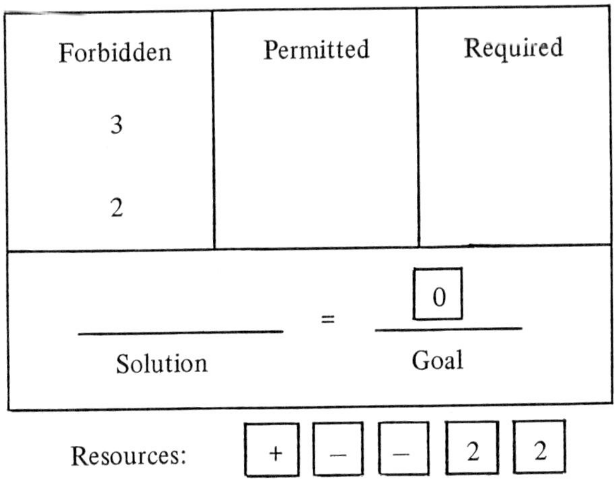

Forbidden	Permitted	Required
3		
2		

$$\frac{}{\text{Solution}} = \frac{\boxed{0}}{\text{Goal}}$$

Resources: $\boxed{+}$ $\boxed{-}$ $\boxed{-}$ $\boxed{2}$ $\boxed{2}$

Figure 13-6.

Notice that if you had permitted a 3 (that is, 3/P) instead of forbidding it, Mate's response (in the 3-row and the P-column) would be P2 (permit a 2). Finally if you had required a 3 (that is, 3/R), you would find (in the 3-row and the R-column) the small letter 'a'. Such an entry (a small letter) indicates that the game has ended. To find out why, you must consult the Alphabetic List of Comments. In that list, next to the appropriate small letter will be a comment explaining why the game ends in that particular situation. In this example, you would consult comment 'a' of the Alphabetic List, which might begin as follows:

Alphabetic List of Comments

a. Mate challenges: Cp. You have violated the possibility claim. No Solution is now possible. There are still some interesting ideas in this game that you have not yet encountered because of the way that the play developed. Play again and try some different moves.

b. That is an incorrect Ca challenge. There is no one-cube Solution. There are still some interesting ideas in this game that you have not yet encountered because of the way that the play developed. Play again and try some different moves.

c. That is an incorrect Cp challenge. A possible Solution is 2 — 2. There are still some interesting ideas in this game that you have not yet encountered because of the way that the play developed. Play again and try some different moves.

Instead of moving a cube to the playing mat, you may wish to challenge. You will find Mate's response to your challenge by observing which small letter appears as an entry in the look-up table for that kind of challenge and consulting the comment listed under that letter in the Alphabetic List. For example, if you challenge, asserting that Mate has violated the A-claim (Ca) in setting the Goal, Mate's answer to the challenge is listed next to 'b' in the Alphabetic List. A response to a challenge is always found in the column labeled **P**.

Second Round

If Mate has moved a cube in the first round, it is your turn to make your play for the second round. Suppose (in our sample game) you move a $\boxed{-}$ cube to Permitted. After a first move of forbidding a 3, the r/c name of this second move is 3—/FP, because the r/c name of a second move is an extension of the r/c name of the first move that preceded it. You might record this move next to your first-round move as follows:

Column

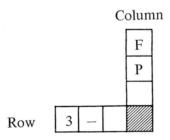

Row

Figure 13-7.

To find Mate's response, you should consult the r/c name of your move in the second-round look-up table; there you should look in the row labeled 3— and the column labeled F.[4]

$$\mathbf{P}$$

If you challenge Mate's first move you should, of course, look

---

[4]To help you find the proper entry, the labels of the columns are in alphabetical order as are the labels on the rows if we stipulate the following order to the alphabet: $+ - \times \div * \sqrt{\ }$ 0 1 2 3 4 5 6 7 8 9. This means that row $+\times 0$ precedes, is above, row $+\times 2$ in the table; that row $+\times 2$ precedes $+01$, etc.

up his response in the appropriate part of the second-round table for the kind of challenge made. In the example, if you want to challenge Mate for violating the P-claim (Cp) after his response to your first round move of forbidding a 3, the r/c name is 3Cp/FP and you can find his response in the row labeled 3Cp and the column labeled F. (The bottom column heading for every chal-
P
lenge response was arbitrarily chosen to be always P.)

Third Round

If Mate has moved in the second round, it is your turn to make your third-round play. Suppose you move a ☐2☐ cube to Required. You have then made a move with the r/c name of 3—2/FPR that you might note as follows:

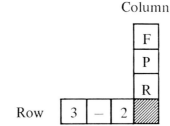

Figure 13-8.

The third-round table has several component tables; Mate's response is found in the table labeled with the symbol of the cube you moved in the first round. In this sample game where your first move was of a ☐3☐ cube, you should consult the table marked '(3)'. Suppose the component-3 tables looks (in part) like this:

3rd ROUND	F F F	F F F	F F F	P ...
	F Γ Γ	P P P	R R R	
	F P R	F P R	F P R	
. . .	. . .	. . .	. . .	
3—+	R— R— a	. . .	. . .	
3——	a h h	R2 P2 P2	P2 P2 a	
3—2	a k k	a d ⎡d⎤	a d d	
. . .	. . .	. . .	. . .	

Figure 13-9.

You should look in the row labeled 3—2 and in the column labeled
F
P. There you find the entry 'd' which sends you to the comment
R
labeled 'd' in the Alphabetic List.

If you wanted to challenge Mate's second-round move, you
would find the answer to your challenge in the appropriate third-
round table. For example, if you challenge Mate for not challenging you (a C-claim violation), Mate's response is found in the row
F
labeled 3-Cc and the column labeled P.
P

If Mate moves a cube on the third round, there will be exactly
one cube left in the Resources. When this occurs you must either
(1) challenge or (2) indicate that a Solution can be built with
the last cube from the Resources and then write such a Solution
on a piece of paper. In either case you should consult the IMP
Kit's last page labeled 'End of game when only one cube is left
in Resources.' In case (2), if you have written a Solution that
matches one mentioned on the final page, you have tied Mate. If
your Solution is not listed, you should find out why (by asking
someone . . . or writing to us).

SUMMARY

A. Anatomy of the Play of a Round

1. Make your play:
   a) Challenge, or
   b) Declare that a Solution can be built with one more cube from the
      Resources, or
   c) Move a cube.
2. Figure out the row/column (r/c) name and make a note of your move.
3. Look up Mate's response in the Mate-Play table for that round.
4. Make Mate's play:
   a) Move a cube, or
   b) Consult a comment in the Alphabetic List of Comments.

REPEAT FOR THE NEXT ROUND (until just one cube remains in Resources or until there is a challenge).

B. What to Do When One Cube Remains in Resources

You must either indicate that a Solution can be built with the remaining Resource cube or you must challenge. In either case, Mate's response is found on the final page of the kit.

C. Some Differences Between IMP Kit Games and Ordinary EQUATIONS Games

Ordinary EQUATIONS Games	IMP Kit EQUATIONS Games
16 — 24 cubes used	usually uses fewer cubes
2 — 5 players; 3 recommended for classroom play	2—player game
bonus move allowed on any play	no bonus moves allowed
statement by a player that a Solution can be built with one more Resource cube allowed on any turn	option for making such a statement allowed only after Round 3

Figure 13-10.

Now, try your hand at playing IMP Kit #1, the one we call MEEMI.

MEEMI—IMP KIT #1

Resources: $+$ $-$ $-$ 0 1 2 2
Goal: 3

It is now your turn to play. Then consult Mate Play #1 below for MEEMI's response.

1st ROUND	F	P	R
+	F0	F1	F1
-	F+	F+	F+
0	F+	F+	F+
1	a	F+	F+
2	F+	F+	F+
Ca		b	
Cp		c	

Figure 13-11. Mate Play #1

2nd ROUND	F F	F P	F R	P F	P P	P R	R F	R P	R R
1 -	.	.	.	a	FO	FO	a	FO	FO
1 0	.	.	.	P-	P-	P-	P-	P-	P-
1 2	.	.	.	PO	FO	FO	PO	FO	FO
1 Cc		.			f			f	
1 Ca		.			b			b	
1 Cp		.			g			g	
2 -	a	PO	PO	a	FO	FO	a	FO	FO
2 0	a	P-	P-	P-	P-	P-	P-	P-	P-
2 1	a	PO	PO	a	FO	FO	a	FO	FO
2 2	a	PO	PO	PO	FO	FO	PO	FO	FO
2 Cc		f			f			f	
2 Ca		b			b			b	
2 Cp		j			g			g	

2nd ROUND	F F	F P	F R	P F	P P	P R	R F	R P	R R
+ -	a	P-	P-	d	d	d	d	d	d
+ 0	.	.	.	d	d	d	d	d	d
+ 1	a	P-	P-	.	.	.	.	.	.
+ 2	a	P-	P-	d	d	d	d	d	d
+ Cc		e			f			f	
+ Ca		b			b			b	
+ Cp		g			h			h	
- -	d	d	d	a	FO	FO	a	FO	FO
- 0	d	d	d	P-	P-	P-	P-	P-	P-
- 1	d	d	d	a	FO	FO	a	FO	FO
- 2	d	d	d	PO	FO	FO	PO	FO	FO
- Cc		f			f			i	
- Ca		b			b			b	
- Cp		h			g			g	
0 -	a	P-	P-	a	P-	P-	a	P-	P-
0 1	a	P-	P-	a	P-	P-	a	P-	P-
0 2	a	P-	P-	P-	P-	P-	P-	P-	P-
0 Cc		f			f			i	
0 Ca		b			b			b	
0 Cp		g			g			j	

Figure 13-12. Mate Play #2

Figure 13-13. Mate Play #3 (+)

3rd ROUND	FFF	FFP	FFR	FPF	FPP	FPR	FRF	FRP	FRR
- - 1	.	.	.	.	.	.	.	.	.
- - 2	.	.	.	.	.	.	.	.	.
- - Cc		.			.			.	
- - Ca		.			.			.	
- - Cp		.			.			.	
- 0 1	.	.	.	.	.	.	.	.	.
- 0 2	.	.	.	.	.	.	.	.	.
- 0 Cc		.			.			.	
- 0 Ca		.			.			.	
- 0 Cp		.			.			.	
- 1 -	.	.	.	.	.	.	.	.	.
- 1 2	.	.	.	.	.	.	.	.	.
- 1 Cc		.			.			.	
- 1 Ca		.			.			.	
- 1 Cp		.			.			.	
- 2 -	.	.	.	.	.	.	.	.	.
- 2 1	.	.	.	.	.	.	.	.	.
- 2 2	.	.	.	.	.	.	.	.	.
- 2 Cc		.			.			.	
- 2 Ca		.			.			.	
- 2 Cp		.			.			.	

3rd ROUND	PFF	PFP	PFR	PPF	PPP	PPR	PRF	PRP	PRR
- - 1	.	.	.	a	P2	P2	a	P2	P2
- - 2	.	.	.	a	P1	P1	a	P1	P1
- - Cc		.			e			e	
- - Ca		.			b			b	
- - Cp		.			g			g	
- 0 1	a	P2	P2	a	k	k	a	k	k
- 0 2	a	P1	P1	P1	1	1	P1	1	1
- 0 Cc		e			e			m	
- 0 Ca		b			b			b	
- 0 Cp		g			g			j	
- 1 -	.	.	.	a	P2	P2	a	P2	P2
- 1 2	.	.	.	a	P-	P-	a	P-	P-
- 1 Cc		.			e			e	
- 1 Ca		.			b			b	
- 1 Cp		.			g			g	
- 2 -	a	P1	P1	a	P1	P1	a	F1	P1
- 2 1	a	P-	P-	a	P-	P-	a	P-	P-
- 2 2	a	P-	P-	a	P-	P-	a	P-	P-
- 2 Cc		m			e			e	
- 2 Ca		b			b			b	
- 2 Cp		j			g			g	

3rd ROUND	RFF	RFP	RFR	RPF	RPP	RPR	RRF	RRP	RRR
- - 1	.	.	.	a	P2	P2	a	P2	P2
- - 2	.	.	.	a	P1	P1	a	P1	P1
- - Cc		.			e			e	
- - Ca		.			b			b	
- - Cp		.			g			g	
- 0 1	a	P2	P2	a	k	k	a	k	k
- 0 2	a	P1	P1	P1	1	1	P1	1	1
- 0 Cc		e			e			m	
- 0 Ca		b			b			b	
- 0 Cp		g			g			j	
- 1 -	.	.	.	a	P2	P2	a	P2	P2
- 1 2	.	.	.	a	P-	P-	a	P-	P-
- 1 Cc		.			e			e	
- 1 Ca		.			b			b	
- 1 Cp		.			g			g	
- 2 -	a	P1	P1	a	P1	P1	a	P1	P1
- 2 1	a	P-	P-	a	P-	P-	a	P-	P-
- 2 2	a	P-	P-	a	P-	P-	a	P-	P-
- 2 Cc		m			e			e	
- 2 Ca		b			b			b	
- 2 Cp		j			g			g	

Figure 13-14. Mate Play #3 (—)

3rd ROUND	FFF	FFP	FFR	FPF	FPP	FPR	FRF	FRP	FRR	PFF	PFP	PFR	PPF	PPP	PPR	PRF	PRP	PRR	RFF	RFP	RFR	RPF	RPP	RPR	RRF	RRP	RRR
0 - 1	.	.	.	a	P2	P2	a	P2	P2	.	.	.	a	k	k	a	k	k	.	.	.	a	k	k	a	k	k
0 - 2	.	.	.	a	P1	P1	a	P1	P1	.	.	.	P1	l	l	P1	l	l	.	.	.	P1	l	l	P1	l	l
0 - Cc		.			e			e			.			e			e			.			m			m	
0 - Ca		.			b			b			.			b			b			.			b			b	
0 - Cp		.			g			g			.			g			g			.			j			j	
0 1 -	.	.	.	a	P2	P2	a	P2	P2	.	.	.	a	k	k	a	k	k	.	.	.	a	k	k	a	k	k
0 1 2	.	.	.	a	P-	P-	a	P-	P-	.	.	.	P-	n	n	P-	n	n	.	.	.	P-	n	n	P-	n	n
0 1 Cc		.			e			e			.			e			e			.			m			m	
0 1 Ca		.			b			b			.			b			b			.			b			b	
0 1 Cp		.			g			g			.			g			g			.			j			j	
0 2 -	.	.	.	a	P1	P1	a	P1	P1	a	P1	P1	a	l	l	a	l	l	a	P1	P1	a	l	l	a	l	l
0 2 1	.	.	.	a	P-	P-	a	P-	P-	a	P-	P-	a	n	n	a	n	n	a	P-	P-	a	n	n	a	n	n
0 2 2	.	.	.	a	P-	P-	a	P-	P-	a	P-	P-	P-	P-	P-	P-	P-	P-	a	P-	P-	P-	P-	P-	P-	P-	a
0 2 Cc		.			e			e			m			e			e			m			m			m	
0 2 Ca		.			b			b			b			b			b			b			b			b	
0 2 Cp		.			g			g			j			g			g			j			j			j	

Figure 13-15. Mate Play #3 (0)

3rd ROUND	F F F	F F P	F F R	F P F	F P P	F P R	F R F	F R P	F R R	P F F	P F P	P F R	P P F	P P P	P P R	P R F	P R P	P R R	R F F	R F P	R F R	R P F	R P P	R P R	R R F	R R P	R R R
1 - -	.	.	.	.	.	.	.	.	.	.	.	.	a	P2	P2	a	P2	P2	.	.	.	a	P2	P2	a	P2	P2
1 - 2	.	.	.	.	.	.	.	.	.	.	.	.	a	P-	P-	a	P-	P-	.	.	.	a	P-	P-	a	P-	P-
1 - Cc		.			.			.			.			e			e			.			e			e	
1 - Ca		.			.			.			.			b			b			.			b			b	
1 - Cp		.			.			.			.			g			g			.			g			g	
1 0 -	.	.	.	.	.	.	.	.	.	a	P2	P2	a	k	k	a	k	k	a	P2	P2	a	k	k	a	k	k
1 0 2	.	.	.	.	.	.	.	.	.	a	P-	P-	P-	n	n	P-	n	n	a	P-	P-	P-	n	n	P-	n	n
1 0 Cc		.			.			.			e			e			m			e			e			m	
1 0 Ca		.			.			.			b			b			b			b			b			b	
1 0 Cp		.			.			.			g			g			j			g			g			j	
1 2 -	.	.	.	.	.	.	.	.	.	a	P-	P-	a	P-	P-	a	P-	P-	a	P-	P-	a	P-	P-	a	P-	P-
1 2 2	.	.	.	.	.	.	.	.	.	a	P-	P-	a	P-	P-	a	P-	P-	a	P-	P-	a	P-	P-	a	P-	P-
1 2 Cc		.			.			.			m			e			e			m			e			e	
1 2 Ca		.			.			.			b			b			b			b			b			b	
1 2 Cp		.			.			.			j			g			g			j			g			g	

Figure 13-16. Mate Play #3 (1)

3rd ROUND	F F F	F P F	F R F	P F F	P P F	P R F	R F F	R P F	R R F
	F F P	F P P	F R P	P F P	P P P	P R P	R F P	R P P	R R P
	F F R	F P R	F R R	P F R	P P R	P R R	R F R	R P R	R R R
2 - -	. . .	a Pl Pl	a Pl Pl	. . .	a Pl Pl	a Pl Pl	. . .	a Pl Pl	a Pl Pl
2 - 1	. . .	a P- P-	a P- P-	. . .	a P- P-	a P- P-	. . .	a P- P-	a P- P-
2 - 2	. . .	a P- P-	a P- P-	. . .	a P- P-	a P- P-	. . .	a P- P-	a P- P-
2 - Cc	.	m	m	.	e	e	.	e	e
2 - Ca	.	b	b	.	b	b	.	b	b
2 - Cp	.	j	j	.	g	g	.	g	g
2 0 -	. . .	a Pl Pl	a Pl Pl	a Pl Pl	a 1 1	a 1 1	a Pl Pl	a 1 1	a 1 1
2 0 1	. . .	a P- P-	a P- P-	a P- P-	a n n	a n n	a P- P-	a n n	a n n
2 0 2	. . .	a P- P-	a P- P-	a P- P-	P- P- P-	P- P- P-	a P- P-	P- P- P-	P- P- a
2 0 Cc	.	m	m	e	e	m	e	e	m
2 0 Ca	.	b	b	b	b	b	b	b	b
2 0 Cp	.	j	j	g	g	j	g	g	j
2 1 -	. . .	a P- P-	a P- P-	. . .	a P- P-	a P- P-	. . .	a P- P-	a P- P-
2 1 2	. . .	a P- P-	a P- P-	. . .	a P- P-	a P- P-	. . .	a P- P-	a P- P-
2 1 Cc	.	m	m	.	e	e	.	e	e
2 1 Ca	.	b	b	.	b	b	.	b	b
2 1 Cp	.	j	j	.	g	g	.	g	g
2 2 -	. . .	a P- P-	a P- P-	a P- P-	a P- P-	a P- P-	a P- P-	a P- P-	a P- P-
2 2 1	. . .	a P- P-	a P- P-	a P- P-	a P- P-	a P- P-	a P- P-	a P- P-	a P- P-
2 2 Cc	.	m	m	m	e	e	m	e	e
2 2 Ca	.	b	b	b	b	b	b	b	b
2 2 Cp	.	j	j	j	g	g	j	g	g

Figure 13-17. Mate Play #3 (2)

Alphabetic List of Comments

a. Mate challenges: Cp. You have violated the Possibility claim. No Solution is now possible. There are still some interesting ideas in this game which you have not encountered because of the way that the play developed. Play again and try some different moves.

b. This is an incorrect Ca challenge. There is no one-cube Solution. There are still some interesting ideas in this game which you have not encountered because of the way that the play developed. Play again and try some different moves.

c. This is an incorrect Cp challenge. The Solution 1+2 is possible. There are still some interesting ideas in this game which you have not encountered because of the way that the play developed. Play again and try some different moves.

d. Mate challenges: Cc. You have violated the Cannot-challenge claim. No Solution was possible after Mate's last move; you should have made a Cp challenge. There are still some interesting ideas in this game which you have not encountered because of the way that the play developed. Play again and try some different moves.

e. This is an incorrect Cc challenge. Mate could not have made a correct Ca challenge because there was no way a Solution could be built with one more cube. Mate could not have made a correct Cp challenge because the Solution $2-(1-2)$ was still possible. Notice how a pair of minus signs can be used to give the effect of addition. Since $1 - 2 = -1$ and $2 - -1 = 3$, the Goal can be achieved even though the $+$ cube is forbidden. Go on to the next IMP Kit.

f. This is an incorrect Cc challenge. Mate could not have made a correct Ca challenge because there was no way a Solution could be built with one more cube. Mate could not have made a correct Cp challenge because the Solution 1+2 was still possible. There are still some interesting ideas in this game which you have not encountered because of the way that the play developed. Play again and try some different moves.

g. This is an incorrect Cp challenge. The Solution $2-(1-2)$ is possible. Notice how a pair of minus signs can be used to give the effect of addition. Since $1 - 2 = -1$ and $2 - -1 = 3$, the

Goal can be achieved even though the + cube is forbidden. Go on to the next IMP Kit.

h. You win. You caught Mate bluffing. No Solution is possible. There are still some interesting ideas in this game which you have not encountered because of the way that the play developed. Play again and try some different moves.

i. This is an incorrect Cc challenge. Mate could not have made a correct Ca challenge because there was no way a Solution could be built with one more cube. Mate could not have made a correct Cp challenge because the Solution $1+2-0$ was still possible. There are still some interesting ideas in this game which you have not encountered because of the way that the play developed. Play again and try some different moves.

j. This is an incorrect Cp challenge. The Solution $2-(0-1)$ is possible. Notice how a pair of minus signs can be used to give the effect of addition. Since $0 - 1 = -1$ and $2 - -1 = 3$, the Goal can be achieved even though the + cube is forbidden. Go on to the next IMP Kit.

k. Mate challenges: Ca. You have violated the Avoid claim by allowing the 1-cube Solution $2-(0-1)$. The cube needed from resources is the 2. You could have avoided this by making the move F2. Notice how a pair of minus signs can be used to give the effect of addition. Since $0 - 1 = -1$ and $2 - -1 = 3$, the Goal can be achieved even though the + cube is forbidden. Go on to the next IMP Kit.

l. Mate challenges: Ca. You have violated the Avoid claim by allowing the 1-cube Solution $2-(0-1)$. The cube needed from resources is the 1. You could have avoided this by making the move F2. Notice how a pair of minus signs can be used to give the effect of addition. Since $0 - 1 = -1$ and $2 - -1 = 3$, the Goal can be achieved even though the + cube is forbidden. Go on to the next IMP Kit.

m. This is an incorrect Cc challenge. Mate could not have made a correct Ca challenge because there was no way a Solution could be built with one more cube. Mate could not have made a correct Cp challenge because the Solution $2-(0-1)$ was still possible. Notice how a pair of minus signs can be used to give the effect of addition. Since $0 - 1 = -1$ and $2 - -1 = 3$, the

Goal can be achieved even though the + cube is forbidden. Go
on to the next IMP Kit.

n. Mate challenges: Ca. You have violated the Avoid claim by
allowing the 1-cube Solution $2-(0-1)$. The cube needed from
resources is the —. You could have avoided this by making the
move F2. Notice how a pair of minus signs can be used to give
the effect of addition. Since $0 - 1 = -1$ and $2- -1 = 3$, the
Goal can be achieved even though the + cube is forbidden. Go
on to the next IMP Kit.

End of Game When Only One Cube Is Left in Resources

(1) You have challenged.
> a. If you have made a Cc, then see comment(s) e, m, on the
> Alphabetic List. One of these comments is applicable in
> this situation.
> b. If you have made a Ca, then you are right that a Solution
> can be built with just 1 more cube from the Resources. It
> will be one of the Solutions in (2) below. However, you
> will be unable to sustain the other half of your burden of
> proof for a Ca—namely, showing that Mate could have
> made a move that did not allow a Solution with one more
> cube from the Resources and that did not violate the Pos-
> sibility Claim. Go on to the next IMP Kit.
> c. If you have made a Cp, then see comment(s) g, j, on the
> alphabetic list. One of these comments is applicable in this
> situation.

(2) You have written a Solution.
The Solution(s) possible when just one cube remains in the
Resources is (are) one or more of these:
a. $2-(1 \; -2)$
b. $2-(0-1)$
c. $1-(0-2)$
Did you have one of these in mind?
> Notice how a pair of minus signs can be used to give the
> effect of addition. Since $1 - 2 = -1$ and $2 - -1 = 3$,
> the Goal can be achieved even though the + cube is for-
> bidden.

Now go on to the next IMP Kit.

Redefinition of the basic EQUATIONS game form has allowed us to demonstrate the close relationships between programmed computer-assisted instruction and well-designed instructional games.[5] EQUATIONS—Auto-Mate Imp Kits are probably the most highly-branched non-computer learning program that has ever been written up to this point in time, and as such they are the first of what will probably be many such solitaire games, each of which will contain a variation upon the subject-matter content of mathematics. The EQUATIONS sequence which includes set theory (ON-SETS) and mathematical logic (WFF 'N PROOF) can all be automated in this manner.

ADVENTUROUS EQUATIONS

Recently, an entirely new variation has been added to EQUATIONS.[6]

This variation is called ADVENTUROUS EQUATIONS and it opens the door for using much more mathematics in the play. ADVENTUROUS EQUATIONS may involve much of what is normally included in the secondary school curriculum plus considerably more. It provides the player with a reason to seek out new mathematical ideas and places a premium on a thorough understanding of such ideas. It also strongly suggests that a game (and designing a game) can be a device for teaching new concepts and may well inspire students (or teachers) to invent their own games.

The Added Rule for ADVENTUROUS EQUATIONS

A single additional game rule converts BASIC EQUATIONS into ADVENTUROUS EQUATIONS. The additional rule is this:

---

[5]See Allen, Layman E.: Games and programmed instruction. In Allen, Layman E., and Caldwell, Mary E. (Eds.): *Communications, Sciences and the Law: Reflections from the Jurimetrics Conference.* Bobbs-Merrill, Indianapolis, 1965.

[6]Professor Phillip S. Jones, Mathematics Department, University of Michigan, will recognize the value of a good question. His, which prompted this extension of EQUATIONS, was: Why don't you have the players invent games? He even suggested how—have the players introduce new rules. Upon reflection, it was apparent that to implement his suggestion, only one change was needed in the original EQUATIONS game: Instead of allowing variations to be merely permissible, make them mandatory by imposing upon the players the obligation to introduce such rules on each roll of the cubes.

Before the cubes are rolled at the beginning of the play of a game, each player is required to write one additional rule to be in force for that particular play of the game. As used here, the term 'play of the game' refers to the total of all the individual moves that the players make on one roll of the cubes. The new rules are introduced in writing on a slip of paper. If a prepared list of potential new rules is being used, then only the number or letter of the rule needs to be written. If no such list is being used, then the proposed new rule itself should be written out in full on the slip.

The category of rules permitted to be added in playing ADVENTUROUS EQUATIONS is intended to be an extremely broad one. Almost every rule that players can conceive of will be permitted. The only restriction is that a rule proposed must not give any of the players an unfair advantage. A rule will not be considered unfair just because one player understands the mathematical ideas involved in that rule better than the other players. One example of an unfair rule would be: *Only Player 2 is permitted to challenge A-claim violations in order to win.* It gives player 2 an unfair advantage. Although the following rule is not unfair, it will not be permitted. *All new rules are hereby (by this rule) excluded from the game.* If such a rule were allowed, it would enable any one player to veto the decision of the group to play ADVENTUROUS EQUATIONS and force them to play BASIC EQUATIONS.

All new rules that are proposed should be unambiguous, and all players should be careful not to write down rules that are ambiguous. If a player proposes a rule that is ambiguous and some other player detects that it is, then the proposing player loses one point and the detecting player gains one point. The proposing player should then clarify the rule; and play should continue.

If two of the rules added impose contradictory requirements, then the most recent rule controls. Player 2's rule is more recent than Player 1's and Player 3's more recent than Player 2's. Two rules are contradictory if there is no appropriate equation for any shake of the cubes which conforms to both rules. For example, rule f. below would be contradicted by a rule which forbids a ✳ to be used in the *solution*.

Some of the added rules may be violated by a player's move. This is called a *blunder*. A *blunder* is a move that does not conform to one or a combination of the new rules added in an AD-VENTUROUS EQUATIONS game but is not a *flub* (as defined by the *flubbing* rule in combination with the additional rules).

If a player thinks that the mover has *blundered,* he can charge the mover with *blundering* by saying, *"Blunder."* A *blunder*-charge, like a challenge, can be made by any player at any time and not merely on his turn to play. The player making the charge then puts the cubes moved back into *resources* and makes a different move to *rectify* the *blunder.* This *rectifying* move is open to the charge of being a *blunder* or to challenge as a *flub;* and the challenge, if made, will be evaluated by the usual procedures for evaluating the validity of the challenges. (If there is a challenge, it is directed at the *rectifier*).

A *blunder* is completely insulated by a subsequent move; in other words, if a *blunder* is not *rectified* immediately, it can never be *rectified.* After *rectification* of a *blunder,* it is the turn of the player who would ordinarily play next had the move not been a *blunder.* If the original move was indeed a *blunder,* then the *rectifier's* move stands and the *blunderer* loses one point. If there was no *blunder* so that the charge was erroneous, then the cubes are replaced as originally moved and the *rectifier* loses one point.

If the original move was a *flub,* but the Mover was charged with *blundering,* then the *rectifier* has *flubbed.* In this respect a *blunder*-charge is treated as having the same effects as a move, and the player making the charge has *flubbed* because he failed to challenge the *flub* when he could have. He will also lose one point for making the *blunder*-charge erroneously because the move cannot be a *blunder* when it is a *flub.*

Examples of rules that are permitted to be added in playing ADVENTUROUS EQUATIONS are the following:

a. All players are forbidden to play any cube in *forbidden.*

b. All players are forbidden to play any numeral in *required.*

c. All players are forbidden to play any cube in *permitted.*

d. Each player is required to make a bonus play on each of his turns, if it is possible to do so without *flubbing.*

e. When a player moves a cube to either the *permitted* or to the *required* section, he may arrange the cube moved and any other cubes in that section into a group. If the cubes so arranged are used in the *solution,* they must be used as so grouped.

f. The *solution* must contain a $\boxed{*}$

g. The $\boxed{-}$ cube may vary and may stand for any operation that is on the cubes, but it must stand for the same operation everywhere that it occurs.

h. The $\boxed{\boxminus}$ cube may designate negative property as well as subtraction.

i. The $\boxed{0}$ cube may vary and may stand for any whole number from 0 to 9, but it must stand for the same number everywhere that it occurs.

j. The $\boxed{\times}$ cube may vary and may stand for any symbol that is on the cubes, but it must stand for the same symbol everywhere that it occurs.

k. At least one operation cube must be used in setting the *goal*.

l. Multiplying or dividing by one is forbidden.

m. Multiplying by zero is forbidden.

n. Adding or subtracting zero is forbidden.

o. Using zero as an exponent is forbidden.

p. A *solution* need not be equal to the *goal,* but if it differs it must differ from the *goal* by a multiple of 6. (Arithmetic of modulo less-than-6 tends to be uninteresting and in some situations may even be unfair).

q. A *solution* need not be equal to the *goal,* but if it differs it must be between the same two adjoining primes that the *goal* is between. (By stipulation a number x is between adjoining primes if and only if: $x \geq$ the smaller prime and $x <$ the larger prime).

Example: If the *goal* is 20, then the *solution* can be any expression that designates 19, 20, 21, or 22; and if the *goal* is 13, then *solution* can be any expression that designates 13, 14, 15, or 16.

r. Both sides of the equation are permitted to be interpreted either as base-8 expressions, or as base-10 expressions, but the *solution* must be interpreted as being an expression of the same base as the *goal*. Also multiple digits equal to or less than nine may be used to build the *solution*.

Example: $[11 + 3]_8 = [14]_8$ is allowed; but $[13 + 4]_8 =$ $[17]_8$ is not.

s. The $\boxed{\sqrt{}}$ cube shall not represent the root operation, but rather it shall represent the minimum operation.

Examples: $5 \boxed{\sqrt{}} 4 = \text{Minimum } (5, 4) = \text{Min } (5, 4) = 4.$
$(1 + 0) \boxed{\sqrt{}} 9 = \text{Min } (1, 9) = 1.$

t. The $\boxed{+}$ cube shall not represent addition, but rather it shall represent the operation of averaging two numbers.

Example: $7 \boxed{+} 9 = \dfrac{7 + 9}{2} = 8.$

u. The ⊡ cube shall not represent exponentiation. Instead it shall represent the operation of least common multiple.
Example: 4 ⊡ 6 = LCM (4, 6) = 12.

v. The ⊟ cube shall not represent subtraction. Instead, it shall represent the operation of highest common factor.
Example: 9 ⊟ 6 = HCF (9, 6) = 3.

w. The ⊡ cube may represent the log operation or the division operation, e.g., a ÷ b may be interpreted as $\log_b a$ or the result of dividing a by b; (a ÷ b) ÷ c may be interpreted as $(a \div b) \div c$, $\log_c (a \div b)$, $(\log_b a) \div c$, or $\log_c (\log_b a)$. Thus, 8 ÷ 2 may be 3 or 4.

x. The ⋁ cube shall not represent the root operation, but rather, the imaginary number i.

y. The ⋁ cube shall not represent the root operation, but rather, the imaginary number i. In addition, if a *goal* is either of the form A—B or A+B, then either the A or the B or both may be interpreted by the player building a *solution* as expressing the corresponding imaginary numbers Ai or Bi. For example 7+2 may be interpreted as $7 + 2i$, as $2+7i$ or $9i$ (as well as 9); 1—(2*2) may be interpreted as $1 - 4i$, as $i-4$, as $- 3i$ or as $- 3i$; and 0—23 may be interpreted as $-23i$, or as -23.

z. When building a *solution,* a player must specify where decimal points occur in the *goal,* but no decimal points are allowed in the *solution*. For example, a *goal* of 20 may be interpreted as 20, 2.0, or .2, and a *goal* of 2* 3 may be interpreted as 2. * 3., 2. * .3, .2 * 3., or .2 * .3.

Discussion of Sample Rules

The first five rules are mainly procedural. Their tendency is to change the ability of a player to constrain the situation. For example, rule e. gives a player more opportunity to steer toward the *solution* he has in mind.

The other rules are more oriented toward the subject matter of the game. Rule f., for example, may rule out many *solutions* that would otherwise qualify. For some shakes of the cubes, rule f. may even lead to a *no-goal* situation such as when no ⊡ appears in the *resources*.

Combinations of rules can make for unexpected results. Rule p. alone tends to allow many more *solutions* than are appropriate in the basic game. The same is true for rule q. Rules p. and q. operating together, however, tend to limit the possible *solutions* to a set that is considerably smaller than the one for either rule alone. See Puzzle 6 for an instance of this.

the list above give an indication of how new concepts can be introduced. Of course, a teacher can at any time add a rule which he
considers fruitful.

The puzzles below show some of the possibilities of ADVEN-
TUROUS EQUATIONS. The new rules added are given before
each puzzle.

One-Cube-Solution Puzzles

PUZZLE 1
Rules added: b, p, 1
Resources: * + 1 2 3
Forbidden: ÷ ÷ 3 2 *
Permitted: 5 7
Required: — *
Equation: _____ = 22 ____

PUZZLE 2
Rules added: q
Resources: 6 + 5
Forbidden: 1 √ ÷ 2 4 6
Permitted: 0 — 4 2
Required: *
Equation: _____ = 34 ____

PUZZLE 3
Rules added: h, r
Resources: 2 0 1 — 3
Forbidden: + * — 6
Permitted: — 2 ×
Required: 4 5
Equation: _____ = 15 ____

Taboo-Move Puzzles

PUZZLE 4
Rules added: f, p, j
Resources: + × 1 3 — 7
Forbidden: 1 √ 2 5
Permitted: 0 + +
Required: * 2
Equation: _____ = 17 ____

PUZZLE 5
Rules added: q, r, s
Resources: $+$ $\sqrt{}$ ` 3 0
Forbidden: $\sqrt{}$ $-$ 4 $+$ 1
Permitted: 5 1
Required: * $\sqrt{}$ 1
Equation: _____ $= 32$

PUZZLE 6
Rules added: p, q
Resources: 1 7 3 $-$
Forbidden: $\div$ * 9
Permitted: $+$ $\times$ 0
Required: 2 2 2 *
Equation: _____ $= 90$

CAP-Claim Puzzles

PUZZLE 7
Rules added: t
Resources: 1 4 9 $\ominus$
Forbidden: $-$ 0 $-$
Permitted: $\times$ $-$ 1 5
Required: $+$ $+$ 2 9
Equation: _____ $= 15$

PUZZLE 8
Rules added: w, k
Resources: 0 $\div$ $\circledast$
Forbidden: $+$ $+$
Permitted: $-$ $\times$ 4 $\sqrt{}$
Required: 8 $\div$ 1 2
Equation: _____ $= 5 + 2$

PUZZLE 9
Rules added: m, x
Resources: 6 $\div$ $\div$ $\oslash$
Forbidden: 0 * $-$ $+$
Permitted: $\sqrt{}$ $+$ $-$ 0
Required: 2 2 $\times$
Equation: _____ $= 5$

PUZZLE 10

Rules added: n, y
Resources: — + 5 ④
Forbidden: * 1 3
Permitted: $\times$ + 7 +
Required: $\checkmark$ $\checkmark$ 2
Equation: $\underline{\hspace{4cm}}$ = $\underline{2+4}$

Some Suggested Answers to the Puzzle Questions

Puzzle 1:

With the $\boxed{1}$ from *resources*, the *solution*, 5 — (1 * 7), can be built. Note that 5 — (1 * 7) = 4 and $4 \underset{6}{=} 22$.

Puzzle 2:

With the $\boxed{6}$ from *resources*, the *solution*, 6 * 2, can be built. Note that 6 * 2 = 36 and $36 \underset{prime}{=} 34$.

Puzzle 3:

With the $\boxed{-}$ from *resources*, the *solution*, (4 $\times$ 2) — —5, can be built. $\left[(4 \times 2) — —5\right]_8$ $=$ $\left[10 — —5\right]_8$ $=$ $\left[15\right]_8$

Puzzle 4:

If either $\boxed{-}$ or $\boxed{1}$ is moved to *permitted* or *required* with just one more cube from *resources* the *solution*, $\left[1 * 0\right]$ — 2, can be built. $(1 * 0) —2 = 1 — 2 = —1$ and $—1 \underset{6}{=} 17$.

Thus, $\boxed{-}$ or $\boxed{1}$ to *permitted* or *required* are taboo moves because they violate the A-claim. Since 7 * 0 = 3 * 0 = 1 * 0, $\boxed{7}$ or $\boxed{3}$ to *permitted* or *required* are taboo moves.

Also, since $\boxed{\times}$ is wild, moving it to *permitted* or *required* is a taboo move.

Puzzle 5:

Moving $\boxed{+}$ or $\boxed{3}$ to *required* or *permitted* are taboo moves, because they violate the A-claim by allowing the one-cube *solution*, 5 * $\left[(1 + 1) \boxed{\checkmark} 3\right]$. $\left[5 * ((1 + 1) \boxed{\checkmark} 3)\right]_8$ $= \left[5 * (2 \boxed{\checkmark} 3)\right]_8 =$

$\left[5 * Min(2,3)\right]_8$ $= \left[5 * 2\right]_8 = \left[5\right]_8 * \left[2\right]_8 = \left[31\right]_8$ and $\left[31\right]_8$

$\underset{prime}{=} \left[32\right]_8$

Moving $\boxed{+}$ to *forbidden* is also taboo, because it makes building a *solution* impossible and is therefore a violation of the P-claim.

Puzzle 6:

Moving $\boxed{-}$ or $\boxed{7}$ to *required* or *permitted* are taboo moves, because they violate the A-claim by allowing the one-cube *solution,* $\left[(7 * 2) \times 2\right] - 2.$ $\left[(7 * 2) \times 2\right] - 2 = 98 - 2 = 96;$ and $96 = \dfrac{90 \text{ and}}{6}$

$96 \underset{\text{prime}}{=} 90.$

Puzzle 7:

Violates C-claim. Mover could have correctly challenged the previous player, because the *solution,* $(9 \boxed{+} 1) \times \left[5 \boxed{\div} (2 - 1)\right]$, could be built with only the $\boxed{1}$ from *resources.*
$(9 \boxed{+} 1) \times \left[5 \boxed{+} (2 - 1)\right] = 5 \times \left[5 \boxed{+} 1\right] = 5 \times 3 = 15.$

Puzzle 8:

Violates C-claim. Mover could have correctly challenged the previous player because the *solution,* $4 - \left[(1 \boxed{\div} 8) \boxed{\div} 2\right]$, could be built with only the $\boxed{\div}$ from *resources.*
$4 - \left[(1 \boxed{\div} 8) \boxed{\div} 2\right] = 4 - \log_2 (1 \div 8) = 4 - -3 = 7.$

Puzzle 9:

Violates C-claim. Mover could have correctly challenged the previous player, because the *solution,* $(2 + \boxed{\checkmark}) \times (2 - \boxed{\checkmark})$, could be built with the $\boxed{\checkmark}$ from *resources.*

Puzzle 10:

Violates A-claim. With the $\boxed{-}$ from *resources,* the *solution* $\boxed{\checkmark} \times (4 - 2 \boxed{\checkmark})$ can now be built.
$\boxed{\checkmark} \times (4 - 2 \boxed{\checkmark})$ $1ix(4 - 2i) = 4i + 2 = 2 + 4i.$

A considerably less adventurous version of EQUATIONS can be played by requiring each player to stipulate an additional rule *chosen by him from a given list of rules* (such as the list above). This is usually necessary during tournament play when the press of time prevents judges from ruling on fairness, ambiguity, and the often complicated ramifications of combinations of rules.

In conclusion, we exhibit several equations that were recently devised by some elementary and junior high school students in a county-wide EQUATIONS tournament in western Pennsylvania. The equations constructed were:

a. $\left[(2 \checkmark 4) \div 3\right] \checkmark \ 4 = 8.$
b. $(1 \div 2)_{\text{six}} = .3_{\text{six}}.$

c. $5 \checkmark \left[1 \div (8 + 2)\right] = .1 * .2.$

These students had only been playing a simplified version of ADVENTUROUS EQUATIONS for a short time. Surely these sample equations are appropriate, not only for the game itself, but also as persuasive evidence that EQUATIONS can be a powerful and useful tool in the teaching of creative mathematics.

CHAPTER 14

CHILDREN'S GAMES: DIAGNOSTIC AND THERAPEUTIC USES

ROBERT W. FREEMAN

INTRODUCTION

THIS CHAPTER begins a set of papers devoted to socialization and diagnostic/clinical uses for game-situations. Robert Freeman points out that child psychotherapy and most social contacts between children and adults rely heavily on games. Presumably, in diagnostic assessment, a child's game-setting activity will display interpretable patterns of behavior. Likewise, one may look forward during clinical treatment to "better" patterns of behavior as "play therapy" goes on. Games seem to serve a different purpose in this set of papers than they do where the purpose is to teach academic content. There, games only facilitate learning. Here, the games actually set up a climate in which a child's attitudes and reactions can develop. It is extremely difficult if not impossible for such attitudes and behaviors to be taught, in the usual sense, by lecture, textbook assignments, and repetitive practice dictated by the teacher. However, social situations can be set in motion within the game-form which help people to face the specific problems that the situation contains. After several similar but not identical experiences, the individual can abstract his/her own conceptualization composed of attitudes, acts and emotions experienced during the games. This conceptualization can contain the child's view of himself in the real world. Each view may be ac-

267

companied by rules for action, level of aspiration and knowledge of the probabilities for success in similar situations. The player's social relations can be seen as events which occur in the real world. In these games children can practice coping in familiar ways as well as innovative ways. This practice takes place under the protection of a game that provides a "distancing effect." It is possible that children can practice behaviors and relationships which can be carried over into real life.

Freeman makes it clear that everyday, readily available games have academic and socialization potential and that games make both tasks easier for the players. He suggests that adults involve themselves with children. He stands ready to advise teachers who face specific problems of child-learning and social-situation teaching.

—Editors

CHILDREN'S GAMES have widespread use in many recreational and therapeutic settings. In fact, there is little work with children which does not include some allusion to or use of games. The types of games may be indoor or outdoor; require many players or just one; use standard equipment or be improvisational; have structure rules or flexible standards; be homemade or commercial; require teams or use variable participants.

Games have been used and sometimes overused as tools for implementing learning. Observing the tester who covers the possible threat of a test by calling it "playing games" and the teacher who blithely trips from spelling "games" to word "games" to number "games," we would gather that children find games appealing. And typically they do.

One appealing feature about games in general is the protected nature which is built in. Aspects of games may be like life—there may be triumph and disaster, cooperation and conniving—but a game has a relatively short time span, it has a beginning and an end, it can be dumped, smashed and the pieces lost; the current of life, on the other hand, goes on in time, win or lose or draw.

Another important feature of playing a game is that it typically involves interaction with one or more other players. This fact is seldom lost on children who know that the request, "Play a game with me," is hard for adults to turn down. With adults or other children, a game has come to mean an accepted form of participation and is often easier for the child to manage than is straight verbal interaction.

It is relative to these two points that I wish to mention the value that certain games can have *in situ*. (That is, there need be no manipulation of rewards, no trickery with the playing pieces, but only a standard use of the standard games.) Beyond the "fun" of playing, a standard game can serve the additional functions of providing diagnostic and developmental information and therapeutic implementation.

Diagnostic/Developmental Use of Games

The following presentation examines simple, standard card games and a few standard boxed games and their uses as diagnostic and developmental activities.

Playing Cards (the standard 52-card pack) can be used as a diagnostic tool, as well as helping children ages 5 and up to learn and practice various "intellectual" functions.

The graduated schedule below shows a few of the simple card games which can be useful in working with children. These games are essentially "match" games. The participant is required to match stimuli on some dimension.

Card Game:	*Learning:*
Red and Black	
Players each have a color (red or black) and a half of a pack of cards. A color match with the simultaneous turn of a card goes to the player who has that color. When not a match, cards are put in a pile and go to the next winner of a match.	Matching Colors
Go Fish	
Players try to get 3 or 4 number matches by drawing or asking other players.	Identifying and matching numbers

Patience

Players try to match two cards by number by turning cards from the pack spread out face down. Remembering the location of previous sets is important.

Matching by numbers; numbers

War

Players gain cards by having a higher card on a simultaneous display.

Discrimination by number: higher, lower or same

Crazy 8's

Players follow suit or number to a discard pile with one card as wild to change suit.

Making public discrimination by suit-match, or by number-match

Rummy

Players try to get at least 3 number matches or a number sequence of 3 by suit.

Making private discriminations of number and sequence, matching number and determining sequence by suit

These card games are played by most children of elementary school age. In a counseling situation they can be used as a diagnostic tool to determine level of functioning. They have the practical advantage that, if the child does not know the game, it can usually be taught in a brief lesson. As listed, these games form a developmental pattern of increased sophistication.

In addition to the card games mentioned, there are simple commercial games which could be viewed in this diagnostic/developmental way as games which teach or drill concepts in the preschool or early school grades.

Game:	*Learning:*

Candyland[1]

Players use color card to move pieces.

Learning and matching colors from a card to a board

Cootie[2]

Players put together a Cootie-bug by selecting pieces with numbers attributed to them to match with a die's numbers.

Recognizing numbers on die and relating them to pieces needed

Twister[3]

A group game where players touch colored circles with a hand or foot to match the spin of a dial.

Matching of colors, but mainly the learning and drill of "right" and "left"

Lotto

Many variations where pictures are matched from a single card to a card with multiple stimuli.

Stimulus matches in various dimensions, from animals, to household objects to more abstract connections such as products of a state

The advantage of using standard games is that no special materials are needed. These traditional games can provide information and faster learning and have the added benefit of being popular with children.

Therapeutic Use of Games

Three standard commercial boxed games will be mentioned here with comments about how they can be used for therapeutic implementation. As presented below the feature of interest is the

---

[1]CANDYLAND is a registered U.S. trademark of Milton Bradley Company.
[2]COOTIE is a registered U.S. trademark of Schaper Manufacturing Company.
[3]TWISTER is a registered U.S. trademark of Milton Bradley Company.

CHAPTER 15

COMMUNITY DEVELOPMENT GAME

R<small>OSE</small> H<small>OUSE</small> F<small>RUTCHEY</small>

INTRODUCTION

R*OSE FRUTCHEY'S game is a mixed-motive game in that cooperation and competition or a mixture of both can characterize any player's attitude for any specific move or round of the game. She has used her game to induce an attitude of cooperation among villagers on the basis of realized interdependence. They can be brought to see that consensus is possible and that they have common and/or complementary goals as individuals. This kind of game illustrates a unique characteristic of simulations; they speed up the time sequence to reveal final outcomes. Thus, particular playing strategies can be carried to their logical conclusions in a short time span. The players can also experience their feelings— for or against—and try out alternative strategies in later rounds of the game.*

Frutchey indicated that there are additional uses for the same game; training for workers in specific, simulatable situations. The workers can forsee problem areas as they work with the villagers if the simulation of their cultural premises is accurate. The author's third application for her game, research, allows comparisons to be made between cultures, grade levels in schools, socio-economic levels and the like. Findings from such research would answer questions concerning differences between groups. It would also yield information about the hows *and* whys *of games like this.*

Frutchey's game serves as a good initial step in social studies

274

projects and in social action settings. This author is interested in results from either situation and offers her help to the innovative teachers who wish to discuss their game experiences with her.

—Editors

T HE COMMUNITY DEVELOPMENT GAME is a simulated village situation designed to overcome some major, well recognized technological development problems. As its basic function the game is designed to impart awareness as opposed to specific technological facts. Achievement of an effective dialogue based on mutual understanding of problems is a necessity prerequisite to effective development. The design should allow the game's use (toward greater awareness) in three specific areas: (1) training of villagers, (2) training of development workers, and (3) research.

The use of the word "game" implies the mood with which participants should approach the use of the technique. To some students of cross-cultural technical change, a lack of sophistication or seriousness of purpose is implied by the word "game." As a stable base upon which comparisons can be made both by the players and the analysts, the "game" is designed as a *test* in the same sense as the well respected Rorschach Tests. The game and its rules become the *picture* to which the participants respond. Responses can then be recognized by the participants or analyzed by researchers.

The Rationale for Game Construction

Community development efforts are designed to speed the natural tendencies of cultures to change. These efforts, however, have been constantly frustrated by lack of success. Unplanned technological changes can be observed in the remotest villages, and yet the planned activities of specialists are seemingly met by unconquerable levels of neophobia or ethnocentrism. Lack of motivation and cooperation on the part of the villagers, compounded by insufficient awareness of cultural and local peculiarities on the part of development workers, have been described among the major problems involved.

The community development concept of self-help implies the necessity for cooperative action by groups of people. Most peoples of the underdeveloped countries of the world do not have a history of sustained cooperative secular activities. Implementation of community development projects has been through the designated governmental authority structure. Participation can be acquired through this channel, but continued maintenance has not been effected. Changes made and facilities constructed through the authority structure are considered by the people to be the property of the government or the group inspiring the action. Research has indicated that projects which are regarded as the property of the villagers are more likely to be maintained if the project is feasible.

Cooperation can take different forms. Each culture or subculture may have its own traditional form of cooperation. For example, the Northern Thai farmers participating in cooperative people's irrigation projects tend to prefer to select a representative in whom they invest the power and the responsibility for implementing the project. His calls for assistance, when necessary, will be heeded by the farmers. Total group participation in decision-making is considered unnecessary and a waste of time (Frutchey, 1969).

Resistance to participation in a self-help development project could prove valuable. It forces clarification of purpose and goals. It may disclose inadequate communication channels or insufficient information. It may even force a more careful study of possible consequences since technological change does mean disorganization of the culture and the social environment.

Each person involved in a group activity is primarily interested in or motivated toward the satisfaction of his own felt needs. The extent to which cooperation can satisfy his felt needs determines the extent to which his behavior will benefit the group. If the behavior demanded by the group is different from the felt needs of the members, the group suffers. Sufficient desire for the fulfillment of a need must be felt for a villager to be willing to break with tradition. Change agents, to be successful, should make possible the achievement of individual felt needs.

Technological justification for change alone is not enough. Technological emphasis needs to be balanced with social and cultural concerns. Culturally oriented cooperative participation in all phases of a project from planning through implementation has been suggested as necessary for long term success. A device which could more vividly display general and specific socio-cultural phenomena would be useful to the achievement of more profound awareness. The following is a list of the basic awareness goals projected for the Community Development Game.

(1) Villager Awareness
 —that the solution of some village problems is possible at a local level.
 —that cooperation is the easiest means of achieving a solution to these problems.
 —that immediate frustrations can be overcome by persistent effort.

(2) Technician Awareness
 (a) Through role playing.
  —that individuals are primarily interested in satisfying their own needs.
  —that cooperation is the easiest means of achieving a solution to these problems.
  —that villagers are confronted by many varied frustrations.
 (b) Through observation or administration of the game in the village setting.
  —that individuals are primarily interested in satisfying their own needs.
  —that cooperation is the easiest means of achieving a solution to problems, but difficult to achieve.
  —that there are specific frustrations confronted by villagers. Some of these frustrations may be specified during the course of the game.
  —that there are specific personalities involved in each village's leadership positions. Many of these leadership positions could be more specifically pinpointed.
 (c) Through comparative analysis of results from administering the game in several villages.
  —that identification of relevant general socio-cultural phenomena is possible.
  —that identification of relevant leadership characteristics and patterns is possible.
  —that identification of development problems of a more general nature is possible.

A Technique for Problem Solution

Community development is an applied social science. Therefore, development workers are more concerned with the practicality and results of techniques rather than the theoretical ramifications involved. Potentially, techniques used in other educational settings could be applied to community development efforts. As a proposed application of a yet untested technique, the indications of potential effectiveness of social simulation exercises are only theoretical or fragmentary research results.

Social simulation has been used in industry since the mid-50's and is now being explored for use in more formal educational settings. Just as a simulated airplane (Link Trainer) allows manipulation, study, and reversal, so do simulated life situations.

Very few research results are available from which accurate predictions of the effectiveness of simulated social situations can be made. Reliable research results from comparisons between different methods of teaching are difficult to obtain even under classroom conditions. However, useful indications can be drawn from game research efforts reported to date:

(1) Player predispositions regarding game participation account for some differences in enjoyment and learning. The important positive predispositions are those that enhanced interest in playing a specific game as opposed to ideas held prior to game participation. (Inbar, 1968).

(2) More than nine (9) players reduces learning and enjoyment. Each game, however, has its own maximum number of participants to achieve enjoyment and learning (Inbar, 1968).

(3) The prevailing group atmosphere during the game play directly influences enjoyment and learning (Inbar, 1968).

(4) Participants are generally highly motivated during game play. However, research has not determined the effect of high motivation on learning. (Cherryholmes, 1966).

Theoretically, simulation could be a very effective teaching method. John Dewey (1928) presented universally accepted principlcs that (1) play itself is functional, and that (2) the most effective means of learning is "learning by doing." Further, most educationalists believe that the following figures are fairly accurate estimates of the rate of learning:

—from READING most people learn and retain about 10-15%,
—from HEARING most people learn and retain about 20-25%,
—from SEEING most people learn and retain about 30-35%,
—from SEEING and HEARING together most people learn and retain 50% or more,

—from ALL THE SENSES together most people learn about 90% if they participate fully in the activity (Noordhoff, 1961).

Other educationally proven properties built into simulation are the ability to: (Plattner and Herron, 1962)

(1) focus attention onto the specific elements of desired learning.
(2) require participation.
(3) provide built-in rewards for participation and accomplishment.
(4) condense large amounts of decision making into a shorter period of time.
(5) integrate the different aspects of the problem into an understandable whole.
(6) provide experience in role playing in an environment similar to reality.
(7) allow play-back and immediate observation of the results of each decision or play.
(8) provide an opportunity for experimenting.
(9) direct attention toward finding the important factors in the situation and relating them to planning.

Other fragmentary research indicates that to augment the influence of a sound theoretical base, attention should be given to implementation features and the administration of the technique. Specifically, effective use of the game technique in community development depends on the ability of the innovators to clarify definitely the goals to be achieved and to construct a situation and a set of rules which will display these goals.

The Game

The Community Development Game attempts to mirror the social setting existing in a typical village. The rules depicting the village situation control basic behavioral responses of the players. Some implicit social rules are also explicitly stated in the game rules.

Rules form the basic framework within the limits of which manipulation and built-in chance channel the players to predetermined general goals and conclusions. Involvement and participation require that the model be as realistic as possible, and that the results of experimentation and the consequences of various moves be easily seen. Basically, the situation models reality, but some compromises are necessary to achieve clarity and simplification.

Some subordinate situations were relegated to chance. However, for village use, chance situations should be reduced to a minimum. Situations over which there was previously little control are widely believed to be responsible for the extensive existing feelings of apathy. The game is designed specifically to demonstrate that participation and cooperation can overcome obstacles. For the training of development workers, the injection of chance situations more clearly points out the causes of villager apathy.

The game is not intended to teach the development worker all he should know about development. It is designed to point out aspects of socio-cultural importance, particularly those of inter-personal relations and leadership patterns. For the villager, the game points out the necessity for cooperation in order to overcome obstacles and achieve satisfaction of his individual felt needs.

Enthusiasm, which is an inevitable by-product of game play, provides a jumping-off point for discussions of the needs of the particular village involved.

Explanation of Game Parts

The Community Development Game consists of five (5) separate items: a map, a sheet of "need" chips, a sheet of food storage chips, a sheet of natural contingency slips, and the game explanation booklet. A single die or set of dice is also necessary, but not included with the game.

Map

The map depicts the actual village layout. The map, localized for Southeast Asian Buddhist cultures, will be used in the explanation, but changes in the pictures can be made to depict any tribal situation. For example, the home positions in each case should show typical homes for the area. The more closely the map simulates a real situation to the players, the greater will be the probability of villager identification with their own real situation.

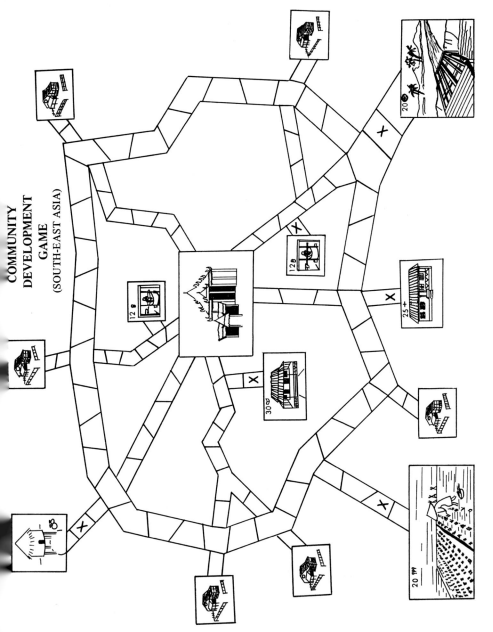

Figure 15-1.
Several different structures appear on the map.

Figure 15-2.
  (a)
    Indicates a HOME posi-
    tion. There are six (6).

Figure 15-3.
  (b)
    Indicates a Buddhist
    PAGODA as the center
    of village activity.

Figure 15-4.
  (c)
    Indicates a WELL.
    There are two (2).
    Twelve (12) "need"
    chips are needed for
    constructing each. (See
    "need" chip no. 3.)

Figure 15-5.

(d)

Indicates a DISPEN-SARY. Twenty-five (25) "need" chips are needed for construction. (See "need" chip no. 2.)

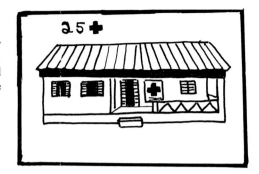

Figure 15-6.

(e)

Indicates a SCHOOL. Thirty (30) "need" chips are required for construction. (See "need" chip no. 1.)

Figure 15-7.

(f)

Indicates AGRICULTURAL IMPROVEMENTS needed. Twenty (20) "need" chips are required to achieve improvements. (See "need" chip no. 4.)

Figure 15-8.
  (g)
    Indicates ROAD RE-
    PAIRS needed. Twenty
    (20) "need" chips are re-
    quired for construction.
    (See "need" chip no. 5.)

Figure 15-9.
  (h)
    Indicates the FOOD
    STORAGE HOUSE.

The illustrations of school, dispensary, wells, road repairs and agricultural improvements have numbers with a figure near them (Ex: Well = 12. Fig. 15-16). This indicates the number of that particular kind of "need" chip necessary to construct that facility. In the example, twelve (12) "need" chips are required to construct a well.

The rest of the map consists of pathways through the village. Each section of the path between two cross lines is a space. It is vital to the success of the game that the number of spaces not be changed. Spacing has been adjusted in such a manner that the game progresses smoothly but with the proper element of frustration.

Wording is omitted from the game map to avoid confusion for illiterate players.

"Need" Chips

The Community Development Game is based on the fact that all village people have needs. Each villager has different needs or different levels of the same needs.

In this game village, the players have five (5) kinds of needs.

Figure 15-10.
1. School Needs

Figure 15-11.
2. Dispensary Needs

Figure 15-12.
3. Well Needs

Figure 15-13.
4. Road Repair Needs

Figure 15-14.
5. Agricultural Improvement Needs

All the "need" chips required to play this game are printed on one sheet. These should be cut into individual pieces.

If the "need" chips designated for use are not representative of a particular situation, changes can easily be made. Substitute other needs in the same place or at other locations on the map.

Also printed on the card with the "need" chips are X chips which are PERMANENT BLOCKS and HOME PAWNS numbered one (1) through six (6).

Food Storage Chips

Food, such as corn or rice, is more valuable to the villager than is money. Food in storage will be used as the medium of exchange in this game. Each area of the world has its own staple food. In Southeast Asia the staple food is rice; therefore, the chips can be more accurately called "Rice Storage" Chips.

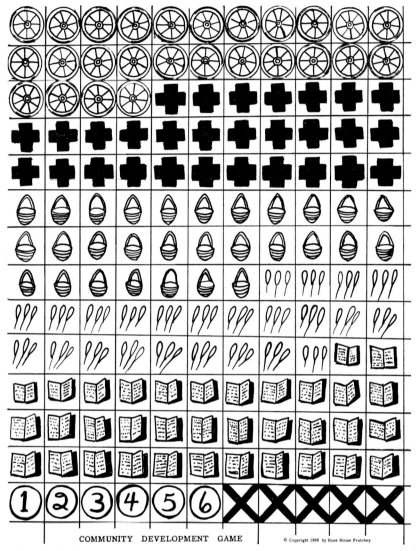

COMMUNITY DEVELOPMENT GAME   © Copyright 1966 by Rose House Frutchey

Figure 15-15.

Natural Contingency Slips

"Natural Contingency" Slips are designed to insert other aspects of the real village situation into the game. These can be used for training purposes only and probably should not be included until the third or fourth playing of the game by a particular group.

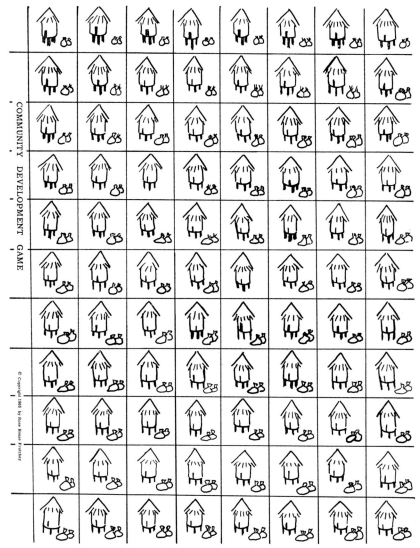

COMMUNITY DEVELOPMENT GAME

Figure 15-16.

Playing the Game

The Community Development Game simulates a village situation with a set of hypothetical but realistic problems or "needs": a school, road improvements, agricultural improvements, a dispensary and two wells. Six players attempt to completely satisfy these "needs" by the construction of appropriate facilities.

Before starting play, the chips should be mixed in a hat and each player allowed to select from the hat (without looking inside). Individual or groups of chips are divided until all are gone. Each player should arrange his "need" chips in front of himself and place similar "need" chips together so that they can be easily seen by all players. These represent his "needs" as a member of the village. In the villages of Southeast Asia everyone knows the needs of his neighbor.

Twelve (12) "food storage" chips are placed in the food storage house on the map at the beginning of the game. This village stores its rice collectively, but this aspect of play can be adjusted to depict a situation where villagers store their own food. For individual storage, each player should be given five (5) "food storage" chips. When an individual player has no more "food storage" chips, he is out of the game. The advantage of having collective food storage is that all players can remain in the game until there are no longer any food stores remaining. The game is then over.

Each complete round of turns (one turn by each player) requires the relinquishment of two (2) "food storage" chips to indicate the passage of time. These can be taken out by the administrator or by any other player selected by a vote of the players prior to the start of the game.

Work in the field can replenish the food in the food storage house. One turn in the paddy will earn one (1) "food storage" chip for the community storage house. However, if agricultural improvements have been completed, one turn in the field will earn two (2) "food storage" chips for the storage house.

Play begins with each villager located in his home position. HOME PAWNS are used to indicate the player's position. Each player must use a HOME PAWN number to coincide with the home position from which he started. The player in home position number 1 can start the game and others follow numerically, or the first player can be selected by drawing straws and other players then follow numerically.

Each player automatically gets 10 energy units for his use each time he has a turn. He may choose not to use some of his energy units; however, energy units are not cumulative. Moving one space requires one energy unit; therefore, a player can move ten (10) spaces if desired. Trading one "need" chip for another "need" chip held by another player also requires the use of one energy unit. A player may choose to trade as many as ten (10) "need" chips, or he can move several spaces and trade with the remainder of his energy units.

Since there are no telephones in the village, talking is allowed only by the two or more players who meet at the same location on the map. Trading "need" chips requires discussion; therefore, players must meet to exercise this privilege. Others can listen but must refrain from comment.

When the specific number of similar "need" chips are accumulated through cooperation or by trading, the facility can be constructed and the "need" thereby satisfied. Construction of a facility requires that all players involved meet at the construction site and collectively deposit their "need" chips. The stated objective of reducing individual "needs" to zero (0) as quickly as possible can be achieved through this means. Extra "need" chips held by any player after a particular facility is constructed are automatically satisfied. All players automatically benefit from the efforts.

Any player can block construction of any facility if he so desires. If a player stops on one of the map positions marked with an X, movement past him is not possible. If the blocker will discuss his reasoning, a compromise may be possible.

To establish a permanent block, one complete turn must be forfeited (10 units of energy) after a player comes to rest on the position. Placement of a permanent block means the block is still in effect but the player can move around.

Rolling one die will depict the chance of removing a block. Any two or three numbers (depending on the odds) can be selected prior to the start of the game. These odds should be adjusted to more closely depict the reality of different situations.

Players soon become aware that cooperation provides the easiest and most certain route to the satisfaction of individual needs. The game may, however, be prolonged if players refuse to cooperate. If so, the administrator may choose to terminate the game before any player actually satisfies all of his needs, or before the food stores are depleted.

Early stages of the game may prove extremely frustrating. This is desirable as it is designed to simulate actual development learning situations and create an optimum mood for learning.

Village Play

The most influential element for success is the administrator/ player. *The administrator must have had previous experience playing the game.* His job is to maintain a good playing atmosphere, which should begin with an enthusiastic introduction to game play. He is also responsible for mediation of discussions concerning game technicalities. As one of the villagers in the game, he can play toward the satisfaction of his "needs" or he can play the part of a disenchanted villager who wishes to prevent the construction of one or more facilities.

The administrator must spend time in the village to build rapport prior to introducing the game. Each village has its own rate of acceptance of outsiders. Therefore, no specific number of visits can be recommended as necessary to achieving satisfactory rapport. In the instances where foreign observers or others are to be present at game sessions, they too must spend time gaining rapport, perhaps even more time than is necessary for a local person. Without good rapport, reactions will be biased and result in less valid conclusions. For best results the administrator in actual village play situations should be a fellow tribesman or someone who speaks the villagers' language or dialect fluently.

To induce a sense of urgency and help speed the game, a time limit should be set. One (1) hour and forty-five (45) minutes or two (2) hours should be adequate. An alarm clock may be set to go off every half hour, or the administrator can inform the players at half-hour intervals.

After the game the administrator explains what happened and discusses how it relates to real life. A complete explanation of the administrator's role is essential, as is a discussion of cooperative versus individual effort.

Replaying the game, with a thirty (30) minute time limit, will point out that cooperation can overcome "blocking" actions and is effective when the majority are determined to participate in the completion of a facility. Any one of the players can play as a "blocker". The "blocker" can be designated by drawing slips of paper, one of which is marked X.

Training Development Workers

The administrator's job is the same as that already described under village play. He has, however, to play the role of a specific village personality who may be opposed to development. The administrator may act as a village chief dubious of and resisting the intrusion of outsiders, a spirit doctor whose methods have been denounced by medical technicians, a disloyal element trying to win the confidence of the people, a villager who has previously worked on a government project for which the promised wages never arrived, or one who irritation has been provoked by disregard for the moral and ethnical codes of the society by outsiders. All of these reasons for opposition are potentially important to future development activities.

Additional replays for training purposes can be useful. Facilities constructed collectively must also be maintained. After each facility is constructed, the group can decide on some means of maintenance, considering both personnel and costs involved. Government assistance can be requested for staffing a facility if three players use ten (10) earned "energy units" each and then toss a die to determine the probability of success.

Capitalism can be introduced as a possible variation. When a facility is constructed by one person alone or by two people, he (they) can charge other villagers for the use of the facility. If charges are to be made for use of facilities (i.e. disposing of their needs), the player should place a solid black marker on the "blocking" position in front of his facility. Specific charges can be designated by the player(s) responsible. If a player's demands are unreasonable and all play ceases, this would be a good point to stop. A discussion of the implications for this kind of action in an actual village situation, or in society in general, would be useful.

Natural contingencies are chance occurrences that significantly affect village life. Floods, droughts, sickness and the opposite optimum conditions are completely out of the control of villagers but influence their ability to participate in community development activities. When used, a "natural contingency" slip must be drawn after the second complete round of play and every second round following. The cards are drawn automatically by the administrator or by another member of the group. The dictations of the slips must be honored.

Other rules for the third playing are the same as those for the first and second.

The various actions and reactions of the players reveal real life problems, views, philosophies and beliefs likely to be confronted in actual development projects. Also, actual village leadership may be revealed if the situations are studied thoroughly. The game provides a stable setting through which many groups can be compared. Indigenous leadership characteristics can be compared through the observations and recordings (tape and charts) of the game in action.

Rules

(Complete for first and second playings)

1. Each player starts from a home position. Position number one starts, etc. Use the chips numbered one (1) through six (6) as markers or "pawns".
2. One turn means that a player automatically gets ten (10) "energy units" which he may or may not wish to use. These energy units are not the same as NEED CHIPS.
   (a) Moving one space requires one unit.
   (b) Trading one "need" chip requires one energy unit.
       All players involved in a trade must be positioned on the same space. EXCEPT: talking is possible with a blocker from the space adjacent to the block.
   (c) Unused units are not cumulative.
3. Talking is not permitted until two (2) or more players occupy the same space. No other player is allowed to join the conversation.
4. Number of chips required for construction are indicated in the upper left corner of each construction site on the map. ALL players participating in the construction of a project must be present on the site. ALL chips required must be deposited all at once.
5. X Blocking
   (a) Any player stopping on one of these positions (X) completely stops movement beyond him.
   (b) Forfeiting one (1) complete turn after coming to rest on a blocking position will allow establishing a permanent block with a chip marked X. This means that the position is still blocked but the player can move again.
   (c) *Removing Blocks*—Thirty (30) energy units can be sacrificed (by one

or more players together) allowing an opportunity to role the die.

6. Food Depletion and Replenishment

    (a) Food stores are depleted by 2 chips for each round of playing.

    (b) Food stores can be replaced by work in the rice paddy.

        One (1) complete turn (10 energy units) in the field earns *one food storage chip*. EXCEPT: if agricultural improvements have been completed, *one turn* in the rice paddy will earn *2 food storage chips*. One or more players may work in the field at one time.

    (c) The administrator makes all additions and subtractions from the food storage house.

7. Game Termination

    (a) The game is won by one person successfully disposing of all his "need" chips.

    (b) When all the food storage chips have been used up the game is over.

    (c) At the expiration of a previously determined time limit.

CONCLUSION

The Community Development Game is perhaps the first effort to utilize the simulation technique for technological change activities. Although seemingly sound theoretical framework, from both an educational viewpoint and from a development viewpoint, the game has not been tested extensively. It is hoped that the ideas presented can be used effectively. However, if this game proves insufficient, it is hoped that other workers will be inspired to test and improve upon the one described. Conclusions regarding the use of simulation in development projects hopefully will be based on unbiased research rather than initial reactions to the title or the idea.

Copies of the game are available from International Voluntary Services, Inc., 1515 Connecticut Avenue, N. W., Washington, D. C. 20036. The cost is $5.25 per copy, plus postage.

REFERENCES

Boocock, Sarane and Schild, E.O.: *Simulation Games in Learning*. Beverly Hills, Sage Publications Inc., 1968.

Cherryholmes, Cleo: Some current research on effectiveness of educational simulations: Implications for alternative strategies. *American Behavioral Scientist, 10*:4-7 (October, 1966).

Dewey, John: *Democracy and Education*. New York, Macmillan Co., 1928, pp. 230-240.

Frutchey, Rose H.: *Socio-Economic Observation Study of Existing Irrigation Projects in Thailand*. Unpublished report for United States Operations Mission to Thailand, Bangkok, Thailand, 1969, p. 134.

Inbar, Michael: Individual and group effects on enjoyment and learning in a game simulating a community disaster. In Boocock, Sarane S. and Schild, E.O. (Eds.): *Simulation Games in Learning.* Beverly Hills, Sage Publications, 1968, pp. 182-183.

Noordhoff, Lyman H.: *The Eyes Have It.* (Federal Extension Bulletin 150.) Washington, Government Printing Office, 1961, p. 10.

Plattner, John W. and Herron, Lowell W.: *Simulation: It's Use in Employee Selection and Training.* (Management Bulletin No. 20), New York, American Management Assn., 1962, p. 5.

CHAPTER 16

NEGOTIATION: A GAME FOR SOCIALIZATION TRAINING AND ASSESSMENT

Loyda M. Shears

INTRODUCTION

*L*OYDA SHEARS *has described a socializing situation in her* NEGOTIATION *game. The game-form upon which this game is based calls for* coalition formation *under open* bargaining *conditions. All* information *is available for the players who deal with a situation similar to that found in a stockholders' meeting. A majority of the stock, not of the people, wins. Such a game facilitates experiences in coping with others. It allows individuals to train in social skills and experience the rewards and disappointments of social interaction. Under these controlled circumstances the individual's experience can be buffered by "as if" distance from real life and a playful attitude.*

NEGOTIATION, like Frutchey's Community Development Game has value chiefly as a vehicle for socialization training and assessment. In the latter role this game has been used extensively in research concerning developmental and cultural norms for competitive behavior. If teachers and counselors wish to share their experiences as they use NEGOTIATION, the author will be happy to respond in kind.

—Editors

Background

T HE WORLD WE LIVE IN is a stimulating and exhilarating place. It is also complex, threatening and full of risks. Some children who grow up in this way of life manage to cope with it better than others. In fact, some of them cope so well that we say that they transcend the limits of their abilities. Then, we call them *over-achievers*.

In the past, youngsters who were not coping well were thought of as defective as individuals. The trait of good or poor coping was associated with the personality of the person. The role of specific kinds of situations in which "good" coping did or did not occur was largely overlooked. The defined role of education was teaching coping skills to be applied in ALL situations, and the children were deemed differently able to learn the skills. We propose an alternative way of looking at coping and suggest that successful coping mechanisms differ depending on the situation and that some mechanisms suit some people better than others. Thus "good" coping will represent an interaction between the individual's style and the nature of the situation.

In line with this idea, a new way of inducing coping in each child has been developed. It takes the situation into account and attempts to define coping within that framework. In order to train a child, situations have been formalized in which the participant makes choices under conditions of uncertainty and in which some people in the situation do not get what they want at each round of decision-making. Over several rounds of choices each child would get what he/she wants a percentage of the time. Of course, it is important for the outcome to be clearly stated and the setting for its occurrence clearly defined. The formal mathematical statement of such situations define a game as stipulated in mathematical game theory. Inasmuch as risk exists and payoff docs not go to everyone in many real-life situations, we may use this formulation as a basic simulation for many life situations.

Children and adults face risky life situations daily, but individuals do not respond to them in identical ways. It is a developmental fact that children face a world that becomes more varied as they extend themselves into the wider world. Likewise, we can assume that they shift about among situations more often as they get older. Some percentage of the situations that they meet are bound to be risky. As a basis for analyzing behavior in risky settings we propose that good coping may be thought of as competent handling of personal threat in risky situations. Furthermore, we propose that "good motivation" means willingness to accept a role in a risky situation in a "positive" way. Finally, we propose that a positive, motivated response is indicated when a person continues to try to win under conditions of uncertainty and limited payoff. A motivated person would come to seek risks and see them as challenging and enjoyable. The ultimate level in such a sequence describes a person so motivated that they have fun taking risks.

When a game situation is defined as one containing risks we may ask about the strategy (set of choices) that will put each participant in the position of winning all he/she can win, that is, all that the situation allows, while protecting his/her position against losing any more than he/she has to. A strategy intended to achieve this goal in mathematical game theory is identified as the min-max solution. It should be a simple matter to arrange this kind of outcome if the participants know what they want and if participants can achieve their goals independent of each other. There are some games that fit this description, but many do not. Suppose each participant can help one or more others to attain an agreed-upon goal. For this situation, coping consists of recognizing the need to cooperate. No such simple solution is available when each person must gain the cooperation of some of the others on the way to beating them all and carrying off the indivisible prize. Competition adds to the complexity of the social situation and poses problems that are not easy for the participants to solve. The game of NEGOTIATION simulates this complex competitive social situation and exposes the participants to the social problems that follow from asking another person to cooperate with him/her now on the way to beating that person later.

The sequelae highlight and expose potential problems within and between the participants. Often individuals do not know whether they want to compete or cooperate, and winning is not always a clear-cut goal even for the most competitive. The personal sense of threat can be considerable whether the participants agree

to cooperate or compete, and it takes considerable skill and effort
to deal with the situation. If the participants cannot develop in-
ternalized defenses and come to an individually acceptable agreement about how to handle the situation, the dissatisfied participant's sense of threat may rise to unbearable proportions. In the
light of these observations it is clear that the process of coping
takes on added dimensions when this commonly occurring threat
is taken into account. Some game situations present choices that
carry differing amounts of risk, and the participant must choose
his/her risk-outcome preference. If the person is satisfied with a
likely outcome, coping is easy and non-threatening. However, selection of an infrequent outcome will require a waiting period.
Waiting, trying again and good humor indicative of a hopeful
attitude constitutes one kind of coping behavior. Lacking a hopeful attitude specific to the situation, a shift out of that situation to
one where the person's preference occurs more frequently would
also constitute good coping. Since higher payoff often attends the
less frequently occurring choices, the latter strategy could be the
superior one. Thus, persistence toward achieving one's goal in a
risky situation logically emerges as the central theme of good
coping.

It is also evident that the participant's attitude under risky conditions is associated with the central theme. This theme is part of
the earlier point of view which affirmed the primacy of personality
traits in coping behavior. It now seems likely that assessing situations and planning a strategy composed of successive choices is
even more important, since the attitude probably follows the selection of a reasonably successful and satisfying strategy. Teachers
can facilitate the development of both attitudes and strategies that
lead to good coping and satisfaction by using games that simulate
the risky life situations. This is a familiar task for educators. It is
only the instructional situation that is redefined when games are
used. The game may be designed to permit psychological distance
and participant-control of the amount and kind of threat.

NEGOTIATION: The Game

The game prepared for presentation here is competitive but
not purely so. For many it is a mixed-motive game, since social

and rational (competitive) objectives become intertwined as it is played. Children who play it have the opportunity to try various points of view in the course of the game(or set of games) with the result that they may decide whether or not they like the risks involved. NEGOTIATION facilitates the learning of various aspects of self-awareness in the social life space. Each individual lives in a social-power matrix that is defined and redefined for each new social context. The child, willy-nilly, has a hand in these definitions since he/she is an integral part of the social contexts.

The child learns, first, to cope with parents as power figures and, later, with siblings and peers. By the time the sibling and peer interactions have developed into a reasonably coherent system, from the child's point of view, he/she has begun to try to change any present status to the most favorable one possible at any given time. In this struggle to gain status in social settings, skills in social intercourse are developed and a sense of self-worth becomes established at some level. This level, too, is constantly being revised upwards or downwards. Each episode has an outcome that conveys information about how skillful self is what others think of him/her. The outcomes are also some kind of reward or punishment in the child's eyes. The persons did or did not get the outcomes they wanted or expected from each social situation and may have gained or lost in self-evaluation as well.

Our game is one of a set of games in which social power may be experienced. It is a competitive, four-person (tetrad) power game. In it the players can face the problems they must cope with when they seek to compete and try to win in social situations. The game presents the problem of facing others within a situation with the objective of securing their cooperation toward an unclear and risky end. In the final outcome even those who cooperate may not win and share in the prize. To soften the impact of this fact, NEGOTIATION should be embedded in a larger situation by carrying on a series of games with the same people or by setting up a tournament. In such a metagame (life situation in which the game is imbedded) the experience of handicapping early winners for later rounds will probably develop in the social system of the game. The relationships within the smaller, intra-game setting may be placed in the perspective of the larger social situation with the result that hope for a delayed reward may be learned, and long-term strategies may be developed. The teacher plays the important role of manager as these events occur.

Rationale for the Game

Our power game, NEGOTIATION, may be adapted to vary the power relationships among the players. It is modeled after a stockholders meeting in which various players have different amounts of voting strength. When the players combine they can form coalitions that have or do not have a majority of the voting power within the game. They cannot lose or gain voting power within a round of the game, but they can combine to form larger blocks of voting power.

A game like this can be designed to accommodate any number of players, and the power weight relationships may be varied to make some players have more advantage (or disadvantage) than others as they bargain to secure a place on a winning coalition. If one player has enough power to claim a majority of the resources or strength he will have no need to join a coalition to win. Anything less than this amount of power makes it necessary for even the strongest player to negotiate for a place in a coalition. It is variations on this latter situation that comprise the power patterns in NEGOTIATION.

Relative Advantage Among Players

The relative advantage or disadvantage among lesser power weights depends on their relative combining powers with respect to the highest weight. Of course, the number of players becomes an important variable which interacts with the size of their respective power weights. Since we are only dealing in our demonstration with groups of a specific size, that is, four players, we will illustrate how combining power of lesser weights influence coalition formation within that size group. When the lesser players hold weights that combine with the highest power equally well as they seek to arrange a majority of their power resources, the relative size of the lesser weights becomes unimportant. Such a game is defined by the power pattern in which players hold 1, 2, 2 and 4. Despite the smaller size of a weight it is not a functional disadvantage of this pattern. The 1, for example, can form a winning pair with 4 as well as either of the 2's. Games so designed permit the teacher or counselor to demonstrate that apparent disadvantage may not be real in the game situation. Hopefully, the notion that this is also true in situations outside of the game will be communicated in the process.

Bargaining

If lesser weights in the 1-2-2-4 pattern can combine to form a majority, the weakest players may be led to see that they do not have to acquiesce to the demands of a strong player. The action necessary to obtain this defense against the strong player's demands is, of course, cooperation among all of the lesser weightholders in forming a coalition against the strong player. As the bargaining to secure coalition members progresses it becomes clear that the strong player has a functional advantage. He can argue that he needs fewer allies to make up a majority of the resources because he brings a larger number of resources to any arrangement he proposes. Furthermore, he can offer some concessions in payoff to the weak player who will join him.

Payoff

The point just made concerning payoff makes it clear that payoff is, itself, an important variable in designing a game of this kind. The NEGOTIATION game we will present uses a fixed payoff, that is, the total payoff amount is the same size under all playing circumstances for any given series of games. (A variable-payoff game is one in which certain actions taken by the players during the game increases or decreases the total payoff size for specific games within a series.) Variable-payoff games may be desirable for later phases of training in power-use, but, at the outset, the fixed-payoff management of the reward system seems to be more effective in teaching the limits of a social system.

Instruction Script for NEGOTIATION or
STICKS AND CHIPS[1]

A script format has been chosen for the instructions of NEGOTIATION. The numbered instructions on the left side of the sheet

---

[1]STICKS AND CHIPS is the children's version of NEGOTIATION.

indicate the actions to be carried out by the teacher or counselor. The instructions on the right are to be spoken. The order in which the actions and spoken portions of the script are to be performed is indicated by the sequential number. Pauses for players' responses are indicated by dashes (———————).

Do This	Say This
1. Place four chairs, two on either side of a table, and place a fifth chair at the end of the table.	2. Will you sit in these chairs, two of you on each side of the table. I'll sit here at the end.
3. From the materials on a small table within easy reach pick up the recording sheets (a pad will do) for use on the game table.	4. Tell me your names and I will write them down.——————— ———
5. Turn first to the person on your left and record his name.	6. You will be player A.
7. Repeat 5 and 6, recording each name and assigning the letters B, C, and D in a clockwise direction.	
8. Present the BANK from the supply table. (See figure 16-1 for drawing of the equipment).	9. The game we are going to play is called *STICKS AND CHIPS*. You will be using this BANK to store the chips you win. There is a slot for each of you in it. We will mark your slot with your name now. This slot (far left) is for you, A.
10. Use A's name and record it on the top of the BANK. Repeat 9 & 10 for B, C, and D.	
11. Take a stack of white CHIPS from the supply table STORAGE BANK.	12. These are the CHIPS we will use. There will be 20 of them for each game. We will

CARDS/PLAYERS

A	B	C	D
4	2	2	1
4	2	1	2
2	1	4	2
2	2	1	4
1	4	2	2
1	2	4	2
2	4	2	1
2	1	2	4

These are "Equal Opportunity" weight assignments for 8 Games

BANK AND CHIPS

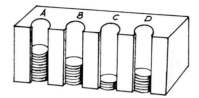

BOARD AND STICKS

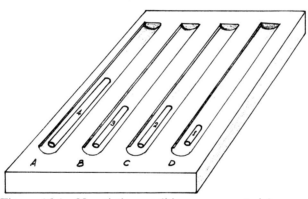

Figure 16-1. Negotiation coalition game materials.

play a set of four games. Then we will declare a winner. The person with the tallest stack of CHIPS in the BANK will win.

13. Take a bag of M & M's from the supply table.

14. The winner will get this bag of candy. If there are two stacks the same height, we will flip a coin to see who gets the candy. You see, there will be only one winner for each set

of four games.

15. If we play another set of four games there will be another bag of candy for the winner.

16. Point to the stack of 20 CHIPS in front of you.

17. Remember, there will be a stack of 20 CHIPS to be won for each of the four games we will play in a set.

18. Present the BOARD from the supply table.

19. This BOARD will help us as we play the game. You can see that there are four grooves in it. There is one for each of you.

20. Record the names of A, B, C, and D at the ends of the grooves, beginning on the left.

21. Take the STICKS from the supply table and set them on end, one beside each player's groove.

22. These are the STICKS we will use in the game. You can see that they are not the same length. This one is four inches long. These two are two inches long, and this small one is one inch long.

23. Lay the STICKS in the grooves for A (4), B (2), C (2), and D (1).

24. Just to see how the game goes we are going to let A have the 4, B and C have the 2's and D have the 1.

25. When a reaction appears for the smallness of the 1, comment on it. There may not be any, but there usually is either comment or gesture from either D or one of the others at this point. If there is none, state 26 without emphasis.

26. Don't think that the 1 is unimportant. You will see that that is a good STICK to have!

27. The idea of the game is to make your STICK longer than

the other STICKS. You see, the longest STICK wins. Who would win right now if nothing else happened?————

28. Point to the 4 STICK in A's groove. The players will see that A will win, because the 4 is the longest stick.

29. Is there anything that you can do, B?————

30. Wait a moment, then place B's stick in C's groove.

31. Will this make a winner? ————

32. Point out the equality of 2+2=4.

33. Is it still possible to make this STICK longest? ————

34. Point to the two 2's in C's groove.

35. Let's look at D's 1. What can he do with it?————

36. Pick up D's 1 and place it first in C's groove, then in A's groove.

37. Which makes the longest STICK?————

38. Repeat 36. If the answer does not identify either combination that includes 1.

39. Is there another way? ————

40. Pick up C's or B's 2 and put it in A's groove. Remove D's 1 to C's groove.

41. You see, any one of the short STICKS can win with the long one. Don't forget that the short STICKS combine to make a long one, too.

42. Pick up the 2 in A's groove and place it in C's groove, again.

43. Which is the longest now? ————You see, there are several ways to make the longest STICK. Now who wins? ————

44. Make it clear that all contributors to the longest STICK win something and that the owner of the groove in which the STICKS lay is not the winner by himself.

45. The people who join together to make the longest STICK win these 20 CHIPS.

46. Pick up and show the players all 20 white CHIPS mentioned in 11 and 12 above.

47. If these are to be stored in the BANK (see 9 above), and you who have joined together to make the longest STICK have won them together; they must be divided. You will have to decide how to divide them as you decide how to make the longest STICK.

48. Present a colored FELT piece from the supply table to each player. Give D red and A green.

49. As you discuss who will join together you will be talking about 20 white CHIPS as though they were yours already. This piece of FELT will help you to talk about them.

50. Present 20 colored CHIPS to match his FELT to each player from the supply table.

51. These 20 CHIPS in your own color will help you to remember that you are talking about the same 20 white CHIPS. They will, also, help you to remember who offered you a share of the 20 white CHIPS and how many he offered. You can compare offers to see whose offer is the best.

52. The idea of dealing in the division of future winnings is not easy at first for young children. The colored CHIPS serve to confirm their right to talk about 20 CHIPS as though they were their own. They also assist with the arithmetic problems in dividing 20 by two, three or four players who may decide to join together. Older children will not need

them, and younger children will need to be reminded to use them appropriately.

53. There is a special way of joining up. Before you get together with someone you ask him if he wants to come over to your side, *and* you offer him some of the 20 CHIPS in order to get him to come. You see, he wants some to put in his BANK.

54. Pick up D's 20 red CHIPS and his 1 STICK. Place both in front of you.

55. Suppose D wants to join with C. He will say to C, "I'll give you so many CHIPS and keep so many." How many CHIPS do you want to offer him?————

56. Count out the number D suggests and offer them to C. If C accepts, put the CHIPS in front of him on the FELT and have D put the 1 in C's groove. If C is reluctant————

57. This is not a game for keeps. Will you pretend that you are willing to accept his offer so we can learn how to play the game?

————————

58. Put D's 1 in C's groove and point to the length of the STICKS together.

59. Is this a winner? What must they do to make a winner?

60. If one of the players does not suggest that A or B be included————————

61. One more is needed.———— ———— Which one of the others is to be included?———— ————Why don't you ask B to join you?————————

62. If at first or after 61, B is suggested have him pick up his 2 and put it in C's groove. Suggest B if he is not proposed by a player.

63. How will the 20 CHIPS be divided?————————Look at the red CHIPS and divide them three ways now, since there are three (two) of you.

64. When the players have settled the division put B's share on the FELT before him.

66. Point to the smallest stack of red CHIPS before one of the players.

68. Count the CHIPS and count out one or two more from A's green CHIPS.

71. Present the STICK AS-SIGNMENT CARDS from the supply table.

73. Show the ASSIGNMENT CARDS, face up, with the numbers and letters showing. (See Fig. 16-1 for the FAIR GAME power weights).

75. Shuffle the cards face down and have A draw one. Have him place the STICKS in the proper grooves.

65. A, can you do anything to get someone to join you now?

66. Point to the smallest stack
67. Can you offer him more than he is getting now? How many does he have?

69. A, say to him "I'll offer you_____(the number of green chips) CHIPS to join me."

70. Now, you see how to offer CHIPS as you try to get someone to join with you.

72. D, did you know that you didn't have to keep that 1 all of the time? Everybody gets it some of the time. Isn't that nice! You all wondered why I called you A, B, C, and D, didn't you? These CARDS have those letters on them.

74. We will give the STICKS to different players each time. I'll shuffle the cards and you will each get a turn to choose. A will be first, then B, and so on.

76. You can begin the game now. Anyone can speak whenever he wants to. You don't have to wait for turns or anything. If you want to stop the game at any time, let me know. The game ends when you have decided who will join together and how many

of the 20 white CHIPS each of you who joined can put in their BANK. Remember it is up to you to tell me when the game is to end.

77. If bargaining does not begin in a reasonable time . . .

78. Who will win if nothing happens?

79. If nothing happens then . . .

80. Do you all plan to let (holder of the 4) put all of the 20 white CHIPS in his BANK? Unless some of you get together that is what will happen.

81. Assist with the division of the CHIPS for triple alliances using the colored CHIPS of the player who offered first as shown in 63.

82. If bargaining goes on for a considerable time and the players seem to be unable to conclude a coalition and end the game . . .

83. When you have decided who will get the 20 white CHIPS we can put these CHIPS in the BANK and begin a new game. Remember it is up to you to tell me when the game is to end. We will play four games before we decide a winner.

84. After four games have been played and the white CHIPS are in the BANK bring the BANK into the center of the table.

85. Do we have a winner?——————Who is he?——————

86. Carefully compare the four stacks of CHIPS. If there is a winner declare who it is and award the prize.

87. Here are the M & M's for winner.

88. If there are ties flip a coin to decide the winner.

89. Repeat 87.

Children's Responses to the Game

Our subjects up to now have been third- to sixth-grade children, and we have only observed boys and girls playing in the same-sex groups. We have made an analysis of game events which sheds some light on how children deal with the competitive task contained in the game. Results of the analysis fall into three broad categories. They reflect the following aspects of the game situation:

1. Cognitive aspect, pertaining to an understanding of what is involved in playing the game;
2. Social aspect, referring to considerations other than competition; and
3. Affective aspect, relevant to the emotional impact of the game upon the players.

Cognitive Aspect

As we consider the components of the cognitive aspect three sub-parts emerge:

1. Learning the situation as a whole, i.e. learning the rules;
2. Learning to apply the rules, i.e. improving one's score; and
3. Learning to do well, i.e. getting the highest score.

These sub-parts may be thought of as a developmental hierarchy in which "Learning the rules" constitutes the most elemental level.

LEARNING THE RULES. Misunderstanding of the rules probably underlies several game behaviors. Some children have difficulty in understanding that the chips remain at the disposal of all the players until a firm alliance is concluded. Such statements as, "I don't have any chips to offer," after another player has made a tentative offer to a third member of the group points to such a difficulty. Such a player assumes that the chips have been used by the one making the offer, and sees them as no longer available to him/her. Arithmetic problems present difficulties at lower grade levels (third and fourth grade) that are commonly solved spontaneously by offering portions close to equality or vastly disproportionate. Seemingly, calculations are easier at the extremes. It is interesting that proposed payoff shares do not seem to be related to the power weight (length of the player's stick). Young children (third- and fourth-graders), also, experience difficulty with the limitations imposed by a fixed payoff. They fail to realize that each coalition-member's payoff is going to be reduced as more players are included in an alliance. Although this difficulty seems to be one of rule-misunderstanding, it may have wider implications. Somehow the general concept of competition is not very clearly understood at the lower age levels. That is not to say, however, that younger children *cannot* understand since some third graders placed in a way that clearly indicated their understanding of competitive strategy. The effect of misunderstanding would be to prevent progress to the second level of development, "Learning to apply the rules." It follows that they do not improve their scores as much or as often as the game situation allows.

IMPROVING ONE'S SCORE. Even though there is a generalized understanding of the notion of competition based on knowledge of the rules of the game, specific information about maneuvering during the game is needed for players to improve their scores. The most obvious maneuver is to get into a winning alliance. When an alliance is formed initially between two players, one of whom holds the high weight, both members probably know how to increase their individual scores. Likewise, when two weak players (both hold low weights) ally and take a third to form a winning coalition they also demonstrate this knowledge. Addition of a third player to the winning pair demonstrates imperfect knowledge of how to increase individual scores—*or* a choice to use a social criterion for inclusion in a coalition. It is often not clear which is the case. Also, a division of payoff that does not reflect the relative powers held by each ally can indicate imperfect knowledge *or* use of social criterion. Both of these game-events bear on the player's effectiveness as he/she seeks to win.

OBTAINING THE HIGHEST SCORE. The most effective strategies (sequences of maneuvers) lead to the highest score. Attempts to use effective strategies represent the most sophisticated level of game knowledge and introduce the notion of control. Since the highest cumulative score wins, each player must seek a coalition and payoff that will increase his own score and at the same time control the increase in the scores of others. It is necessary to understand the maneuvers necessary to secure both results. There are two such maneuvers available for the 1-2-2-4 power pattern. Two players who are behind in total score may ally if one of them holds the highest weight. When the highest weight is also held, the weak, winning triple (three holders of low weight) is needed to simultaneously increase the players' own scores and control the score of the player in the lead. Although adults understand these maneuvers and use them, none of the school children (third through sixth grades) succeeded in actually using them. This finding occurred even though the maneuvers were demonstrated after the first round of the game had been played. Despite considerable reference to the principle among fifth and sixth grade children none of them were able to overtake the player ahead after the first round. In the second set of games, the winner of the first round was likely to be excluded, but this seemed to be either social reprisal or due to the retreat of the early winner from the competition.

Social Aspect

The small group situations lends itself to the development of social relations among group members. This may inhibit competitive responses during the game if competition assumes threatening proportions. Several game events seem to be purely social. Sometimes the players sought to prolong the game as a social event. In some groups bargaining became ritualized and the players would make offers in turn without regard for the weights they held; and again, solidary pairs would make offers disproportionate to the weights they held. They even offered to form coalitions in which one member received all the payoff. This behavior was especially prominent among fourth grade boys. In some cases there would be a barrage of offers directed toward the high scorer. There seemed to be social value in being associated with the "leader." In other instances the barrage would be directed toward the holder of the highest weight for that round. Perhaps this is another definition of "leader" among school children. Often coalitions included more players than were needed to win, and it is not clear whether this behavior occurred because game knowledge was inadequate. Either the objective of social solidarity or a defense against threat were also possible. In any case children in grades three through six formed more such coalitions than did adult males. Child behavior is more like adult female behavior in this regard. Children in school had a tendency to share their prize of chocolate candies (M & M's) after the games were over. This is a form of solidarity that is expressed outside of the game proper and represents what is called "side-bets" in game theory. Sharing can be selective (include few players) or general (include all players). When it is selective it probably serves a competitive goal, while general sharing can serve social ends.

Affective Aspect

While the exact nature of the affective response may be in doubt, it is very clear that the game situation often evokes strong emotions. The affective responses found in game behavior may be conceptualized as a bifurcating function. At the low end of the continuum there is *disinterest*. Children showing this emotional response were apathetic—seemingly completely uninvolved and lacking either a sense of threat or pleasure in what they were doing. Children who were judged to be disinterested complied minimally with the mechanical acts of the game. At the lowest point the children seemed not to understand the rules of the game at all. However, some children seemed to understand the rules and elected to remain uninvolved in the situation. Moving up the interest scale, the children were more alert to game details but it was not possible to say whether they viewed the game *positively* or *negatively*. As the observed degree of involvement increased, it was possible to identify which view the child was taking. Some players verbalized their interest while others expressed it by tense posture, standing up and gesturing. In the excitement of the game there often was excessive talk and raised voices. The excitement rose as winning or losing became imminent. For children who behaved in this way we assumed a positive attitude toward the game, at least for the moment.

Negative emotional responses represent the second branch of the bifurcated function and indicate a subjective sense of stress. When a child responds in this fashion one may assume that he/she either cannot cope with the stress now and may not wish to take the risks entailed in the game at a later time. Negative responses may be covert or overt. When interest is followed by virtual withdrawal from the game and/or actual withdrawal (e.g. going to the restroom) the child's response is probably negative. Overt negative responses can be as clear as "No, no, no." Further, a variety of ploys may be used: playing on the sympathies of others, calling attention to one's unfortunate lot and threats of reprisals outside the game situation. Verbal rejection of the situation may occur in the clear statement, "I don't like this game, it's silly," and the negative player may threaten to leave or actually leave.

SUMMARY AND RECOMMENDATIONS

In summary, we may ask, "How may such a game be used to help children to grasp and cope with social situations?" We must, first, summarize some objectives. Then, we will tentatively suggest a series of training games.

The most obvious objective to be sought in competitive game experiences would be to teach competitive behavior. It is, also, too limited and simple an objective to be undertaken for its own sake. Two other objectives have been suggested: (1) to obtain general self-knowledge concerning subjective feelings about the competitive situation, and (2) to provide an opportunity for the individual to work out skills and attitudes for coping with the competitive situation. Let us briefly explore the ramifications of these objectives. The child may be pleased with and enjoy the game situation. On the other hand, he may be uncomfortable and dislike it. These feelings and attitudes may appear regardless of whether or not he wins or loses or they may be contingent upon winning or losing. Knowing his own point of view will permit him to take appropriate action about his continued participation in the situation.

Moving on from the affairs of single individuals to those of the aggregate of individuals who comprise the group, suppose there is substantial agreement among the players, and suppose that they can play either competitively or accommodatively (according to their agreement). Their single problem will be to maximize the satisfaction of group members in terms of their consensus. Under these circumstances they may concentrate on their unambiguous goal. On the other hand, should there be disagreement among the players the likelihood of their achieving either subjectively or situationally maximized outcomes is greatly reduced. Presumably the effectiveness of skillful management of the situation would be made more difficult and probably reduced when a mixture of motives exists among the several players. From the individual player's point of view he could size up the group climate and "play" accordingly. Given self-knowledge, game knowledge and skill he would know when to stay and play and when to quit and leave for his own greater satisfaction.

Since the four-person competitive game is clearly quite complex, in the hands of children it has served to separate component concepts used in our example from the finished and assembled whole of adult play. We will now present a simpler, stepwise, set of experiences calculated to teach the component concepts. The gradations are undoubtedly gross and would require considerable exploration and refinement before the ends sought by their use could be obtained. The basis of the arrangement is the increasing size of the groups. Listed in sequence they are as follows:

1. Two-person groups, dyads, could inform the child of his preference for accommodative or exploitative game behavior and about the possibility of maximizing payoff available in a variable-payoff situation.
2. Three-person groups, triads, could generate skill in negotiations, knowledge of the limitations of a fixed-payoff, and the principle of holding the high-powered participant in check.
3. Four-person groups, tetrads, could give the high status player a notion of how to hold his own and overcome attempts to hold him in check. On the other hand, weak status players could learn about the difficulty and expense-in-payoff associated with larger alliances in a fixed-payoff game-situation.
4. Five-person groups, pentads, could be used to give the weak players a sense of their own power, again. The odd player, left out after two pairs are formed, would probably command a high payoff-share in those game situations where he holds the winning supplement to either alliance. Under these circumstances the notion of timing, which probably is subtly involved in all of the earlier levels of this series, could be made explicit.

The contributions proposed for these sizes of groups are dependent on many other aspects of the situation besides the size element. For the most part it was the essential, negotiable, fixed-payoff zero-sum game that was intended. The exception is the dyadic game which in this case has a variable payoff. Direct negotiation may or may not be permitted between the dyadic players. Negotiation takes place anyhow if a series of games are played since earlier decisions become the basis for later expectations.

CHAPTER 17

A MODEL FOR THE DESIGN OF ACADEMIC GAMES

PERRY GILLESPIE

INTRODUCTION

*P*ERRY *GILLESPIE'S chapter provides detailed instructions for creating games to be used in the classroom—or in any other setting. His model for creating games is spelled out with illustrations and his rationale to support each step in the process. As the user follows his instructions and creates his own game his points will come to life and provide the innovative teacher with a sense of freedom not otherwise available in this teaching modality.*

His limitations which apply to children's use of games serves to illustrate that restrictions exist and that they are lawful within existing theories of child development. As Gillespie describes the limits, the game-user can identify the desirable effects that attend the use of games. Otherwise they might be missed. Furthermore, the user can diagnose unwanted side effects, identify the sources of the trouble and probably find ways to eliminate them.

Gillespie's illustrative game came into being in response to a need for such a game to teach course material related to curriculum planning. The age level of his students and the relevance of his model for his task leads us to the conclusion that his model can be generalized far beyond the two age levels he used in his discussion. Teachers are encouraged to venture into equally unlikely areas armed with his model. He will be interested in any informa-

tion about such excursions and is willing to help with advice and further theory when teachers contact him.

—Editors

The Use of Games

RESEARCH ON THE USE OF GAMES for academic purposes can be traced to the Rand Corporation in Santa Monica, California and the Massachusetts Institute of Technology. Their initial work and that carried on by their sister educational institutions was done primarily for the military and business worlds. In recent years, the early success in the use of games at more advanced levels of learning prompted a number of educators to think in terms of using academic games in the secondary and even the elementary schools.

Several notable academic centers have devised and tested the use of games at these levels. Among those most often mentioned are the Western Behavioral Science Institute in La Jolla, California which conducted *Project Simile,* testing the use of simulation games used in the Elementary Project of the Social Studies Program; and the Johns Hopkins Center, where a number of games were conducted by James S. Coleman and Sarane S. Boocock in cooperation with the Baltimore City School System.

There seems to be little doubt that the use of games is increasing in formal educational settings. They are used because they: allow children to experience the consequences of their actions immediately; focus attention by requiring active physical and mental participation; allow the child to experience a sense of controlling his own future; remove the teacher from the position of having to judge children on the basis of teacher expectations; actively interest students in the formal educational process; and accommodate a wide range of student abilities with only minor modifications (Coleman, 1967, pp. 69-70; Boocock and Coleman, 1966, pp. 215-236).

Early reports on the use of games in the schools are favorable, but there is little formal research to support their success as a better means of organizing the learning process than the present curriculum. However, their use is increasing and with it a need for new games designed specifically to meet educational objectives set for them. Hence, the need for a model to serve as a guide in the design of academic games.

Models

A model is a set of principles or statements which describe patterns of relationships holding among the units and variables of a system. Models are useful for description, explanation and prediction. They represent essential features of the real world; they

TABLE 17-I
STEPS OF GAME DESIGN

	START	MAJOR VARIABLES
STEP 1	Determine the Age Group of the Intended Players (see pp. 320-324)	Age 7-12 12+
STEP 2	Determine the Primary Function of the Game (What is it to do or represent?) (see pp. 324-326)	Socialization Disguise Decision-making Transmit Knowledge
STEP 3	Establish the Context of the Game World (see pp. 326-329)	Rules of Relevance Rules of Irrelevancy Transformation Rules Space Time
STEP 4	Formulate the Internal Structure of the Game (see pp. 329-338)	Role Player Interaction Plot Goals (Objectives)
STEP 5	Determine the Procedural Rules Needed to Govern the Operation of the Game (see pp. 338-344)	Initiation & Termination Deployment & Disposition Communication Arbitration Intervention Enforcement Outcome
STEP 6	Write the Instructions Necessary to Administer the Game (see pp. 344-350)	Pre-game Game Post-game

describe arrangements holding among the components which shape the system; they depict the logical order and flow of events and

TABLE 17-II
CONSIDERATIONS FOR GAME DESIGN

Age Four to Seven

1.	Stages of develop-ment according to Piaget	Last half of the egocentric stage
2.	Practice of observance of rules	The child shifts from individual acts to reciprocal actions
3.	Understanding of obligation of rules	Rules apply to all players and are obeyed as given and are hence unalterable
4.	Typical social behavior exhibited by child	Children carry out actions together but often miss one another's intentions. No winner is required
5.	Type of activity engaged in	Quasi-games Example games: *Cowboys & Indians* *Doctor*
6.	Characterization of activity	May meet some of the functional and structural requirements of a game, but not all

		Age Seven to Twelve	*After Twelve*
1.	Stages of develop-ment according to Piaget	Cooperative stage	Codification stage
2.	Practice or observance of rules	Reciprocity	Actions are reciprocal with differentiated responses to initiatives of other players
3.	Understanding of obligation of rules	The individual is concerned with the mutual control and unification (regularization) of rules	Rules are established by mutual consent of all participating players. They may be altered by common consent at any time
4.	Typical social behavior exhibited by child	Activities are coordinate, i.e. actions are relative to other players. Each child seeks to win. Competition is limited	Activities are inter-dependent and fully coordinate. Full range of social behavior is possible
5.	Type of activity engaged in	Central-person games. Example: *Red Rover*	Team games Example games: *Football, Crisis*
6.	Characterization of activity	Satisfies all of the definitional requirements of a game. (see page 133ff.)	Same as for age seven to twelve

yield information about structural changes over time; and they allow for the effects of such changes to be predicted. Since a structural-functional approach was used to identify the component properties of games (See Chap. 8), a similar framework has been adopted for the design paradigm. It outlines the makeup of the model and illustrates how the parameters of the model can be used to create academic games. The model is illustrated with examples drawn from existing games. Six steps forming the design model used in the construction of academic games are presented in summary form in Table 17-I. At each major step in the design process, the choice of variables and their pattern of relationships are discussed. Examples selected from existing games illustrate the constraints imposed upon game design by age for two groups—a seven to twelve year old group and a post-twelve year old group. The steps are used by a series of successive approximations. First, run through the steps once, outlining the general framework of the game. Then repeat the process defining the structure more clearly with each successive consideration of the steps until the game is completed. Follow the same procedure in *revising* a game already in existence.

STEP 1: DETERMINE THE AGE GROUP
FOR WHICH THE GAME IS INTENDED

Games are primarily social in nature, facilitating the integration of the individual into the group. Since groups are governed by rules or norms of behavior, participants must learn to abide by social rules. The child's ability to understand the meaning and use of rules is a prerequisite behavior for gaming, and this, in turn, places limitations upon the structuring of games (see Table 17-III).

Piaget asked two questions of children about the meaning and use of rules:

> (1) how the individuals adapt themselves to the rules, i.e. how they observe rules at each age and level of mental development; and (2) how far they become conscious of rules, in other words, what types of obligation result (always according to the children's ages) from the increasing ascendancy exercised by rules (Piaget, 1965, p. 24).

TABLE 17-III

THE FUNCTION OF GAMES

	From Age Seven to Twelve	*After Age Twelve*
Prototypic Games	Central person games Example games: *Red Light, Green Light* *Marbles* *Black Tom* *King of the Mountain*	Team games Example games: *Cowboys and Indians* *Crisis* *Inter-Nation Simulation* *Dangerous Parallel* *Football* *Baseball*
Primary Function(s)	1. To aid in the social-ization process by modeling different patterns of social organization, control, and interaction.	1. To structure inter-dependent social situations in which the child may practice decision-making under varying conditions of conflict, e.g. interest, perspective, and values.
	2. To introduce the child to features of the real world which he is unable to accept, by disguising or softening them.	2. To transmit knowledge under conditions which permit the child to discover and make application of it.

Development From Age Four to Seven

Somewhere after four years of age, the child moves into a transition period which includes the latter half of what Piaget terms the *egocentric stage* of development. Children engage in a form of quasi-game in which very little risk, if any, is involved; there is neither climax nor plot (Peller, 1954, p. 186). There is an increase in order and coherence, a desire for an exact imitation of reality, and a differentiation and adjustment of roles (Piaget, 1951, p. 135). As the child becomes more socialized, there is a shift from egocentrism to reciprocity, a prerequisite for participation in any social game. The child's consciousness of rules alters as well. Rules ". . . are regarded as sacred and untouchable, emanating from adults and lasting forever. Every suggested alteration strikes the child as a transgression (Piaget, 1965, p. 28).

Peller observing children ranging in age from three to six found that they sought to imitate adults. They engaged in quasi-games which more closely approximated events in the world around them. For example, they play *House, Doctor, Cowboys and Indians, Fireman,* etc. Plots emerge and roles increase in number and type. The child pretends to possess privileges reserved for adults as is re-flected in the variety of roles, disguises and settings for his games. There is an increase in his tolerance for ambiguity and risk as seen in the uncertain outcomes of dramatic games. Plots may be involved and tell complete stories. Children make attempts at shar-ing a common plot and may carry out actions seemingly together, but often miss one another's intentions. Yet at this stage of de-velopment they still have not quite grasped either the use for or the meaning of rules necessary for successful participation in social rule games (Peller, 1954, pp. 183-189).

Development From Age Seven to Twelve

Somewhere around seven years of age the child moves into what Piaget terms the *stage of incipient cooperation.* The individual sub-stitutes games involving rules for those of egocentric play. With the addition of rules, both a regularity and the concept of obliga-tion (reciprocity) which accompanies the coordination of the ac-tivities of two or more individuals is imposed upon games (Piaget, 1951, pp. 140-143). The individual is concerned with the mutual control and unification of the rules governing games. Each child seeks to win, i.e. to triumph over others in a similar act, and, hence, is acting relative to the actions of others. Winning and losing are now possible.

Maccoby, in his study of Mexican children's games, found that skill games increased in the eight to twelve age group. In a similar study of American games, Sutton-Smith noted that central-person or "It" games characterized the nine to twelve age group (Maccoby, Modiano and Lander, 1964, p. 159; Sutton-Smith, 1961, pp. 17-46). A central-person game is one in which a single player opposes a group or "pack" of players. In it he must coordinate his own actions with the members of the pack. The power or control over the actions of others built into the central role is usually increased for children under twelve.

Development After Age Twelve

During the final stage of development after eleven or twelve years, which Piaget termed the *codification of rules stage,* children practice rules which have become codified. Rules are recognized as being ". . . due to mutual consent, which you must respect if you want to be loyal but which is permissible to alter on the condition of enlisting general opinion on your side" (Piaget, 1965, p. 28). Rules can be altered before the game by common consent or after it has begun if all players agree. In more sophisticated games rules may become vague and ambiguous, thus introducing greater risk into them. As the individual grows older, he assumes roles in which built-in power is decreased. After twelve, team games predominate.

Implications of Prerequisite Gaming Behavior for the Design of Games

The seven to twelve year old child practices rules which impose regularity on games. Players coordinate their actions so that plots utilizing multiple roles are employed. Players mutually control the rules which establish and govern the context of the game, its operation, and its administration. Roles are differentiated and numerous, with the behavior for each prescribed in advance. Because coordinate action is possible, games require criteria for determining a winner. As a result some type of reward must also be determined for the winner. Uncertainty is built into the game since the child is more tolerant of ambiguity and the risk it entails. Central roles are needed which provide additional control over the actions of others. With coordinate action, competition is possible and is increased gradually in intensity and importance. Games suitable for this stage of development are central-person games, for example, *Red Rover,* in which one player is pitted against the combined physical and mental skills of a pack composed of two or more players.

The post-twelve age group is ready to participate in the most complex social games. Common action is possible, permitting a diversity of roles and tasks to exist simultaneously. The behavior, resources, and power ascribed to each role may thus vary within the game and from role to role. Players may enact roles as they see fit, offering their own particular solutions to a given task or problem. Many games of this period are team and task oriented. *Football* exemplifies team effort in which each player performs a specialized task contributing to the team's winning or losing the game. The conditions under which games are enacted become more realistic. Player interaction may vary from within-group cooperation to between-group competition. The functional range of games is more extensive than for the earlier age group.

STEP 2: DETERMINE THE PRIMARY FUNCTION OF THE GAME

The game designer must determine the primary purpose or function of the game, i.e. what it is to do or represent. Games serve: (1) as expressive models for the various patterns of social control, organization and interaction found in a culture; (2) to soften or disguise the more stringent features of the real world so that a child may gradually accustom himself to the demands of everyday life in a protected environment; (3) to structure social encounters in which individuals make decisions under varying conditions of conflict—interest, perspective, and values; and (4) to transmit knowledge leading to a more complete understanding of one's culture. The first two functions are typical of games practiced by the seven to twelve year old group, while the last two functions are common to games of the post-twelve year old age group (see Table 17-III).

The Function of Socialization and Disguise in Games for Ages Seven to Twelve

Central-person games emphasizing socialization and/or disguise introduce the seven to twelve year old to the many patterns of social relationships he will likely encounter in the adult world. Each type of game reflects a different pattern or style of social behavior. By participating in such games the child learns to differentiate one style from another. In them, he may continue to test his personal concepts of appropriate social behavior until he finds the one best suited to his needs and acceptable to the group. Thus, games of this period may aid in the socialization process.

In early central-person games the child may learn to control the actions of others while filling a leadership role as is found in *Red Light, Green Light*. He may encounter limited competition in games like *Marbles*. As he grows older, he may face increasing competition, and even conflict, in such games as *King of the*

Mountain where the child must defend his position against the competitive behavior of his peers.

Games of this period also serve to soften or disguise the more stringent aspects of the real world. Children who are immature or suffer from psychological problems often find it impossible to accept social controls in their adult form. They must be softened or disguised, i.e. modified, before such children can bear to cope with them (Sutton-Smith, 1955, pp. 228-229; Redl and Wineman, 1952, pp. 110-114). Other children who lack physical or mental skills cannot enter into activities in which the pattern of interaction is highly competitive and which requires well-developed skills.

Redl reports that children will accept rules which control their social behavior in games but refuse to accept societal rules governing similar behavior in the real world. For example, children who are hyperaggressive under ordinary conditions will accept *game imposed rules* controlling aggression while playing games like *Monopoly.* Significantly, the participants themselves enforced the rules (Redl and Wineman, 1952, pp. 110-116). It is also reported that unskilled children will engage in games in which the pattern of interaction is softened. *Black Tom* is an example. The central player is given additional power to control the actions of other children thus offsetting his lack of skill. This in turn has the effect of reducing the element of skill competition among the players. Under such conditions of reduced competition even the most inept children will participate in games (Gump and Sutton-Smith, 1955, p. 3).

The Functions of Decision-Making and the Transmission of Knowledge in Games After Twelve

Games which commonly appear in the post-twelve age group stress the functions of decision-making under varying conditions of conflict found in the social group and the transmission of knowledge. After twelve, organized team games first appearing around nine or ten years of age, take on an ever-increasing importance. In such prototypic games as *Cowboys and Indians,* multiple social relationships are stressed. In later appearing games the child develops skills in working with others toward a common goal. He may learn to respond differentially to each player according to the prevailing set of conditions and the problem faced. More recently, educators have created such games as *Dangerous Parallel* which combine both functions (Nesbitt, 1969, pp. 16-18). In it, the student is introduced to a situation in which he must make decisions based upon his personal assessment of the consequences both for himself and the other players. It also provides him with factual information about international relations which he can use to make his assessment.

STEP 3: ESTABLISH THE GAME WORLD

The game world is partitioned off from the real world by rules

TABLE 17-IV

ESTABLISHING THE GAME WORLD: PARTITIONING RULES

Rules of Relevancy	*Age Seven to Twelve*	*After Age Twelve*
1. Indicate those features of the real world to be included or maintained in the game world.	Material features of game would closely approximate those of real world, e.g. roles, titles, names, equipment, clothes, props, settings. Motifs and relationships should be simple.	Any attributes to the real world may be included except those which dissolve the imaginary partition between the real and the game world.
Rules of Irrelevancy		
2. Indicate those features of the real world to be excluded from the game world.	Inappropriate social behavior is not to be penalized. Stringent features of real world, e.g. pure conflict situations, are excluded. All players are to be treated equally in the game. Non-material attributes such as wealth, status, exceptional abilities or skills are set aside or offset by handicap rules.	Exact representation of the real world attributes is not required. Instead they may be symbolically represented. Any real world attribute may be declared inessential to the game.
Transformation Rules		
3. Indicate those features of the real world to be retained, but modified in the game world.	Certain aspects of the real world are to be relaxed or disguised. Temporal and spatial dimensions are to be scaled down to fit the capabilities of seven to twelve-year-olds.	Real world features may be abstracted to meet the availability of personnel, resources, time or space, or research requirements such as replication.

of relevancy, irrelevancy and transformation. The designer must first indicate those features of the real world which are to be included; second he must state those aspects of life which are to be consciously excluded, and third, he must declare what modifications are to be made in order to relax or disguise the more severe requirements of ordinary life. In effect, partitioning rules determine the degree of correspondence between the two worlds (see Table 17-IV).

The Use of Partitioning Rules for Ages Seven to Twelve

First, the age of the group restricts application of the rules' relevance. The motifs and movements transferred from life must be simple enough for a young child to understand. Rituals and rhymes are used in such early, central-person games as *London Bridge.* Subsequently, limelight roles appear requiring the use of names, titles, clothing, equipment and other trappings from life. Children learn to use those game trappings much as they would the social trappings of real life (e.g. prestige, status symbols). In leadership games which follow, children learn the meaning of superior-inferior relationships as well as the duties and responsibilities of a leadership position. For example, a child may learn either to give or follow the instructions of a leader in *Simon Says* (Sutton-Smith, 1959, pp. 157-159).

Second, the more stringent features of the real world such as pure conflict, cut-throat competition, or ostracism are cancelled out. Games of the pre-twelve age period are structured to provide security for the individual child who is learning to differentiate among the many patterns of social behavior found in adult society. In such games as *Poor Pussy* where a child is teased or harassed in order to make him do something which the rules prohibit, the child must learn to control his personal emotions and abide by the rules in order to remain in the game.

Finally, the designer is concerned with rules of transformation which determine the modifications to be made on attributes drawn from the real world. Such rules are used to establish the temporal and physical boundaries of the game world. Children of the seven to twelve age group are concerned with closely approximating the real world in all of its dimensions. Fast moving games of short duration are appropriate since the child, although he would like to do what the adult can do, cannot match the adult in attending or in endurance. Both time and space need to be set aside in order to give younger children a chance to catch their breath. For example, the end zones in *Red Rover* provide a safe area in which the players can rest. For the most part, games of this period take place on actual physical terrain and not on symbolic game boards. Once the external boundaries have been laid out, the internal boundaries must be considered such as home base, taboo areas, safety zones. Such special areas as the "Mountain" (base) in *King of the Mountain* must also be designated. In addition, the players need to know in what direction and how far they can go, as in *Hide and Seek*.

The Use of Partitioning Rules After Age Twelve

The rules for establishing the game world for the older age group are generally the same as for the younger group. However, their application is subject to fewer restrictions. Features brought into the game world very closely approximate those of the real world. For example, in the *Inter-Nation Simulation* developed for use in junior high schools, high schools, and colleges, five national units are represented by teams composed of three players— a central decision maker, an external decision maker, and an aspiring decision maker. Each decision-maker has at his disposal capability units which can be used to wage war either offensively or defensively, or for improvement in the standard of living of the game populace. Each decision-maker must satisfy the populace enough to remain in office. In such a game we see both rules of relevance, irrelevance, and transformation at work. For example, the position of leaders and the task of decision-making are relevant features of international political life, whereas, exact titles, numbers of offices or powers are not. Hence the relevant features were transformed, i.e. roles and powers were combined. Although much simplified, the final roles and attendant duties and responsibilities could be found in the executive branch of any government. In other games, the actual offices with names, titles, personalities and powers may be made relevant or irrelevant as the need arises. In the *Inter-Nation Simulation* game-time is used rather than every-day time units. Events occurring over a period of several months in real life are handled in 75 minute periods. All the physical dimensions of the real world apply except the distance between decision-making units of the countries which are actually a "table distance" away from one another. Time lags are built into the structure of the game to account for the actual physical distance between countries (Guetzkow, 1963, pp. 43-68).

Because the age, ability and experience of the post-twelve group, game scenarios can be employed which describe in detail events leading up to game time. Affect-laden roles such as "The Russians," "The Red Chinese," or "The Viet Cong" have meaning for players who are old enough to follow what is going on in the real world, and hence, have relevance in games for this period. Intangible features such as wealth, social position, status, and prestige are meaningful to this age group and thus can be used effectively. There is also an increase in the use of symbolic representation such as a chess board to represent the deployment of warriors on an actual terrain. Rest periods and areas can be reduced or eliminated. Instead, time and space can be set aside for critiques to be held periodically during the game. Finally, handicap rules are used less because the older youth can handle roles of unequal power.

STEP 4: FORMULATE THE INTERNAL STRUCTURE OF THE GAME

In order to establish the internal structure of a game, the designer must keep four general design principles in mind: (1) the identification of roles maintaining the minimum number of two *bona fide* roles, type, power, and resources; (2) an indication of the manner in which the players are to interact; (3) a description of the plot outlining the sequence of action and major decision-points; and (4) a statement of goals.

Role

Number of Bona Fide Players

There must be at least two *bona fide* roles in a social game (see Table 17-V). The only exceptions are activities in which a player is competing with his own prior score or against nature and then comparing his final score with other players. *Hopscotch* and *Jacks* are examples of such games. *Bona fide* players are those decision-makers who receive payoffs and make choices from among the possible moves in a game (Rapoport, 1966, pp. 18-21).

TABLE 17-V
ROLE

	Age Seven to Twelve	*After Age Twelve*
Prototypic Game Number:	Central-person games	Team games
	There must be a minimum of two *bona fide* players in a social game.	

Types:	*Individual*: Central player takes initiative against the group (pack). No differentiation of roles within group. Players are simply members of the pack. Central role models in their order of appearance are
	    1. Subordinate—*In and Out the Window*
	    2. Limelight—*Ten Little Indians*
	    3. Leader—*Mother May I*
	    4. Dramatic—*Tag*
	Individual: Central player defends his role from members of the group (pack). No differentiation of roles within the group. Central role models in their order of appearance are
	    1. Defensive—*King of the Mountain*
	    2. Scapegoat—*Blind Man's Bluff*
		Each player fills an individual, task or maintenance role. Roles may be interdependent and differentiated both within and between teams.

Power:	Control over other players is a function of a player's ability to say who may move and when, where, and how other players may move. Additional control may be obtained from the recognition a role receives due to expert, legitimate, reward and coercive power.	Sources of power are similar to those found in central-person games. However, they may be more abstract and symbolic.
Resources:	Materials, equipment, trappings used in the game closely approximate those found in the real world. Helpers or assistants are live players.	Both physical and human resources may be abstract and symbolic.

Role Types

Roles are of three types: maintenance, task, and individual

(McDavid and Harari, 1968, p. 302). The latter predominates in the seven to twelve age group. Each child is learning to act in relationship *to* others in the group rather than *with* others as is the case of the later appearing team games in which specialized task roles appear. In the central-person games of this age period, the key role is individual. Individual roles are those in which the person filling it is allowed to enact his own behavior and if it is appropriate and he wins using it, he alone reaps the rewards of the payoff. An example of such a role is "King" in *King of the Mountain*.

The relationships established between role types in central-person games change over the span of time covering the seven to twelve year old group. The types of central-person games which appear during this period are especially useful to the game designer as models, since the sequence of their appearance in real life suggests the appropriate time for introducing children of this age group to newly created games expressing similar relationships and problems. In the earliest central-person games, a child must learn to obey a rhyme or ritual pattern, as found in *In and Out the Window*. If he is able to do so, he succeeds in that individual role. Following such games, limelight roles appear which permit a child to experience a position relative to others in which he enjoys greater prestige, status, and so forth, with all the attendant benefits. Such roles are protected by both song and ritual ceremony as found in *Ten Little Indians*. Appearing next are dominating or leader roles as is found in *Mother May I* and *Simon Says*. Following these central-person games are those in which the central role has dramatic features or special powers such as those of the "It" in *Tag* or *Hide and Seek*. At about ten years of age appear roles in which the central person must defend his role from other players as the "King" does in *King of the Mountain*. Finally, scapegoat roles appear in which the youngster is blindfolded and must then do something or guess the identity of a player who does something to him or near him while the remaining players make fun of his mistakes. Examples include *Blind Man's Bluff* or *Pin the Tail on the Donkey* (Sutton-Smith, 1959, pp. 157-159).

Sutton-Smith notes that in all but the last two types of individual roles, the group is on the defensive protecting themselves from the central role. In effect, in the early central-person games, the newcomer to the social group is placed in a role which gives him much support in his relationship to the other members of the group. As he gains in experience with increased age, ability and experience, he is placed in a role which he must defend from the members of the group. Role types naturally occurring in central-person games thus suggest themselves as models useful in the construction of games performing analogous role functions.

In the older group, all three types of roles are found. More advanced students may help administer the game, filling maintenance roles such as director, analyst, or messenger. Task roles call upon the individual to do a specific job which together with his teammates will lead to a win. Examples of task roles are a guard on a football team and a banker in the game of *Monopoly*.® Generally, roles for this age group permit the youngster to enact a role he is likely to fill in life itself.

Role Power

Role power is an important variable. By its manipulation, the game designer can alter the control a player wields over other players. The designer can adapt the power of the role to suit various needs which individual players bring to the game. Role power can be increased or decreased as needed. For example, Gump and Sutton-Smith studied ways of inducing inept (unskilled) players to enter into game activities with more skilled players. They used the "It" of the central-person game called *Black Tom* (similar to *Red Rover*). The variable they worked with was the power assigned to the "It" role. The power

> . . . was shaped by a number of game provisions: *It's* prerogatives in determining which pack member he will engage in competitive encounter and when this encounter will begin; his "trappings," for example, his game name *or* his power symbols; his protection against the combined efforts of pack members against him; and so forth. Power of this type resides entirely in the *It* role and is separated from the skill of the player occupying the *It* role (Gump and Sutton-Smith, 1955, p. 5).

Additional powers can be built into the "It" role. The ability to reward or punish while occupying a role is a very powerful means of increasing the confidence of children who seldom fill leadership positions in everyday social activities. The younger child will accept legitimate power built into a role, but has trouble understanding expert power since few, if any, children are experts in any given field of endeavor.

The ability of the players to control their actions and those of other players is much greater in games found in the post-twelve age group. The quarterback in *Football* calls the play for the entire team, controlling the basic plan of the game. However, each player carries out his task role (e.g. left end) which often alters the original game plan.

There is a greater differentiation of type of power i.e. *expert, legitimate, reward* and *coercive* and its use in games of this period. Specialized human and physical resources are employed. One finds offensive and defensive squads on a football team. Equipment is also specialized.

Role Resources

The materials, equipment, helpers, trappings, which a player has available serve as an additional source of power. In the younger group, such items as roles and trappings are drawn from real life and are altered very little since the child at this stage of development is trying to approximate more closely what is going on in the real world. For example, in *Cowboys and Indians,* realistic firearms, outfits, and other simulated period trappings are used.

Resources used by the older age group are more abstract and symbolic in nature. For example, war games such as *Chess* and *Go* are played on symbolic battlefields, using boards instead of being played on actual terrain. Also, symbolic players or pieces are used to represent human forces that one can command. The material aspects of physical and human resources do not have to be physically represented; only the abstract concept behind them. Thus, many items such as chips, financial units, or capability units may replace the actual use of money, industrial production, or the gross national product.

The Structure of Player Interaction

The structure of player interaction determines the manner in which a player is to relate to other players in the game (see Table

17-VI). It is, therefore, used to pattern different types of social behavior. The game designer must indicate whether interaction is to be physical or non-physical; whether live or symbolic players are to be used; and whether interaction is to be cooperative or competitive.

TABLE 17-VI
PLAYER INTERACTION

Age Seven to Twelve	*After Age Twelve*
What one player does is relative to what another player does.	Same.
Physical interaction predominates.	Interaction is unrestricted. It may be physical or symbolic.
The physical presence of live players is required.	Symbolic or live players may be used.
The intensity of competition must be reduced or softened. Example game: *Black Tom.*	Interaction may range from pure conflict to complete cooperation or coordination of activities.
The two-person game predominates.	Two-person game with more than one member on each team or games with three or more players (N-person) predominate.
A simple one-to-one relationship exists, i.e. central player reacts to a single player or the group treated as a single unit. A central person role and a "pack" in the role of other person ought to be used as the model for this age group. Example game: *King of the Mountain.*	Multiple patterns of relationships may be developed with players responding differently to different individuals in the game, e.g. cooperation within the team and competition between teams. Example game: *Inter-Nation Simulation.*

Games for the pre-twelve age group generally structure a physical type of interaction, i.e. children are allowed to do something with their bodies. In *Tag,* for example, players must intercept and tag another player. The physical presence of live players is also typical of games of this period. Because games introduce the child to different patterns of social behavior, competition is not as intense as it is in games for the older adolescent. Interaction in central-person games can be used as prototypes for the construction of new games since they pattern different types of behavior encountered when an individual relates to the group. He either responds to the initiatives of the group, or it responds to him. A central-person game is a two-person game with the pack in the role of the other player. Player relationships remain simple enough for the child to handle considering his limited experience in dealing with other people in group activities. The powers ascribed to roles are equalized so the child will not refuse to enter an activity because of overwhelming odds. *Black Tom* or *Red Rover* are typical of central-person games in which interaction is softened.

In games designed for the older group, interaction is unrestricted. The child is introduced to social encounters under conditions closely approximating those found in adult society. The protective safeguards built into central-person games of the younger age group are dispensed with. Interaction may be either physical or non-physical; and the players are either live or symbolic. For example, in the *Inter-Nation Simulation,* the decision-makers are live, but the problems they encounter arc abstract and fictitious. The players interact verbally rather than physically. Armies clash on symbolic plot boards rather than on the playing fields. Roles are differentiated; players wield different powers; and they seek different goals (Guetzkow, 1963, pp. 43-68). Thus, in games with three or more players within the group cooperation and competition may occur simultaneously, i.e. competitively with his opponents and cooperatively with his allies. Hence games for this age period structure multiple patterns of relationships and permit complex social behavior.

The Game Plot

The game designer must write a plot or scenario which tells the key actors and counter-actors what they are to do (see Table 17-VII). In effect, the plot is an outline of what takes place. The manner in which the plot is carried out is left to the individual players to enact as they see fit or is prescribed by the rules.

For the younger group, the plot is generally very simple and brief. For example, in *Black Tom,* a game similar to *Red Rover,* a rectangular field is laid out with two safety zones at each end. The players must run from one end zone to the other across an intermediate zone upon signal from the player occupying the central-person role. The player designated as "It" must tag three players in order to win and move out of the role. The plot is even simpler for early team games. In *Cowboys and Indians,* two teams oppose each other—the *good guys* and the *bad guys.* An ambush and ensuing gun battle takes place. In order to win, the Cowboys

TABLE 17-VII
PLOT

Age Seven to Twelve	*After Age Twelve*
Plots are codified and given.	Plots may be given or developed during the game as each team seeks to achieve its goals.
They are simple and brief, but tell complete stories.	They may be complex and detailed.
Outcomes or uncertain.	Same.
A moderate degree of ambiguity and risk can be used.	Much ambiguity and risk may be purposely built into the game.
Decision points and their sequence are outlined, but the plan of action (strategy) may be either prescribed or left to each player to decide.	Decision points and their sequence may be outlined in detail or left to the players to develop during the course of the game.

must "kill" more Indians than the Indians kill Cowboys. In *Hide and Seek,* a player becomes "It" and covers his eyes while the remaining players hide within a prescribed area; he counts to one hundred and then calls out: "Here I come, ready or not." He seeks out the hidden players who, if they get the chance or if discovered, must run and tag home base before the "It" player tags them. Not many game plots are more complex than those mentioned above for this group.

Few restrictions are placed upon plots for the post-twelve group. Plots can range from a highly detailed scenario in which the sequence of action is carefully laid out to open-ended plots in which the players indicate what the sequence of events are to be. For example, in *Crisis,* decision forms containing a set of nine alternative moves from which the player selects one are handed out at designated intervals. The history and prescribed behavior for each country is found in the scenario. In some current games testing hypotheses about social behavior at the international level, the players write their own country's history, the manner in which it wants to act toward other countries, and its goals. Thus, in the latter type of game it is impossible to set out the exact sequence of events which will occur. Games with "open-ended" plots are engaged in only at the more advanced levels of social and intellectual stages of development.

Game Goals

In games the actions of players are carried out in pursuit of a goal. Goals are either material or non-material such as the payment of money or the sheer joy of winning under adverse conditions (see Table 17-VIII).

TABLE 17-VIII
GOALS

Age Seven to Twelve	*After Age Twelve*
Goals must be clearly identified and be recognized by all players.	
Goals may hold the same meaning for each of the participating players.	
Goals ought to be	Goals ought to be
Tangible (material)	Tangible or intangible
Short-term	Short-term or long-term
Written in advance of game—i.e. prescribed	Prescribed in advance or written as part of the initial part of the game
Primarily individual	Individual, team, or task
Single goals	Multiple and contingent, i.e. several goals may be written up which are contingent upon the resulting consequences of actions taken by other players

Goals for the younger group should be tangible and short term. They must be clearly identified as a goal and must be recognizable as such by all of the players. Most importantly, if bitter disputes are to be avoided, the goals ought to have the same meaning for each of the players. In *Black Tom,* for example, the goal for the central role is to tag a minimum of three players caught between the two safe end zones. Each player knows what the player designated "It" must do. Thus, his goal has the same meaning for everyone. In *King of the Mountain,* the "King" must stay in his position atop the base (usually a high mound of dirt) and not be forced off by the other players. The "pack's" goal is the reverse—to lure him off or push him off. All players recognize this as the goal of the game.

For the older group, goals may be intangible, that is of a social, psychological and long-term nature. As with the younger group, the goals must be clearly identified and recognizable. However, they do not have to be met at the end of a single game, but may be deferred until the end of a series of games as occurs in a tournament. In a more complex and advanced game such as the *Inter-Nation Simulation* the goals a team hopes to achieve are written by the members of that team as a part of the game process. For example, goal number seven for the country of Utro in the game of *Inter-Nation Simulation* might read: "Utro is favorable to a world organization and will cooperate with other countries to achieve it (Guetzkow, 1963, p. 237). In advanced games goals can be multiple and contingent, i.e. several goals may be written up in the policy plans of a country which are contingent upon what other countries do and the resulting consequences of inter-dependent action. After the results for a period of play become available, the goals may be rewritten. The same conditions of identification and mutual recognition still apply for any goals formulated during the game.

STEP 5: DETERMINE THE PROCEDURAL RULES NEEDED TO GOVERN THE OPERATION OF THE GAME

All games have rules which govern their operation or procedures. The game designer may or may not find it necessary to employ every type of procedural rule which exists. His decision whether a rule is used is influenced by constraints placed upon the use of procedural rules by age (see Table 17-IX). There are seven

TABLE 17-IX

AGE CONSTRAINTS PLACED UPON THE
USE OF PROCEDURAL RULES

Before Age Four:	See the "rules of play" covered in Chapter 8 under *Play*
Age Three to Seven:	Rules are provided by adults as given. They are viewed by the child as sacred, untouchable, and unalterable. As yet, most children do not understand that they bind the actions of others as well as themselves.
Age Seven to Twelve:	Rules may be generated by children or provided by adults as given. They are viewed by the child as mutually controlled and unified. They can be distinguished on the basis of function and degree of control they exert over each player. Each child recognizes that they are binding upon the actions of each game participant.
After Age Twelve:	Rules are generated by the participants or handed down in codified form from one generation of players to another. They can be altered by the mutual consent of all participants at any time.

classes of procedural rules: (1) initiation and termination; (2) deployment and disposition; (3) communication; (4) arbitration; (5) intervention; (6) enforcement; and (7) outcome (see Table 17-X).

TABLE 17-X
RULES REGULATING GAME PROCEDURES

Rules	*Age Seven to Twelve*	*After Age Twelve*
Initiation & Termination	Players decide when to start and stop the game.	Written rules state when a game will begin and end as well as its duration.
Deployment & Disposition	The movement of players is spelled out in detail.	Deployment and disposition of players is either detailed as in board games or left to the players to decide during the game as in "open-ended, reality" games.
Communication	Rules are simple. Few, if any, restrictions are placed on communication between players.	Communication is either permitted or not; direct or indirect; restricted or free; symmetrical or asymmetrical.
Arbitration	Adults mediate problems which cannot be resolved by referring to written procedural rules.	Either a neutral party mediates problems arising from the play or detailed rules state what to do. (Application of the rules may lead to prolonged debate among the players).
Intervention	In both age groups a specific person or team is designated to act as Fate, Nature, or Chance. Chance cards or dice may also be used.	
Enforcement	Minor infractions are resolved by applying a rule of restitution.	Minor infractions are resolved by applying a rule of restitution (the play of the game reverts back to the state of the game immediately prior to the infraction).
	Major infractions are resolved by an adult.	Major infractions which do not threaten the game are resolved by applying a rule of repression (the game continues, but the player breaking the rule is penalized.)
		Infractions which threaten to destroy the game world itself are resolved by applying a rule of expulsion (the player disrupting the game must leave it).
Outcome	Players may compete with their own prior score or with other players for the highest or lowest score.	Players may compete as a team with their own prior team score or with other teams for the highest or lowest score. They may also compete within the team

	against their own prior score or against fellow team members for the "best" score. Competition may center around lower than "best" positions in the score values.
Win/lose criteria are clearly spelled out in advance of the game. A winner is declared immediately upon the termination of the game.	Win/lose criteria may be determined during the initial period of play as part of the game process. The winner(s) may be declared at the end of a series of games, or a winning trend identified which indicates a *probable* win.
Scoring criteria are objective, i.e. stated in a rule applicable to every player. Points are awarded or taken away from players for certain actions or outcomes specified in advance of the game.	Scoring criteria are subjective, i.e. points are awarded or taken away from a player according to the judgment of some previously designated person or persons.

Rules of Initiation and Termination

The initiation and termination of a game are dependent more upon the wishes of the players during the pre-twelve years. A game generally begins when somebody says, "Let's play 'X'," and the rest of the group agrees. The actual game time begins after the boundaries have been laid out, e.g. a circle in *Marbles* or the rectangular field with zones in *Red Rover*; the roles have been assigned; and the players are in their starting positions. It is over when the players declare, "Let's stop," or "We quit." Central-person games typically end when pre-determined criteria for winning have been met. For example, in *Black Tom,* a player must tag two of the three pack members before the game session is over.

For the older age group the initiation and termination of games is usually determined in advance. Either a set of predetermined conditions for winning or losing have to be met or a prescribed period of time must elapse. Games usually begin when the first move has been made. However, in an advanced type such as *Crisis,* the game director decides when it begins and when it is over.

Rules of Deployment and Disposition

Rules of deployment and disposition indicate who, when, where and how a player moves in a given role and state who can initiate and control such movement. For example, in *Black Tom*, a game for younger children, the "It" player can move only within the central zone between the two end zones. The other players can run anywhere within the external boundaries but only upon a signal from the "It." The "It" player in the central-person role chooses who can run, when they can run and his own position relative to the chosen player.

In games for the post-twelve group, the rules of deployment and disposition are less restrictive except for board games in which the players are told exactly how and where to move. In *Chess*, for example, each piece moves in a straight line or diagonally, and for a prescribed distance. In other games such as the *Inter-Nation Simulation*, the movement of the players is determined by the person filling the role, i.e. behavior is enacted (free). In *Hockey*, the players generally move into an area corresponding to the position they fill. For example, a goalie in *Hockey* positions himself in front of the net and rarely moves outside the goal-tending area. In such games as *Baseball*, the players in the field are not penalized if they do move out of positions in which they customarily operate.

Rules of Communication

Communication rules for the pre-twelve age group are seldom restricted. Everybody can talk with everybody else. Communication is therefore all-channel, face-to-face, and direct. Occasionally a player is limited in the information he can pass on to other players due to ritualized lines, songs, or signals accompanying roles in early central-person games. In *Simon Says*, for example, the central player must say "Simon Says" before the remaining players can legitimately move in that game, and more importantly, the central player is the only person who can say it.

For the older groups, communication may be permitted or not; direct or indirect; restricted or free; symmetrical or asymmetrical. Because adolescents have reached a more advanced stage of development, communication rules are more complex and detailed. Each player or team must handle different communication problems such as inaccurate or falsified information, one-way communication, restrictions on the verbal exchange of information, etc. In the *Inter-Nation Simulation,* for example, certain country teams are not permitted to communicate in order to simulate such problems as the breaking of diplomatic relations.

Rules of Arbitration

If an unanticipated situation arises or a dispute breaks out in games for younger children, it is usually handled in one of two ways. The activities of the game are temporarily suspended while the players mutually arrive at an agreeable solution to the problem, or an adult is sought out to mediate the dispute and render a decision binding on all the players. If neither of these solutions is used, or works, the game ends.

In the post-twelve group, the same methods are used. In lieu of seeking out an impartial adult, however, a referee or a game director resolves such disputes. In *Crisis* the game analyst handles problems which arise in the actual play of the game such as the interpretation of feedback information while the game director resolves those problems violating game procedures.

Rules of Intervention

In both age groups, the intervention of Fate, Chance or Nature is left to the discretion of the adult game director or a person designated to act in that capacity. For both groups, dice or chance cards are used in those situations where a person does not represent one of the three environmental forces. In most cases, the intervention of any one force is a purely administrative and arbitrary decision.

Rules of Enforcement

Rules of enforcement are simple and direct and usually cover infractions of procedural rules such as moving out of turn or the improper use of a song, ritual, rhyme, or signal. It is difficult for younger children to distinguish between inappropriate behavior for which a player is penalized but remains in the game and situations where inappropriate behavior is of such magnitude that a player is excluded from further participation. Therefore, decisions regarding repressive action or expulsion are left to the adult in charge of the game. When children are playing without supervision the game is likely to be abandoned under these circumstances.

Adolescents are able to distinguish between degrees of inappropriate behavior. Hence, rules indicating punishment to be meted out for certain types of infractions are quite explicit. Rules of restitution, repression and expulsion are formally stated in a games's set of directions. In *Basketball,* for example, a player is automatically expelled from the game if he accumulates five personal fouls.

Rules of Outcome

Outcome rules tell the players whether they are competing with themselves or with the other players. They also state the conditions which have to be met in order to win the game, and whether they will be paid off at the end of each game period or at the end of a series of games as occurs in tournament play.

In central-person games which predominate during the years from seven to twelve, children compete either with themselves or compare their scores with other players at the completion of the game, as in *Hopscotch* or *Jacks.* They may also compete as opposing groups in games similar to *Cowboys and Indians.* In both types of games, a win is achieved by doing *better than* the other players. A winner, i.e. a person receiving the payoff, is declared immediately upon termination of the game. *Run, Sheep, Run* serves as an example. In it, team members hide, and then try to get home safely before the members of the other team find them. The team getting the most members home safely wins.

In advanced games for adolescents, outcome rules range from detailed and precise to ambiguous and unstated. *Football* represents a game with a set of well defined outcome rules. In it, scoring criteria for a win are clearly spelled out. The payoff is made at the end of the game. However, in simulation games such as Giffin's *Kashmir 1966,* scoring criteria are not defined, nor are criteria for winning or losing. At the beginning of the game, each team writes up a set of objectives which they hope to achieve for their respective countries. No specific win/lose criteria are possible until the country's objectives have been written. The determination of a win is left to the game director or analyst who studies each team's objectives, determines if they have been met, and then declares a winner. Satisfaction from having accomplished as many of the team's objectives as possible constitutes the payoff in "open-ended" games.

STEP 6: WRITE THE INSTRUCTIONS
NECESSARY TO ADMINISTER
THE GAME

Instructions tell the game administrator and his aides what they must do to operate the game. There are three general classes of instructions: pre-game briefing, administrative and post-game de-briefing.

In the pre-game briefing, the game administrator assigns individuals to respective roles; covers the goals for each role; explains the rules which govern the behavior of persons filling each role; and reviews the rules controlling the operation of the game. The Plot (scenario) for the game is handed out as are the materials for the game. The persons who act as gaming staff are told separately their jobs (game maintenance roles) and what they are to do in the game (Abt, 1966, p. 5).

Instructions to the game director are presented in the form of a script. An example is adapted from the game of *Negotiation* by Shears.

> The numbered instructions on the left side of the sheet indicate the actions to be carried out by the game director. The instructions on the right side are to be spoken. The order in which the actions and spoken portions of the script are to be performed is indicated by the sequential numbering (Shears, 1967, pp. 6-11).

For example:

DO THIS:	SAY THIS:
1. . . .	2. . . .
3. . . .	
4. . . .	

During the game each of the gaming staff members will need to be told where he is to be and what he is to do to assist the operation of the game. He should also be told what he can and cannot tell the players when they ask questions. Usually this material is contained in the game director's script.

The post-game debriefing session gives both players and game staff a chance to analyze and criticize what happened in the game. Abt sees this as a time to ask such questions as:

> . . . what kinds of decisions were made? What were the effects of such decisions which became immediately apparent? What influenced the decisions made? What kind of interactions occurred between the teams and players? What did the players learn from the game? What did they feel they had done wrong? What course of action might they choose next time? How closely did the game situation approximate a real one? What kinds of uncertainties were experienced in the game? What personal reactions did players have to each other within the context of the game? (Abt, 1966, p. 3).

In other words, the debriefing session is used to recapitulate what happened in the game and why.

THE ROCKY MOUNTAIN CURRICULUM GAME

Step 1: Determine the Age Group for Which the Game is Intended

The Rocky Mountain Curriculum Game is designed for upper division education students, experienced teachers, and curriculum specialists. The age of the participants makes it possible to incorporate the most complex types of social interaction—unstructured encounters and unprescribed behaviors.

Step 2: Determine the Primary Function of the Game

The Game is a decision-making game, the purpose of which is to simulate problems encountered in the design and implementation of curriculum programs in small city school systems.

Step 3: Establish the Context of the Game World

The external boundaries of the game, constituting its static, formal bounds, are established by three sets of rules—relevancy, irrelevancy, and transformation. The first type deals with those features of the real world which are to be maintained intact in the game-world. In order to make the game as natural as possible for the participants, all the socio-cultural norms, conventions, etc., operative in the western provinces of Canada are operative in the game. The second type considers those features of the real world which are to be consciously excluded from the game world. Such features are normally those which are not essential to the operation of the game. Thus the city chosen for the game is fictitious as are its schools. Rocky Mountain is a composite of typical small cities and their attendent education problems. Finally the third type deals with those features of the real world which are to be retained in the game world, but require certain modifications before they can be introduced into the game world. Both time and space are altered. The players are expected to devise a curriculum plan in game hours as opposed to the days or weeks it would normally take. Players operate in the same room as opposed to the actual separation that would take place in real life. All of the requisite features of the game world are presented in the scenario.

Step 4: Formulate the Internal Structure of the Game

Further definition of the formal, static bounds of the game are determined by the number of players and roles. The game is played by eight or more persons: one School Board team composed of two or more players and three curriculum teams composed of three or more players. The role of game director is non-participatory. It is included to administer the game. There are two individual types of roles: as a member of a curriculum team and as a member of the School Board team. Participants bring their personal experience, educational philosophies, attitudes and values to the roles they fill.

The remaining variables determining the internal structure— player interaction, plot and goals, constitute the functional, dynamic aspects of the game. The game, in its basic form, is two-person (dyadic), with two curriculum teams competing with one another. From a game standpoint, the School Board team was included merely to determine the winner. All encounters are face-to-face and direct. The plot is simple: Each of the curriculum teams devises a curriculum plan independent of the other. Both plans are presented to the School Board team in an open meeting. The School Board team evaluates each proposal in terms of the city's educational needs, and selects the winning plan. Each of the curriculum teams is given an opportunity to defend their ideas and a chance to criticize constructively the plan of the other team. The sequence of events for the School Board team will serve to illustrate plot design:

1. Be assigned by the game director to a constituency, i.e. a specific section of the city.
2. Examine the city map and locate the designated school.
3. Examine the history of the school in order to get a picture of what has happened at the school in the past.
4. Examine the profile of the city to gain an understanding of the needs and problems of the community surrounding the school and the specific needs of the student population they represent.
5. Examine the proposed physical plan for the school to determine what changes would have to be made in order to accommodate different design proposals (optional).
6. Examine the claims profile to determine the desires of various influences or pressure groups upon the school board and the curriculum.
7. Prepare a brief plan of action and set of procedures for conducting an open School Board meeting. The plan should reflect the *general* features (criteria) of a curriculum design acceptable to the Board.
8. Hold an open meeting to consider the proposals.
9. Select a *single* design proposal and announce the Board's decision. (A majority vote is needed for selection, and in case of a tie, the chairman casts the deciding vote). The curriculum team whose plan is accepted wins.

The goals (objectives) for the curriculum teams are: (1) to formulate a tentative curriculum plan for a designated school and (2) to cause the School Board to approve its design. The objectives of the School Board team are: (1) to satisfy the various claims placed upon the Board and the curriculum by different factions of the community and (2) to select a curriculum design which best meets the needs of the city school district and its student population.

Step 5: Determine the Procedural Rules Needed to Govern the Operation of the Game

Procedural rules also constitute functional, dynamic aspects of the Rocky Mountain Curriculum Game. Play begins when the game director states that the game has begun and it ends when he declares the game over. The amount of information a player receives regarding the resources available to other players is the same for all players. Changes in the rules must be decided before the game begins and must be followed until it is over.

Communication among the players is governed by the following rules:

1. Curriculum teams may communicate with other curriculum teams only during the School Board meeting;

2. School Board members may communicate with anybody at any time;

3. Board deliberations are to be treated as confidential unless the chairman of the School Board declares the meeting "open;"

4. Other than rules 1-3, no other restrictions are placed on communication among the players.

Any questions are to be referred to the game director for the *final* decision. The game director also fills the role of Fate, Chance, and Nature. He may delegate this responsibility to an individual or group. Finally, if the rules are broken by a player, the director will determine the penalty.

The outcome criterion for the game is simple. The two curriculum teams compete with one another and a winner is selected by the School Board team.

Step 6: *Write the Instructions Necessary to Administer the Game*

Instructions to the Game Director

Your primary job is to make sure that the game runs smoothly. The steps which follow are guides to assist you in this task. They are not foolproof or ironclad. Filling the role of game director calls for a good deal of ingenuity; an ability to get the "big picture;" and to occasionally "play it by ear" or "wing it." Exercise your *own* judgment. Remember you are in command of all that happens in the game and your word is *final*. Read through the game carefully several times before you attempt to lead it.

Game Director's Script

The numbered steps indicate the sequence of things to do and say. The left hand column indicates what to do and the right hand column states what to say:

DO THIS	*SAY THIS*
1. Set up tables and chairs	

DO THIS	SAY THIS

for the required number of teams.

e.g.

Game Director	School Board
Curriculum Team #1	CT #3
CT #2	

2. Form the teams and assign team leaders. Try to place a person who is experienced or a person who has prepared in advance as the team leader.

3. Would the players take their seats.

4. Pass out the game instructions and materials.

5. Please read through the game carefully.

6. Allow time for players to read about the game carefully.

7. Are there any questions?

8. Answer any questions about game procedures. Make sure each player knows what to do.

9. If it appears that the teams are ready to play, begin the game.

10. Are there any further questions? . . .

You have one hour to prepare your design proposal.

Please tell the game director when your team is ready.

If all teams are ready before one hour has elapsed, we will take a break and

DO THIS	*SAY THIS*
	then go on to period two. Period One begins *now!*
11. Move about the room helping individual players or teams as needed.	
12. When all the teams have finished or one hour has elapsed declare Period One over.	13. Period One has ended.
14. Take a break at this point if desired.	15. At this point we will take a ———— minute break. Please be back in your seats at ————.
16. When everybody is seated start Period Two.	17. Period Two has begun. Make your presentations to the school board. The board chairman is responsible for procedural rules to be followed during the board meeting. You have up to one hour for the total meeting, including time for the board to reach a decision.
18. After the board has announced its decision (the accepted design is the winner), declare the game over.	19. The game is over. The critique period is now open. Let's critique the game. Your remarks should include both the good and bad features of the game. Also please pass in all game materials to the director.
20. Collect the materials.	

SUMMARY

A model was formulated which educators can use for the design of academic games. Game components identified and described earlier were utilized as the building blocks for the model. Examples were drawn from actual games to illustrate the use of the model.

The prerequisites of gaming behavior were considered first. As children move from central person team games, they become increasingly capable of using rules. The concept of reciprocity develops and with it the capacity for mutual action. Competition increases and becomes more intense. Simple relationships between the individual and the group typify central person games for the younger child. As the child grows older he engages in increasingly competitive team games which structure more complex social relationships requiring differential responses to various players. From age seven to twelve central person games function to aid the socialization process and to soften or disguise the more stringent features of the real world. After age twelve, practice in decision-making under varying conditions of conflict and the transmission of knowledge predominate as the major function of team games.

The external boundaries of games are established by partitioning rules which indicate features of the real world to be included, excluded, or modified. In effect, they determine the degree of correspondence between the real and game worlds. Four parameters control the internal structure of games: role, player interaction plot, and goals. Individual roles are most numerous in central-person games while both individual and task roles are found in team games. Interaction between players includes individual-individual, within-group, and between-group with cooperation or competition among player-units. In addition, interaction can be physical or non-physical; symbol or actual; verbal or non-verbal. The plot is an outline of what takes place in a game and indicates the sequence of major decision points for each role. Plots are simple in central person games but become increasingly complex as the child develops and eventually engages in team games. The goal describes what a player in a given role is to accomplish and the conditions under which he must do it. Seven classes of rules regulate the procedural operation of games: (1) initiation and termination; (2) deployment and disposition; (3) communication;

(4) arbitration; (5) intervention; (6) enforcement; and (7) outcome. They constitute the total class of procedural rules from which the game designer selects those required for his particular game. Lastly, the writing of administrative instructions was discussed. Taken as a whole, the model described can be used by educators as a guide for the design of academic games.

REFERENCES

Abt, Clark C.: "Twentieth Century Teaching Techniques," *The Faculty.* XXX, August, 1966.

Boocock, Sarane S. and Coleman, James S.: "Games with Simulated Environments in Learning," *Sociology of Education. XXXIX,* Summer, 1966.

Coleman, James S.: "Learning Through Games," *NEA Journal. LVI,* January, 1967.

Guetzkow, Harold *et al.*: *Simulation in International Relations: Developments for Research and Teaching.* Englewood Cliffs, Prentice-Hall, 1963.

Gump, P. V. and Sutton-Smith, Brian: "The 'It' Role in Children's Games," *The Group. XVII,* 1955.

McDavid, John W. and Harari, Herbert: *Social Psychology: Individuals, Groups, Societies.* New York, Harper and Row, 1968.

Maccoby, Michael, Modiano, Nancy and Lander, Patricia: "Games and Social Character in a Mexican Village," *Psychiatry. XXVII,* 1964.

Nesbitt, William A.: *Simulation Games for the Social Studies Classroom.* New York, The Foreign Policy Association, 1969.

Peller, L. E.: "Libidinal Phases, Ego Development, and Play," *The Psychoanal Study Child. IX,* 1954.

Piaget, Jean: *Play, Dreams, and Imitation in Childhood.* New York, W. W. Norton, 1951.

Piaget, Jean: *The Moral Judgment of the Child.* New York, The Free Press, 1965.

Rapoport, Anatol: *Two-Person Game Theory, The Essential Ideas.* Ann Arbor, The University of Michigan Press, 1966.

Redl, Fritz and Wineman, David: *Controls from Within.* New York, The Free Press, 1952.

Shears, Loyda M.: "Negotiation," paper presented at the NIMH workshop on the Utilization of Games in the Ego and Educational Development of Children, May 24-25, 1967, Bethesda, Maryland.

Sutton-Smith, Brian: "The Psychology of Children's Games," *National Education. XXXVII,* 1955.

Sutton-Smith, Brian: *The Games of New Zealand Children.* Berkeley, University of California Press, 1959.

Sutton-Smith, Brian: "Sixty Years of Historical Change in the Game Preferences of American Children," *Journal of American Folklore. LXXIV,* 1961.

APPENDIX TO CHAPTER 17

ROCKY MOUNTAIN CURRICULUM GAME[1]

T HE ROCKY MOUNTAIN CURRICULUM GAME simulates problems encountered in the design and implementation of curriculum programs in small urban school systems. Increasing responsibility on the part of field personnel such as teachers for the production of new curricula has necessitated devising a means of providing decision-making experience vis-a-vis curriculum design and implementation. The Rocky Mountain Curriculum Game provides the requisite experience.

The city of Rocky Mountain is fictitious yet is representative of a typical small city of 20,000 located in the southwestern portion of Canada. All the socio-cultural norms, conventions, etc., operative in the western provinces of Canada are operative in the game. The time context of the game is the present.

The educational development plan for the Rocky Mountain School District calls for the overhauling of the curriculum prior to the next school year. With the approval of the School Board, the district superintendent has directed that Louis Riel High School, St. Michele Junior High School, and Kanai Elementary School be designated as target schools for curriculum revision. Each school will serve as a model school for future curriculum changes in the remaining district schools. Because of the importance of the project for the entire district, the superintendent has authorized the formation of a number of curriculum teams composed of school personnel drawn from various schools in the district. The goal of each curriculum team is to produce a new curriculum design for the schools. Each plan is to be developed independently for presentation to the School Board team. The School Board team will listen to each of the design proposals in an open meeting, evaluate each in terms of the city's educational needs, and select a final design.

1©Copyright by Perry S. Gillespie, 1973.

Each curriculum team is given the opportunity of defending their plan and a chance to criticize constructively the plan of the other teams.

Specific Rules Governing the Operation of the Game

Play begins when the game director states that the game has begun and it ends when he declares the game over. The amount of information a player receives regarding resources available to other players is the same for all players. Changes in the rules must be decided before the game begins and must be followed until it is over.

Communication among the players is governed by the following rules:

(1) Curriculum teams may communicate with other curriculum teams only during the School Board meeting;
(2) School Board members may communicate with anybody at any time;
(3) Board deliberations are to be treated as confidential unless the chairman of the School Board declares the meeting "open";
(4) Other than rules 1-3, no other restrictions are placed on communication among the players.

Any questions are to be referred to the game director for *final* decision.

The game director fills the role of Fate, Chance, or Nature. He may delegate this responsibility to an individual or group. Finally, if the rules are broken by a player, the game director will declare that:

(1) play will revert back to the state just prior to the minor infraction;
(2) the offending player will be penalized for major infractions (the penalty being determined by the game director); or,
(3) the offending player will be expelled from the game if the offense is serious enough to threaten the game.

Number of Players

The game is played by eleven or more persons: 1 School Board team composed of 2 or more players and 3 curriculum teams composed of 3 or more players.

Roles

Two types of roles are found in the game: (1) member of a

curriculum team and, (2) member of the School Board team. Participants bring their personal experience, educational philosophies, attitudes and values to the role they fill.

The Curriculum Team(s)

The members of the curriculum team have available to them:

1. A map of the district indicating the location of the three schools;
2. A brief history of each of the three schools outlining its specific needs and problems;
3. A profile of the city outlining the socio-cultural, economic, religious, political, and educational needs and problems for different sections of the city;
4. A plan of the physical layout of each of the three schools.

The objectives of the curriculum team are: (1) to formulate a tentative curriculum plan for the designated school and (2) to cause the School Board to approve the design. The curriculum team whose plan is accepted wins.

The plan should be brief and concise. It should include the subject matter content of the program and its organizational pattern (e.g. core, interdisciplinary, separate disciplines, or theme/problem); definition of the role(s) of the teacher and the learner in interaction (e.g. the teacher as *provocateur* and the learner as the ultimate chooser of what he wants to learn); and an instructional strategy (method) which best suits such a set of roles. Current research findings in education should be brought to bear upon the final design. The curriculum and instructional methods currently found in the Province of Alberta should be taken as the "starting curriculum."

The sequence of events for the curriculum team are:

1. Study the map of the city to determine the location of the school.
2. Study the brief history of the school in order to get a picture of what has happened at the school in the past.
3. Study the profile of the section in which the school is located to gain an understanding of the needs and problems of the community surrounding the school and the population from which the study body is drawn.
4. Study the plan illustrating the physical layout of the school in order to determine what changes would have to be made to accommodate the proposed curriculum design.

5. Devise a curriculum plan which meets the needs of the student population in the section in which the school is located.

SCHOOL BOARD CONSTITUENCIES

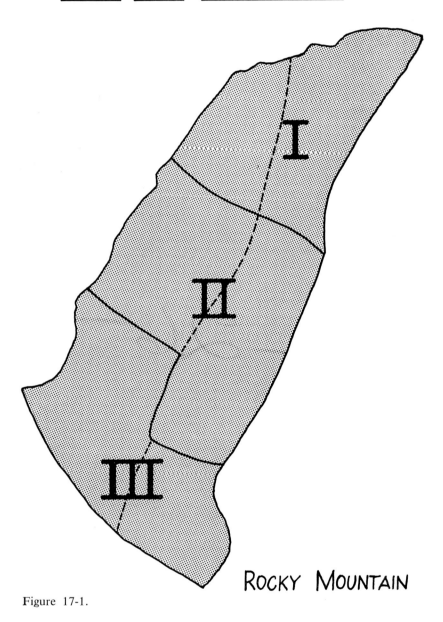

Figure 17-1.

6. Present the design proposal at an "open" School Board meeting. Every curriculum team is permitted to listen to all design proposals; make rebuttal statements after each team's presentation; and attempt to convince the School Board that their proposal best suits the needs of the designated school.

The optimum size of a curriculum team can vary from 3-6 persons.

The School Board

The members of the School Board team have available to them:

1. A map of the district indicating the location of the three schools;
2. A brief history of each of the three schools outlining their specific needs and problems;
3. A profile of the city outlining the socio-cultural, economic, religious, political, and educational needs and problems for different sections of the city.
4. A plan of the physical layout of each of the three schools.
5. A city map outlining the boundaries of each School Board constituency.
6. A claims profile indicating the claims placed upon the School Board and the curriculum by various influence or pressure groups (e.g., the *A.T.A.*)

The objectives of the School Board team are: (1) to satisfy the various claims placed upon the School Board and the curriculum and (2) to select a curriculum design which best meets the needs, of the city school district and its student population.

The School Board team is a non-competitive, decision-making unit in the game. However, there may or may not be competition among Board members due to the differing needs of the constituency they represent.

The sequence of events for the School Board team are:

1. Be assigned by the game director, to a constituency, i.e. responsibility for a section of the city.
2. Examine the city map and locate the designated school.
3. Examine the history of the school in order to get a picture of what has happened at the school in the past.
4. Examine the profile of the city to gain an understanding of the needs and problems of the community surrounding the school and the specific needs of the student population they represent.
5. Examine the proposed physical plan for the schools to determine what changes would have to be made in order to accommodate different design proposals.

6. Examine the claims profile to determine the desires of various influence or pressure groups upon the School Board and the curriculum.
7. Prepare a brief plan of action and set procedures for conducting an open School Board meeting in which the various design proposals are to be considered. The plan should reflect the general features of a curriculum design acceptable to the Board.
8. Hold an open meeting to consider the proposals.
9. Select a single proposal and announce the Board's decision. (A majority vote is needed for selection, and in case of a tie, the chairman makes the final decision.) The curriculum team whose plan is accepted wins.

Profile of Rocky Mountain

Rocky Mountain is located in the southwestern portion of Alberta. The early history of Rocky Mountain was much like that of other foothills communities, passing through several successive phases of an outpost fort, a trading post, a mining community, a transportation hub for the shipment of farm produce, cattle, sheep, and hogs, and finally, as a small commercial and industrial center. Because of its proximity to the Rockies, it has recently become a tourist center. The city has rapidly grown in the last ten years. The city is presently the site of the Rocky Mountain Community College, and has been designated to be the site of Rocky Mountain University in 1973.

The present mayor and city council were instrumental in the rapid growth of the city and its being chosen as the future university site. Many enemies were made of people who did not want to see their nice, quiet community become the bustling city that it is. The opposition has charged that a few have benefited from the growth, while the ordinary citizen has not. They point to the slum area of the Northwest and Northeast sections of the city as a "malignant sore." The mayor has countered that low cost housing is slated to replace the present dwellings in 1970-71. In addition, the crime rate has increased, particularly among the Indian minority. Again the opposition has charged that the present administration of the city has ignored the needs of the community. Recreation facilities for the city's juvenile population has been identified as another glaring problem. The *Rocky Mountain Herald* on its editorial page has run a series on the needs of the city. One article was critical of the schools for not helping correct some of the city's

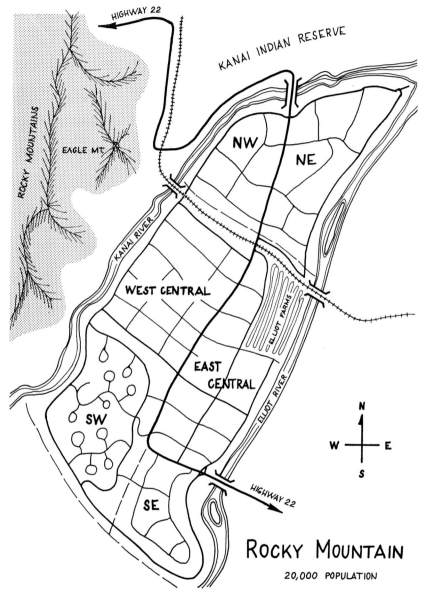

Figure 17-2.

problems, and even hinted that the schools may have caused some of them. The white community has demanded that the "Indian Problem" be taken care of and now!

The Northwest and Northeast sections of the city are very much alike. Both sections are occupied by a large Indian population which has not been well assimilated into the predominantly white Canadian culture. The sections are zoned for small industry. Most of the families that live here are very poor. The breadwinner is usually a factory worker, seasonal or transient laborer, or an unemployed, welfare recipient. In many cases the male head of the house is away from the city for long periods of time. Family dwellings are old and run down, and have been called "slums." The small factories are located in a strip just north of the CPR lines and in a strip along the Elliot River. The median age of residents for the two sections is under 20 years of age. The median income is under $3,000.00. About 80 percent of the parents have a 7th grade or less education. The median value of homes is less than $5,000.00. The highest crime rate in the city exists in these two sections. The divorce/separated rate is likewise the highest in the city.

Both the West Central and East Central sections of the city are much alike. They are composed of mainly blue collar workers, lower middle-class income families, and small businessmen living with their families above and behind their stores. The newest dwellings and stores are located in the West Central section. Both sections are zoned mixed residential and commercial. Many young couples live in this area because of the low rent housing and apartments. They are for the most part interested in the community and the schools. A young parents group was chiefly responsible for a clean up and improvement program in the two sections. The median age of the residents of both sections is under thirty. The median income is under $7,000.00. More than 70 percent have a 7th grade education or better. The crime rate is about average for a typical Canadian city. The divorce/separated rate is average for Western Canada.

The Southwest section of the city is made up of wealthy, retired ranchers and farmers, and successful leaders of the professional and business community. The homes in this area are new with some falling into the $50,000-$70,000 class (River Hills Estates). Parents in the exclusive River Hills Estates have organized an association devoted to the individualization of learning. Some have even suggested a "free school" approach if the local School Board, the Alberta Department of Education, and the Minister of Education would give them approval. Several of the residents are friends of the Minister. The median age of the section is 45 years of age. The median income is over $20,000.00. About 20 percent of the residents have completed a degree program at a university. The median value of homes is $30,000.00. There have been many acts of vandalism and breakings and enterings in the area, and so it is heavily patrolled. The divorce/separated rate is slightly above the Canadian average.

The Southeast section of the city is composed mainly of middle-class income families. These are the white collar workers of the city. The residents believe in the values of the urban middle-class. They are stable and conservative in their basic approach to life. The homes in the area are not new, but they are well kept. The area is zoned residential. The median age for the section is 35 years of age. The median income is $7,000.00. About 50 percent of the residents have a 12th grade education. The median value of homes is $20,000.00. This area has experienced the least number of criminal acts and has the lowest divorce/separated rate in the city.

Kanai Elementary School

Kanai Elementary School is located in the Northeast section of the city of Rocky Mountain. A number of different ethnic groups reside in the city, most of whom have been well assimilated into the Canadian culture. However, there is a sizable Canadian-Indian minority group residing in two sections north of the CPR lines, which have failed to become fully assimilated into the Canadian culture. The parents of the children going to Kanai Elementary School are mostly workers, transient or seasonal laborers, and unemployed welfare cases. Low cost housing has been proposed for the area in the 1970-71 Municipal Budget. The area has been termed by some City Councillors as a "slum" and a disgrace to the city. Most of the factories are located in a strip along the north side of the railway tracks and a strip along the Elliot River. Few parents ever come to the schools and then only when their children had gotten into trouble with school authorities.

One hundred and ninety students attend Kanai Elementary

School. Over 60 percent of the students are Indian. The program
of studies is that prescribed by the Alberta Department of Education. Vandalism and discontent prevail at the school, and the curriculum program obviously does not suit the needs and interests
of the students. Most of the teachers are older, about ready for re-
tirement, and disinterested, while the remainder are new, eager,
but inexperienced. Three of the new teachers are rapidly losing
any enthusiasm they may have had for teaching. Two have indicated they will quit unless something is done to improve the conditions at the school. There are a total of ten teachers on the staff
including the principal. The physical plant is old and district plans
call for the construction of a new school on the same location in
1970-71. The district is deeply interested in improving the conditions at the school and the superintendent is willing to lend his
complete support to this task.

St. Michele Junior High School

St. Michele Junior High School is located in the West Central
portion of the city of Rocky Mountain. A number of different
ethnic groups reside in the city, most of whom have been well assimilated into the Canadian culture. The children going to St.
Michele Junior High School are drawn from the Southeast, Southwest, and East Central sections of the city. The Southwest section
is composed mainly of wealthy retired ranchers and farmers, professional people, and white collar workers. The Southeast section
of the city is composed of middleclass income families. The West
Central section of the city is predominantly blue collar workers,
lower-middle class, and some business families living above or
behind their stores. There are mainly apartment complexes in this
latter section. Both the West Central and the southern half (south
of the rail yard) of the East Central section are zoned residential
and commercial. Many of the homes in the area are old, but well
kept.

Five hundred students attend St. Michele Junior High School.
The school population represents a microcosm of the city's population. Sixteen teachers staff the school. In addition, there is a
principal, vice-principal, and school librarian. Most of the teachers
at St. Michele are traditional, experienced, and competent. They

have exhibited a concern for providing a good education for all the students, and have experimented with a number of educational innovations with moderate success. Several teachers have expressed a desire to team teach next year. Both non-grading and the individualization of learning have been discussed at staff meetings in the past. The principal is in his fifth year and is anxious to try something new. His brother is the Superintendent. There is, however, an articulate group of residents from the Southwest section who feel that the school is not moving fast enough. In addition, some people resent the frank, direct approach of the new principal. District plans call for the construction of a new school on the site in 1971-72.

Louis Riel High School

Louis Riel High School is to be located in the Southwest section of the city of Rocky Mountain. A number of different ethnic groups reside in the city; except for an Indian minority most have been assimilated into the Canadian culture. Children who will attend Louis Riel High School will be drawn from the Northwest, West Central, and Southwest sectors of the city. Louis Riel will absorb half the load being carried by the old Michener High School. The Southwestern section is composed mainly of wealthy, retired ranchers and farmers, professional people, and young professionals. The West Central section of the city is predominantly blue collar workers, lower-middle class income families, and small businessmen living above and behind their stores. The Northwest section is occupied by workers, transient or seasonal laborers, and unemployed, welfare cases. About sixty percent of the people living in the Northwest section are Canadian-Indians. Low cost housing has been proposed for this area in the 1970-71 Municipal Budget. The area has been termed by some Councillors as a "slum" and a disgrace to the city. About half of the factories are located in the strip just north of the CPR lines. Students from this section have been a constant headache to school authorities.

Twelve hundred students are to attend Louis Riel High School when it opens in 1971-72. The staff will be composed of forty teachers. Half of the staff is to be new, with most of them just out of university. The remainder are to be hand picked from the rest of

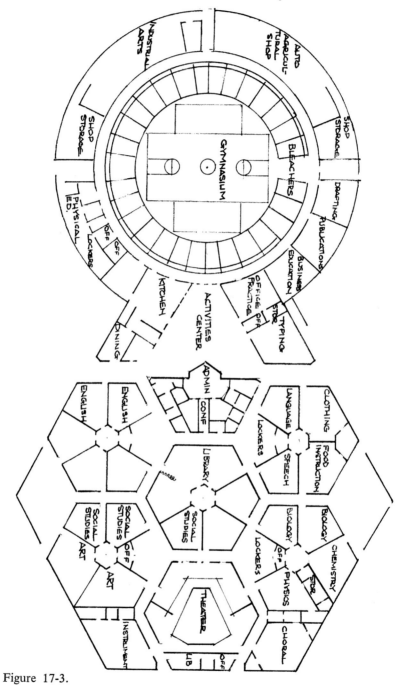

Figure 17-3.

the district. Parents in the exclusive River Hills Estates located in the Southwest portion of the city have organized an association devoted to the individualization of learning. Some have even suggested a "free school" approach.

Claims Profile for the School Board

The School Board is limited in its actions by constraints or claims placed upon it by various influence or pressure groups. Six categories of pressure groups are recognized in the Rocky Mountain Curriculum Game : (1) EDUCATIONAL, (2) ECONOMIC (Occupational/Business), (3) POLITICAL, (4) SOCIAL, (5) RELIGIOUS, and, (6) MASS MEDIA.

Cards are made up indicating the goals of differing pressure groups. From a deck of such cards, six are drawn by the game director, (after being shuffled) and given to the chairman of the School Board. These cards together represent the claims profile or constraint upon decisions made by the School Board.

Six example claims cards are:

(1) EDUCATIONAL: The Alberta Teachers' Association has stated as one of its objectives that: "Every child has the right to educational opportunities in a publicly-supported educational system structured to develop his individual potentialities."

(2) RELIGIOUS: Various church groups seek greater emphasis on moral teachings in the schools. Teachers should act as moral exemplars for their students.

(3) ECONOMIC: Organized labor seeks increased vocational and Industrial Arts offerings in school curriculum programs.

(4) POLITICAL: The RCMP seeks the inclusion of educational programs on drugs, driver training, and safety in school curriculum programs.

(5) SOCIAL: There is pressure from parents of low-social economic standing for more "real learning" in the schools, i.e. "Reading, Riting, & Rithmetic."

(6) MASS MEDIA: The schools are old-fashioned and need to be adapted to the needs of the 20th century.

AUTHOR INDEX

A

Abrams, R.D., 21
Abt, C.C., 344, 345, 352
Adelberg, R., 43, 54
Alexander, F., 33, 53
Allen, L.E., 59, 73, 217, 219, 220, 255
Allen, R.W., 219
Allport, G., 48
Ames, L. B., 39, 53
Ammar, H., 106, 117
Arieti, S., 121, 126
Armbruster, F., 158, 160, 161
Arth, M. J., 57, 142, 152

B

Bales, R.F., 152
Bally, G., 105, 117
Bandura, A., 43, 46, 53, 54
Barker, R.B., 45
Bavelas, A., 140
Beaumont, F., 186, 197
Beilin, H., 125, 126
Beiser, H. R., 44, 54
Bender, L., 54
Berlyne, D.E., 43, 47, 50, 54
Biller, H.B., 24, 41, 54
Block, J., 46, 54
Bobbitt, R.A., 39, 56
Bolton, H.C., 21
Boocock, S., 293, 294, 317, 352
Borgatta, E.P., 152
Bower, E.M., 5, 59
Brewster, P.G., 15, 21
Bronson, G., 45, 54
Brown, F.C., 21
Bruegel, P., 105
Bruner, J.S., 120, 126
Brush, C., 73
Buhler, C., 31, 54, 114, 117
Burgers, J.M., 25, 27, 54
Bush, R.R., 57, 142, 152

C

Caillois, R., 13, 14, 22, 129, 130, 131, 132, 151

Caldwell, B.M., 42, 54
Caldwell, M.E., 255
Call, J.D., 39, 54
Campbell, D., 45, 54
Capobianco, R.J., 40, 54
Carlson, E., 219
Challman, R.C., 40, 54
Champion, W., 164
Cherryholmes, C., 219, 278, 293
Cockrell, D.L., 39, 54
Cole, D.A., 54
Coleman, J.S., 139, 141, 151, 219, 317, 352
Cousinet, R., 24 , 54
Cox, F.N., 45, 54

D

Danielian, J., 143, 144, 151
Dembo, T., 45, 54
de Meyers, V., 105, 117
Dewey, J., 278, 293
Dobbs, D., 199
Dodwell, P.C., 125, 126
Doland, D.J., 43, 54
Dundes, A., 21

E

Eifermann, R.R., 75, 78, 101, 102, 119, 155
Emrich, D., 21
Erickson, E.H., 22, 24, 33, 41, 54, 55, 102
Evans, P., 21

F

Fales, E., 39, 55
Feitelson, D., 103, 106, 117, 119
Finneman, J., 39, 55
Flanders, J.P., 41, 55
Flavell, J., 34, 42, 55, 123, 124, 126
Fortes, M., 105, 117
Franklin, A., 186, 197
Freeman, R.W., 73, 267
Freud, S., 25, 31, 52
Freyer, J.L., 41, 55

SUBJECT INDEX